Contents

Dedication

Keith Randell (1943–2002)

The *Access to History* series was conceived and developed by Keith, who created a series to 'cater for students as they are, not as we might wish them to be'. He leaves a living legacy of a series that for over 20 years has provided a trusted, stimulating and well-loved accompaniment to post-16 study. Our aim with these new editions is to continue to offer students the best possible support for their studies.

access to history

Mao's China 1936–97

MICHAEL LYNCH

SECOND EDITION

HODDER
EDUCATION
AN HACHETTE UK COMPANY

The Publishers would like to thank Robin Bunce, Sarah Ward and David Ferriby for their contribution to the Study Guide.

The Publishers would like to thank the following for permission to reproduce copyright material:

Photo credits: p7 Bettmann/Corbis; **p12** FPG/Getty Images; **p21** HS Wong/Getty Images; **p22** Keystone/Getty Images; **p81b** AFP/ Getty Images; **p92** Bettmann/Corbis; **p105** Sovfoto/UIG via Getty Images; **p110** Bettmann/Corbis; **pp136, 138** Keystone/Getty Images; **pp141, 153** Ullsteinbild/TopFoto; **p167** Bettmann/Corbis; **p178** Topham/AP; **p192** CNN via Getty Images.

Acknowledgements: Belknap Press, *Mao's Last Revolution* by Roderick Macfarquar and Michael Schoenhals, 2006. Cambridge University Press, *An Intellectual History of Modern China* by Merle Goldman (editor), 2002. Foreign Languages Press, *Fundamental Issues in Present-Day China* by Deng Xiaoping, 1987; *Selected Works of Mao Tse-tung* by Mao Tse-tung, 1975. HarperCollins, *The New Emperors Mao and Deng: A Biography* by Harrison Salisbury, 1992. Hodder & Stoughton, *Mao: A Life* by Philip Short, 1999. Interlink Books, *Mao and the Chinese Revolution* by Yves Chevrier, 2004. Ivan R. Dee, *Mao: A Reinterpretation* by Lee Feigon, 2002. John Murray, *Hungry Ghosts* by Jasper Becker, 1996. Jonathan Cape, *Mao: The Unknown Story* by Jung Chang and Jon Halliday, 2005. Macmillan, *Stalin: A Biography* by Robert Service, 2004. Mentor Books, *Mao Tse-tung: An Anthology of His Writings* by Anne Freemantle (editor), 1962. New Left Review, Wang Shi-wei in *New Left Review*, July–August 1975. W.W. Norton, *The Search for Modern China* by Jonathan Spence, 1990; *The Search for Modern China: A Documentary Collection* by Pei-kai Cheng and Michal Lestz (editors), 1999. Penguin, *Mao Tse-tung Unrehearsed: Talks and Letters, 1956–71* by Stuart Schram (editor), 1974; *Red Star Over China* by Edgar Snow, 1972; *The Courage to Stand Alone: Letters from Prison* by Wei Jingshen, 1997. *The People's Daily*, 26 April 1989. Routledge, *Mao* by Michael Lynch, 2004; *Was Mao Really a Monster?* by Gregor Benton and Lin Chun (editors), 2010. Sutton Publishing, *Mao Zedong* by Delia Davin, 1997. Tagman Press, *Hostage in Peking* by Anthony Grey, 2008. University of California Press, *Spider Eaters: A Memoir* by Rae Yang, 1977.

Orders: please contact Bookpoint Ltd, 130 Milton Park, Abingdon, Oxon OX14 4SB. Telephone: +44 (0)1235 827720. Fax: +44 (0)1235 400454. Lines are open 9.00a.m.–5.00p.m., Monday to Saturday, with a 24-hour message answering service. Visit our website at www.hoddereducation.co.uk

© Michael Lynch 2015

First published in 2015 by
Hodder Education
An Hachette UK Company
338 Euston Road
London NW1 3BH

Impression number	10	9	8	7	6	5	4	3	2	1
Year		2019	2018	2017	2016	2015				

Cover photo © Camera Press
Produced, illustrated and typeset in Palatino LT Std by Gray Publishing, Tunbridge Wells
Printed and bound by CPI Group (UK) Ltd, Croydon CR0 4YY

A catalogue record for this title is available from the British Library

ISBN 978 1471838972

Nationalists and Communists

In 1936, two parties competed for power: the Nationalists led by Chiang Kai-shek and the Communists led by Mao Zedong. Intermittently in alliance in a national struggle against the occupying Japanese, the two parties remained mutually hostile. Mao ruthlessly imposed himself on his followers in a way that Chiang, although nominally head of the Chinese Republic, was never able to do on his followers. When the Japanese occupation ended in 1945 the Communists were better placed to win the civil war that ensued.

These developments are described in the following sections:

★ Introduction: China in 1936

★ The Communists under Mao

★ The Guomindang under Chiang

★ The Sino-Japanese war and the second United Front

★ Mao's 'rectification of conduct' campaign 1942–4

★ The impact of the Japanese occupation

Key dates

1931	Japanese occupation of Manchuria		1941	Pearl Harbor attack brought USA into Pacific war
1936	Xian Incident			
	Formation of second United Front		1942–4	'Rectification of conduct' campaign
1937	Start of Sino-Soviet war		1944	Ichigo campaign
	Rape of Nanjing		1945	End of Sino-Japanese war
1940	100 Regiments campaign			Soviet–GMD friendship treaty

1 Introduction: China in 1936

▶ *Why, in 1936, were the two main revolutionary parties in China opposed to each other?*

In 1911, China had undergone the first of its modern revolutions when the ruling Qing dynasty collapsed. The imperial system was replaced by a republic, which claimed authority over the whole of China, but in reality lacked real power. As a consequence, China entered the warlord era, a time when conflicting groups and interests fought to impose themselves on their regions. The general hatred of the warlords and of the continuing subjection of a weak China to foreign

Guomindang (GMD) The Nationalists. A revolutionary party created by Sun Yat-sen that wanted the modernisation of China and the ending of foreign domination. From the early 1930s, at its stronghold in Nanjing, it claimed to be the legitimate government of the Republic of China.

Chinese Communist Party (CCP) A revolutionary party, formed in 1921 with support from Soviet Russia.

United Front A GMD–CCP military alliance that defeated the warlords in a series of campaigns from 1926 to 1928.

Long March The CCP flight from Jiangxi to Yanan in 1934–5. It began as a rout, but its eventual success turned it into one of the great formative experiences of Chinese communism.

Soviet A Communist-controlled area in which life is structured along communal, socialist lines.

influence expressed itself in a driving desire for Chinese regeneration. It was in this atmosphere that two main revolutionary parties developed. One was the Nationalist **Guomindang (GMD)**, founded by Sun Yat-sen and led after 1925 by Chiang Kai-shek; the other was the **Chinese Communist Party (CCP)**, whose leader from the later 1920s was Mao Zedong.

At first, the two parties co-operated in a **United Front** in order to break the warlords. After this had been achieved by 1927, Chiang turned savagely on the Communists. He intended their complete destruction, an aim in which he nearly succeeded. By 1934, the Communists were on the point of extinction, having being penned in their Jiangxi base by surrounding GMD forces. However, the Communists survived by a desperate break-out and flight in 1934–5, known as the **Long March**. In the new northern base of Yanan, reached in 1935, Mao began to construct a **soviet** in defiance of the GMD and of the Japanese who had begun to occupy parts of China in 1931.

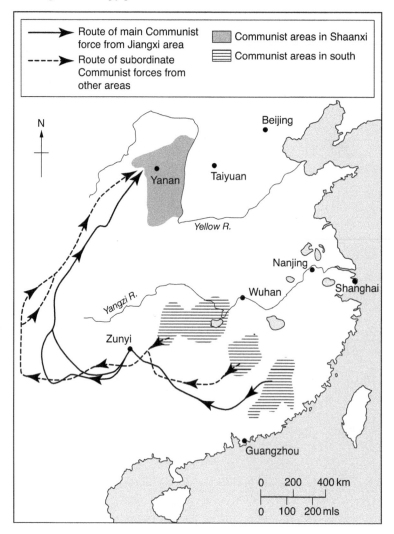

The route of the 1934–5 Long March.

The Communists under Mao

▶ *How did Mao's political ideas condition the way he led the CCP before 1945?*

Mao's concept of leadership

Mao Zedong, a peasant from Hunan province, had grown up an intensely patriotic young man, angered by China's failings and much impressed by Sun Yat-sen's revolutionary ideas. Between 1912 and 1919, Mao had witnessed scenes of great violence as rival Republican factions had fought for supremacy in his home province of Hunan. He recorded that the experience deeply affected him and led him to conclude that to be a leader and to gain success politically or militarily required total commitment and a willingness to use extreme methods. This helps to explain why throughout his career he was so ready to employ the toughest means to crush political opponents. One of his most revealing sayings was that 'all power grows out of the barrel of a gun'.

All Mao Zedong's experiences as a young revolutionary convinced him that unless he was prepared to use brutal, unyielding methods he could achieve little. He was a **dialectician**, which was why he had become a **Marxist** and a founder member of the CCP in 1921. He held that all change, all progress, resulted from suppression of the weaker by the stronger.

Mao's ruthlessness

Moving to Beijing, Mao became attracted to Marxist ideas and developed the conviction that if China was to regain its greatness it would have to undergo a profound social and political revolution. To further this aim, Mao in 1921 became one of the founder members of the CCP. When Chiang's **White Terror** in 1927 forced the Communists to flee to Jiangxi province, Mao began his first endeavour to build a Chinese soviet. It was at Jiangxi that Mao revealed the ruthlessness that he regarded as essential to effective leadership and which characterised his whole career. In 1930 he ordered the torture and execution of some 4000 **Red Army** troops whom he accused of plotting against him. His written instruction read: 'do not kill the important leaders too quickly, but squeeze out of them the maximum information'. Mao showed a similar unwillingness to compromise in establishing his leadership over the party during the Long March.

Mao's ideology

Once established in Yanan in 1935, Mao, over the next decade, turned the camp into a Communist soviet; it served as both a protective base and a haven to which Communist sympathisers flocked. It was at Yanan that Mao developed and formalised his revolutionary ideas. This involved him in an ideological

 **KEY TERMS**

Dialectician A believer that life is essentially a struggle between opposites in which the more powerful always wins.

Marxist A believer in the theories of Karl Marx (1818–83), who used the notion of the dialectic to explain history.

White Terror Chiang's 1927 campaign of annihilation of the CCP.

Red Army The name adopted for the CCP's military forces.

battle to enforce his leadership in the face of opposition from within the CCP and from the **Comintern**. It is important to stress that it was because he was an ardent nationalist that Mao had adopted Communism. He saw in Marxism–**Leninism** a set of principles that he could turn into a practical programme for restoring China to its original greatness. Mao was never a slave to Marxist theory; he interpreted the ideology to suit his purposes for China. The persistent theme in his actions and his writings was that Chinese considerations always had primacy. Since foreign communists, no matter how eminent, could not truly understand actual Chinese conditions, it was not for them to dictate policy.

SOURCE A

From 'Problems of Strategy in China's Revolutionary War' 1936, in *Selected Works of Mao Tse-tung*, Foreign Languages Press, 1975, vol. I, p. 181.

China's revolutionary war is waged in the specific environment of China and so it has its own specific circumstances and nature ... Some people say that it is enough merely to study the experience of revolutionary war in Russia ... However although we must value Soviet experience ... we must value even more the experience of China's revolutionary war, because there are many factors specific to the Chinese revolution and the Chinese Red Army.

Mao was also concerned that to give too much consideration to the opinions of foreign communists as expressed through the Comintern would damage his claim to personal authority in China. His conviction was that 'correct leadership should be based upon careful, detailed study of local conditions which can only be done by each of the Communist parties in its own country. The Comintern, far away from the actual struggle, can no longer provide proper leadership.'

The urban versus rural dispute

Mao's ideas brought him criticism from the pro-Moscow elements in the party who accused him of ignoring Comintern instructions and taking an independent line. A particular point of contention was Mao's insistence that the distinct conditions in China determined that revolution must first come in the countryside. He rejected the Comintern's demand that the CCP direct its efforts into preparing risings in the urban areas. His central belief was that China's revolution must be a peasant revolution. This was heresy in the eyes of the Comintern theorists. They asserted that:

- Mao was ignoring the laws of the **dialectic** whose stages followed a predetermined, ordered path and thus could not be bypassed.
- Peasant revolution was not an end in itself; it was merely the precursor of the final proletarian revolution.
- China lacked an **urban proletariat** and was, therefore, incapable of achieving a genuinely proletarian revolution.
- The best that the CCP could accomplish would be to help bring about the **bourgeois stage** of revolution by merging with the Nationalists.

? On what grounds does Mao argue in Source A that the Russian Revolution is not the model for the CCP to follow?

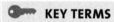
KEY TERMS

Comintern The Communist International, the body set up in Moscow to organise international revolution by requiring foreign Communist parties to follow Soviet instructions.

Leninism The revolutionary theories of class war first formulated by Karl Marx and subsequently developed by Lenin.

Dialectic The dynamic force that shapes the historical development of class war.

Urban proletariat The industrial working class, destined, in Marxist analysis, to be the final victor in the dialectical struggle.

Bourgeois stage The period in Marxist theory when the middle class, having overcome the previous feudal system, dominates society until the working-class revolution occurs.

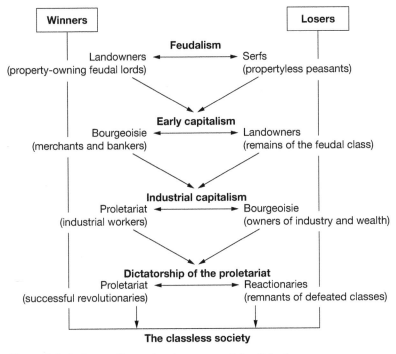

Figure 1.1 A diagram illustrating the pattern of the dialectic.

According to the diagram, what are the principal stages in class conflict?

Mao rejected this analysis and stressed that Marxist theory had to be interpreted in the light of the actual conditions in China. The stark reality was that China did not possess an urban proletariat large enough to mount a revolution. Furthermore, he dismissed the notion that genuine revolution could be achieved only by the industrial workers and countered it by asserting these convictions:

- In China, urban industrial workers accounted for less than four per cent of the population, whereas the rural peasants made up 88 per cent. It followed that a popular revolution would have to be the work of the peasantry.
- In China, therefore, a peasant revolution would be sufficient to fulfil the demands of the dialectic.
- Mao redefined the term proletarian to mean not so much a social class as an attitude. Those who were genuinely committed to revolution were by that very fact members of the proletariat. Anyone who had suffered oppression at the hands of class enemies could be counted a member of the proletariat.
- There was, therefore, no necessity to wait for the growth of an industrial proletariat in China. Genuine revolution would be achieved by the peasants: 'no power, however strong, can restrain them'. He told his followers that it was their task to unleash the huge potential of the peasantry: 'The peasants are the sea; we are the fish. We live in the sea.'

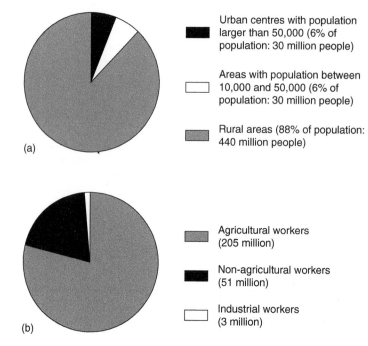

(a)

Urban centres with population larger than 50,000 (6% of population: 30 million people)

Areas with population between 10,000 and 50,000 (6% of population: 30 million people)

Rural areas (88% of population: 440 million people)

(b)

Agricultural workers (205 million)

Non-agricultural workers (51 million)

Industrial workers (3 million)

Figure 1.2 (a) Location of the population of China in 1933 (500 million people). (b) Labour sectors for a total workforce of 259 million in 1933.

KEY FIGURE

Li Lisan (1899–1967)
A Moscow-trained CCP member who held the orthodox Marxist view that peasants could not be a truly revolutionary force.

KEY TERM

'Twenty-eight Bolsheviks'
A group of CCP members who had been trained in Moscow and returned to China with instructions to make the party conform to Soviet concepts of urban revolution.

CCP opposition to Mao

Mao's particular interpretation of the dialectic put him at variance with the orthodox Communists, such as **Li Lisan**, a Moscow-trained Marxist, who continued to follow the Comintern line by insisting that the Chinese Communists concentrate their revolutionary activities in urban areas. Throughout the 1930s, Mao was involved in a battle to assert his authority within the party. His major opponents were a faction known as the **'Twenty-eight Bolsheviks'**, who followed Li Lisan in criticising Mao for ignoring Comintern instructions and acting independently. Mao was accused of 'reckless adventurism' for assuming that the stages of proletarian revolution could be skipped at will. Mao survived such criticism thanks largely to four key factors:

- His selection in 1934 of the correct northern route to follow on the Long March, in opposition to the pro-Moscow faction who had argued for a different western route, had given him a moral superiority over them.
- As a result of his own field research, Mao had an unrivalled knowledge of the Chinese peasantry, which meant he dominated any discussion of the party's peasant policy.
- His intense self-belief and determination allowed him to silence opponents and browbeat waverers into line.
- He was indispensable as a military planner.

Mao Zedong: career to 1949

1893	Born in Hunan province
1912	Joined anti-Qing army in Hunan
1919	Worked as a librarian at Beijing University
1921	Founder member of the CCP
1927–34	Created the Jiangxi soviet
1934–5	Led the Long March
1935–45	Created the Yanan soviet
1945–9	Led the CCP to victory in the civil war
1949	Founded the People's Republic of China

Background

A natural dialectician, who believed in violence, Mao developed the conviction that if China was to be regenerated it would have to undergo a profound social and political revolution. In 1921, he became a founder member of the CCP and over the next few years helped to organise the GMD–CCP United Front against the warlords. Then, to avoid being destroyed by Chiang Kai-shek, Mao fled to Jiangxi where he established the first Chinese soviet. He frequently rejected the orders from Moscow which instructed the CCP to base its activities in the towns rather than the countryside.

Leader of CCP

In 1934, facing extermination by surrounding GMD forces, the Jiangxi Communists undertook the legendary Long March. It was during the year-long march that Mao began to assert his authority over the CCP, an authority that he then ruthlessly consolidated at Yanan, where the Communists established their main base between 1935 and 1945. While at Yanan, Mao developed his theories of revolution based on the peasantry as the major dynamic of revolutionary change in China. Mao's Communists gained a not-entirely deserved reputation for being foremost in resisting the Japanese who occupied China between 1931 and 1945.

Civil war victor

With the surrender of Japan at the end of the Second World War in 1945, the GMD–CCP civil war that had lasted intermittently since 1927 was renewed. A four-year struggle ended with the complete victory of the Communists. Chiang's GMD was driven from the Chinese mainland to the island of Taiwan. In October 1949, Mao triumphantly declared that a new Communist society had come into being: the People's Republic of China (PRC). Mao was destined to rule this new nation for the next quarter of a century until his death in 1976.

Mao's ideological dominance

Mao defined the revolution he was leading not as a class movement but as a national one. Faced with the Japanese occupation of China after 1937 (see page 17), Mao declared the aim of his party to be 'long-term co-operation with all those classes, strata, political groups and individuals who were willing to fight Japan to the end'. He appealed to all Chinese of goodwill to unite against the enemies of the nation.

Helped by Yanan's geographical distance from Soviet influence, Mao was able to dominate the urban-orientated members of the CCP and bring the party to accept his line of thinking. He was acting very much in the Chinese tradition of taking from a foreign ideology those elements considered to be of practical value for China. He made Marxism fit the Chinese situation, not the Chinese situation fit Marxism. For some years he had to contend with opposition from within the party over his reshaping of revolutionary Marxism, but by outmanoeuvring and, where necessary, removing opponents he was able to establish an unmatched authority and so impose his ideas.

Mao's peasant policy

Mao gave practical form to his concept of revolution by sending out Red Army units from Yanan to occupy neighbouring regions. The method was for the troops, having occupied a particular area, to round up the landowners, who were then driven out or shot. That done, the land was immediately reallocated to the peasants, who were invited to co-operate in reorganising the village or region into a soviet. The hope was that such treatment would persuade the local people to become CCP supporters.

Mao urged the soldiers who did the liberating to regard themselves as ambassadors carrying the Communist message to the peasants. Until the Yanan period, Chinese armies by tradition had invariably terrorised local populations. The imperial and warlord forces had ravaged and plundered. But the Red Army was instructed to behave differently. Its duty was to aid and comfort the people. Mao laid down a code of conduct for his troops (see Source B for an extract).

SOURCE B

? What message is being conveyed to the troops in Source B?

From Mao's instructions to the Red Army, 1937, quoted in Anne Freemantle, editor, *Mao Tse-tung: An Anthology of His Writings*, Mentor Books, 1962, p. xxxiii.

Be courteous and help out when you can.

Return all borrowed articles.

Replace all damaged articles.

Be honest in all transactions with the peasants.

Pay for all articles purchased.

Be sanitary and establish latrines at a distance from people's houses.

Don't take liberties with women.

Don't kill prisoners of war.

KEY TERMS

Liberated The CCP's term for the areas brought under its military and political control.

Usury Charging exorbitant interest on money loans.

Mao's instructions provided a simple guide which, when followed, endeared the Red Army to many in the rural population. To win further supporters from the peasants in the **liberated** areas, the Red Army introduced a number of schemes, including:

● the creation of local peasant associations, which were invited to work with the CCP in improving their own conditions
● a programme for ending **usury**, which had so often blighted the lives of the peasants
● the introduction of literacy and education programmes
● the provision of basic medical services.

This evident sensitivity to the wants of the peasants was the most popular of the CCP's land policies and played its part in the growth of the party from 40,000 in 1937 to one million by 1945. It was from this expanding membership that the volunteers for the Red Army came. However, it was not all harmony, there was a darker side to Communist land policy.

Repressive land policies

Mao was certainly prepared to be moderate at times, but all the moves that the CCP made under him had the essential purpose of strengthening Communist control. The removal of the landlords in the areas where the Red Army held sway was often a brutal process. Moreover, despite its feeling for the peasants and its genuine popularity with many of them, the Yanan regime was fiercely authoritarian. In the liberated areas, villages that would not conform to the demands of the CCP's land programme were subject to harsh penalties such as having all their crops and livestock confiscated and ruinous taxes imposed on them.

What the CCP's occupation of 'liberated areas' actually entailed was described in 1937 by **Edgar Snow**, who travelled with the Red Army.

SOURCE C

From Edgar Snow, *Red Star Over China*, Penguin, 1972, p. 220, first published in 1937. Snow was an American admirer of Mao and lived with the Communists in Yanan. In his book, Snow described what he witnessed.

While theoretically the soviet was a 'workers and peasants' government, in actual practice the whole constituency was overwhelmingly peasant in character. Various committees were established under each of the district soviets. An all-powerful revolutionary committee was elected in a mass meeting shortly after the occupation of a district by the Red Army. Under the district soviet, and appointed by it, were committees for education, co-operatives, military training, political training, land, public health, partisan training, revolutionary defence, enlargement of the Red Army, agrarian mutual aid, Red Army land tilling, and others.

The work of all these organizations and their various committees was co-ordinated by the Central Soviet Government, the Communist Party, and the Red Army. The aim of soviet organization obviously was to make every man, woman, or child a member of something, with definite work assigned to him to perform.

KEY FIGURE

Edgar Snow (1905–72)
A US Communist, who became a confidant of Mao. Although his writings are now sometimes criticised for having been too pro-Mao in their bias, they helped greatly in the West's gaining of an understanding of Chinese communism.

How controlling of the local population were the CCP methods as described in Source C?

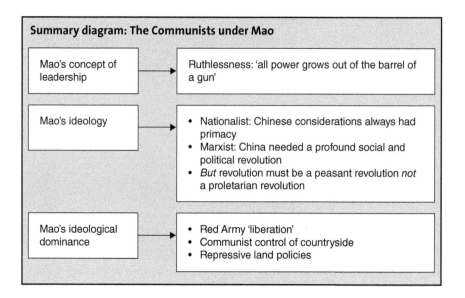

Summary diagram: The Communists under Mao

| Mao's concept of leadership | → | Ruthlessness: 'all power grows out of the barrel of a gun' |

| Mao's ideology | → | • Nationalist: Chinese considerations always had primacy
• Marxist: China needed a profound social and political revolution
• *But* revolution must be a peasant revolution *not* a proletarian revolution |

| Mao's ideological dominance | → | • Red Army 'liberation'
• Communist control of countryside
• Repressive land policies |

(3) # The Guomindang under Chiang

▶ *What strategy and principles did Chiang Kai-shek adopt in his leadership of the GMD?*

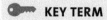 **KEY TERM**

Whampoa Military Academy A military base in Guangzhou dedicated to the training of GMD army recruits.

Such was the violence and lawlessness of warlord China that a party needed an army if it was to survive. That was why Sun Yat-sen, as well as developing his party's political ideas, devoted his attention to the construction in 1924 of the **Whampoa Military Academy**. This proved of major significance since from that point on, the GMD became essentially a military organisation. All the party's leading figures, most notably Sun's successor, Chiang Kai-shek (Jiang Jieshi), were products of the academy, branches of which were later established in other Nationalist strongholds, such as Nanjing and Chengdu.

Chiang Kai-shek had fought his way to the leadership of the GMD in a power struggle that followed the death of Sun Yat-sen in 1925. Before this, Chiang had gone to the USSR in the early 1920s to receive revolutionary training, but his experiences there, rather than drawing him to Marxism, did the opposite. He returned to China with an abiding detestation of communism. This became the motif of his political career. He remained convinced that China could not progress towards true modernity unless it first destroyed Mao's Communists.

Chiang's life was dominated by military considerations. He thought of politics in militaristic terms. At its starkest, this meant that he approached issues not by discussion and concession but by destroying opposition. In this respect he was very similar to his great adversary Mao, who thought in terms of dialectical struggle.

Chiang Kai-shek's ideology

The defeat of the warlords by the United Front and the near destruction of the Communists in the White Terror appeared to give Chiang Kai-shek the freedom to shape the new China according to the GMD's policies. From Nanjing, which in 1928 officially replaced Beijing as China's capital, Chiang planned to build Nationalist China on the basis of the Three People's Principles, first enunciated by Sun Yat-sen.

There is no doubt that Chiang was sincere in this, but, as he saw it, China's instability as it struggled to adopt modern ways did not permit him to introduce democracy immediately. There were too many difficulties in the way. That is why he turned to Sun Yat-sen's definition as a guide. Sun had taught that the circumstances in China meant that the Three People's Principles (see box) could not be put into effect until China had gone through three stages of development:

- A preliminary stage which would witness the overthrow by the Nationalist armies of China's internal and external enemies.
- An intermediate stage of GMD dominance during which the people would be educated in political knowledge and values.
- A final stage in which the now enlightened people would play their part in turning China into a full democracy.

Chiang claimed that the preliminary stage of development had been achieved by the defeat of the warlords. China was now at the second stage, which required that the GMD take on the role of government and teacher and instruct the Chinese people in political understanding. What this meant in reality was that Chiang's Nationalist government claimed the right to govern until such time as it considered China ready for democracy. It provided a justification for authoritarian control by Chiang and the GMD. A symbol of this was the dismantling of the remnants of the republican regime in Beijing, which was renamed **Beiping** to indicate that authority had passed south to Nanjing.

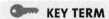 **KEY TERM**

Beiping Meaning 'northern peace' to distinguish it from Beijing, which meant 'northern capital'.

The Three People's Principles

National Sovereignty

The re-establishment of China's lost sense of national pride by ridding it of the remnants of foreign control and restoring its position as a sovereign state.

Democracy

Not individual freedom, as in the Western sense, but collective freedom of the people to build the nation. 'Personal freedom should never be too excessive. In fact, in order to win national freedom, we should not hesitate to sacrifice our personal freedom.'

People's welfare

The adoption of a form of socialism in order to end the poverty of the Chinese people. Private property should be limited and government-owned enterprises encouraged. 'We should have the political power to protect our native industry so that it will not be encroached upon by foreign powers, enchained by foreign powers.'

Chiang Kai-shek

1883	Born to a middle-class family
1906	Entered military academy
1912–18	Began developing contacts with Shanghai's underworld
1918	Joined Sun Yat-sen at Guangzhou
1925	Become GMD leader
1927	Launched the White Terror
1928–34	Head of the Nanjing government
1936	Kidnapped at Xian and obliged to re-form the United Front
1937–45	Led the struggle against Japan
1945–9	Defeated by the Communists in the civil war
1949	Fled to Taiwan

Emergence

Born into a well-to-do family, Chiang was a rebellious student who became quickly attracted to revolutionary ideas. Trained as a soldier, he retained a military attitude to politics, believing that compromise was necessary only when one could not enforce one's will. His gangster links compromised the party's claim to moral leadership. His desire for reform was sincere but he believed China's people needed to be politically controlled if China was to progress. He returned from training in Moscow with a deep distaste for communism and, after seizing the leadership of the GMD in 1925, devoted himself to destroying the CCP. However, the survival of the Communists meant that he was never in full control of China, despite his internationally recognised claim that the GMD was the rightful government of China.

Record

In an obvious sense, Chiang Kai-shek's record before 1949 was one of failure. He had failed to crush the Communists and, having been the dominant force in China for over a decade, he had then lost the civil war and had been forced to escape to Taiwan. Yet, prior to his defeat in 1949, Chiang had triumphed over the Japanese, and been acknowledged as a world statesman. In the face of huge problems he had begun the process of modernising China and freeing it from foreign domination. Against that has to be set the argument that he was essentially a ruthless warlord, who ran a corrupt government in league with gangsters and was reliant on foreign capital. Chiang's constant willingness to compromise his principles meant that the conditions of the Chinese people deteriorated rather than improved. He had failed to meet any of the high expectations with which he and the GMD had come to power.

Chiang's leadership

Of considerable value to Chiang in attempting to exercise personal control over the GMD was the fact that the party had been structured along Leninist lines. This was a result of the Comintern's having had a major influence on the development of the party in its early days. The Comintern believed that the GMD met the criteria of a bourgeois revolutionary party playing its role in the dialectical process. That was why it had urged the CCP to join forces with the Nationalists and work towards a bourgeois revolution, which China had to go through before it could move to the proletarian stage. Comintern agents in 1924 had drafted a new GMD constitution that was clearly Leninist in character. The key element was the insistence that the party should operate on the principle of **democratic centralism**. Chiang found this a convenient justification for demanding conformity from the party. It has to be added that although the GMD and CCP ran on the same leadership principle, Chiang never attained the same degree of authority over his party that Mao did over his.

 KEY TERM

Democratic centralism
The principle, originally introduced by Lenin in Soviet Russia, that in a truly revolutionary party the members owed absolute loyalty and obedience to the leaders.

Chiang's economic and social policies

In keeping with his assumption that the Nationalists had the right to govern without challenge, Chiang introduced a number of reforms from the top. These included the following:

- China's civil service was modernised by the creation of special administrative departments and training colleges.
- Measures to improve the quality and availability of education were implemented.
- Chinese banks were brought under the central control of the Bank of China.
- The Shanghai stock exchange became an international financial market.
- A national resources commission was set up to develop Chinese industry and negotiate foreign trade deals.
- Schemes were adopted to improve urban transport and communication. Modern buses and trams appeared in major cities, and railways and airlines spread across China.
- Government subsidies were provided to help the Chinese film industry, based mainly in Shanghai, which became internationally renowned.
- Similar government support enabled fashion houses in Shanghai to compete with Paris and Milan.

One of Chiang's aims was to reassert some degree of control over the **foreign concessions** whose presence had angered Chinese revolutionaries for decades. Efforts were made to restructure the legal system within the concessions so that Chinese law played a more central role. Foreign commercial companies were required to pay higher export and import duties. However, because of the constant presence of foreign troops, Chiang was not in a position to attempt the physical removal of foreigners.

Chiang was also handicapped by the hard truth that many Chinese people depended for their livelihoods on being employed in the diplomatic offices and commercial agencies within the concession areas. Such reliance on foreigners, particularly in financial matters, was one of the great problems that prevented the Nanjing government from achieving the Chinese independence that the Three People's Principles advocated. Chiang's dislike of the foreign presence in China was real enough but he had to be circumspect in the way he dealt with the issue. His various schemes for boosting China's economic and financial standing indicated that he needed foreign support. This became increasingly so after the Japanese threat to China began to grow following the occupation of Manchuria in 1931 (see page 17).

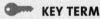

KEY TERM

Foreign concessions
International settlements within Chinese cities in which foreign laws operated and China had no authority; dating from the intrusion of the powers into Chinese affairs in the nineteenth century, they were in effect foreign mini-states.

German influence in Nationalist China

China's foreign ties were also very evident in relation to Chiang's development of the Nationalist army and police forces. In planning to modernise his army,

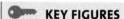
Chiang formed close links with the **Third Reich**, which sent military advisers to train the Nationalists' armies.

A further striking example of German influence was the organisation of Chiang's secret police, the **Blue Shirts**, on similar lines to the *Gestapo*. It was such associations that led to the suggestion that Chiang Kai-shek's regime merited the description **fascist**, since in its authoritarianism, nationalist ideology and policing methods it paralleled the **right-wing governments** of 1930s' Europe. A central figure in the development of the Blue Shirts was **Dai Li,** whose fearsome leadership of the GMD's secret police earned him the nickname the 'Chinese **Himmler**'.

Dai Li built up the innocuous sounding Investigation and Statistical Bureau (ISB) into a highly effective and feared security organisation. By the mid-1930s, Dai had some 1800 agents working for him. Operating outside the law, they were free to arrest and hold suspects indefinitely without having to bring charges against them. They regularly used torture to extract information concerning the names and whereabouts of Communist sympathisers. CCP members were Dai Li's main targets but his agents also used intimidation and threats to prevent even moderate criticism of the Nationalist regime being voiced in the press.

The New Life Movement

Despite his Nationalist regime's preoccupation with economic and military affairs and state security, Chiang Kai-shek always spoke in terms of his party and government leading a moral revolution. In this period there were two main themes in his speeches and writings:

- the need for the Chinese people to unite and crush the Communists
- the duty of the Chinese people to elevate the ethical standards of their country by returning to **Confucian values** of social harmony and by living lives of moral integrity.

Chiang appealed to the people to expose and fight public corruption and called on youth organisations, such as the Boy Scouts and the **YMCA**, to set an example in teaching the young to behave responsibly, especially in sexual matters. To inculcate a sense of shared Nationalist values, he encouraged couples to include a pledge of loyalty to the GMD in their marriage vows. This programme of moral improvement was formalised in 1934 with Chiang's launching of the New Life Movement, intended as a rejection of both communism and Western capitalism and a reassertion of Confucian values. Chiang's wife, **Soong Meiling**, regarded the New Life Movement, which she defined as 'a direct attempt to compete with the Communist platform of economic and social reform, substituting a retreat to Confucius for an advance to Marx', as being 'the only path for the salvation of the country'.

The weakness of the New Life Movement

For all the moral uplift that Chiang and his wife sought to encourage among the people, the reality was that his government had compromised itself from the first by its need to deal with some of the most disreputable elements in Chinese society. This was apparent, for example, in its attempts to control the use of drugs. Chiang's sincere aim was to bring the opium trade under state control, and provide treatment for addicts. But the GMD had received considerable illicit funding from gangster organisations, such as the **Green Gang**. The Nationalists were reluctant to forgo such income. It was also the case that Chiang had received crucial assistance from the drug-dealing underworld in his campaigns against the Communists; he owed the gangs a large favour.

The same contradictions applied to Chiang's attempt to follow a socialist path and end China's reliance on capitalism. His need for inward foreign investment and the heavy costs of his military campaigns meant he could never genuinely abandon capitalism. Despite his professed adherence to the party's policy of ending China's dependence on foreign money, Chiang could not discontinue his association with Western commercial and financial interests. The character of the GMD party in government was determined by the manner in which it acquired its finance.

The GMD's basic problems in government

The underlying political weakness of the GMD was that the social composition of its membership meant that it could never become a mass party. The GMD claimed that its revolutionary purpose was to serve the Chinese population as a whole by implementing the Three People's Principles, but in reality it became the representative of particular minority interests. Chiang Kai-shek's GMD party was largely drawn from the merchants and businessmen who operated in the ports and cities. Such men had little sympathy for the rural peasants, which meant they were no more interested in improving conditions in the countryside than they were in paying for welfare in the urban areas.

Here lay the GMD's crippling limitation as a political party. China's most pressing problem was the poverty of its people. In the years 1934–5 another of China's recurrent famines caused the death of 30 million people. Yet, notwithstanding the Nationalists' commitment to honouring the third of Sun Yat-sen's principles – the people's welfare – no sustained attempt was made to tackle the issue. There was little in the Nationalists' approach to government that allowed it to make a genuine effort to introduce the land reforms they had originally promised. Among the measures that Chiang's government had failed to implement were the following:

- ending of landlord control and exploitation of the peasants
- extension of property rights to the peasants

 **KEY TERM**

Green Gang Shanghai racketeers who dealt mainly in prostitution and drug running and who were notorious for bribing police and government officials to co-operate.

- protection of the peasants against excessive rents
- guarantee of fair prices to the peasants for their produce.

At no time did Chiang's government control more than one-third of China or two-thirds of its population. It is true that these were quite substantial proportions in themselves, but, given the strength of Chinese regionalism and the distribution of the population, the authority exercised by the GMD was far from complete. Resistance from local ruling factions was a major obstacle, preventing the Nanjing government from carrying out its declared policies of land reform. Moreover, the warlords still held sway in a number of provinces. The limitation this placed on GMD control was increased after 1937 when Japan occupied large tracts of territory (see page 17), a humiliating reminder of how far China was from being an independent nation.

The Nationalist record

Nationalist supporters could claim that in its first period of government the GMD under Chiang Kai-shek had:

- overthrown the warlords
- gained international recognition
- taken steps towards the creation of workable governmental and legal systems.

Yet while these were not insignificant achievements, it could be argued that they were far outweighed by failures:

- The Nationalist government had proved unable to tackle China's most urgent social and economic problems.
- The GMD had betrayed its own sense of moral purpose by aligning with some of the worst elements of the Chinese underworld.
- The GMD had turned to coercion and authoritarianism in order to consolidate its power.
- The Nationalists had been powerless to prevent or alleviate the suffering of the victims of widespread famine.
- Chiang's preoccupation with crushing his Communist opponents had diverted vital energies away from the structuring of an ordered civil society.
- Such progress as had been made towards removing foreign dominance from China had been undermined by the Japanese occupation of China that began in 1931.

Summary diagram: The Guomindang under Chiang

GMD aims
- To implement GMD rule as the intermediate stage of China's modernisation
- To fulfil the Three People's Principles
- To achieve moral regeneration of Chinese people
- To reassert Chinese independence

GMD methods
- Suppression of opposition
- Reforms: legal, economic, administrative, diplomatic and military
- The New Life Movement

GMD's record
- Important internal reforms
- International recognition

But

Gap between aspiration and achievement
- New Life Movement undermined by GMD's alliance with gangsterism
- Reliance on foreign money and employment prevented true independence
- Land policies ineffectual – peasants worse off
- Chiang's preoccupation with crushing the Reds diverted resources from social and economic reforms

---

 # The Sino-Japanese war

▶ *Why did the Chinese suffer so severely at the hands of the Japanese?*

▶ *Why was the Second United Front not able to offer effective resistance to the Japanese?*

The Japanese had occupied Manchuria in 1931. Over the next six years they used it as a base for extending their control over many other Chinese areas. In 1937, the Japanese turned their occupation into a full-scale war that was to last until 1945.

The Sino-Japanese war can be divided into two distinct phases:

- 1937–41. During this first phase, Japan made rapid advances down the eastern seaboard (see the map on page 19), to which the Chinese responded with a mixture of courageous resistance, retreat and appeasement.
- 1941–5. The second phase saw the Chinese struggle become part of the Second World War, in which China as an ally of the USA recovered to gain victory over the Japanese.

The Marco Polo Bridge incident

On 7 July 1937, a relatively minor clash between Chinese and Japanese troops occurred at the **Marco Polo Bridge** near Beijing. The confrontation had been deliberately planned by the Japanese to create trouble. Using the clash as a pretext, Japan demanded that, in order to prevent further trouble, the GMD

 **KEY TERM**

Marco Polo Bridge An important crossing point, 16 km (10 miles) outside Beijing.

government yield even greater authority to the occupying forces in China. On this occasion, Chiang Kai-shek refused to make concessions. He declared to the Chinese people that their country was now in a state of total war against Japan. 'If we allow one inch more of our territory to be lost, we shall be guilty of an unpardonable crime against our race.'

The second United Front

Chiang's appeal for national unity may be regarded as the start of the second United Front between the CCP and GMD, a commitment by both parties to suspend their differences and ally against the Japanese aggressors. In doing this, they were activating an agreement they had made seven months earlier following an extraordinary event known as the Xian incident.

The Xian incident

Undoubted patriot though he was, Chiang's response to Japan's occupation of parts of China between 1931 and 1936 had been unambitious. He believed that China was too large a country for the Japanese to occupy without exhausting themselves; a protracted occupation would mean war and the eventual defeat of Japan. He defined his approach as **trading space to buy time**. However, the policy of avoiding direct conflict with the occupier proved uninspiring and his supporters frequently found it difficult to maintain their loyalty. In 1933, it took Chiang over a year to suppress a rising among his troops at Fujian who were reacting against his failure to confront the Japanese.

The culmination of this deep dissatisfaction with Chiang's strategy came in December 1936. During a visit to Xian in Shaanxi province, which, ironically, Chiang had undertaken in order to berate his forces for their slowness in crushing the CCP, he was seized by mutinous GMD troops and handed over to the Communists, whose chief representative at Xian was **Zhou Enlai**, Mao's closest colleague. Zhou offered to spare his prisoner's life if he would promise to end his persecution of the CCP and lead a genuine resistance against the Japanese. Finding himself in an impossible position, Chiang Kai-shek gave in; he agreed to the formation of the second GMD–CCP United Front, pledged to wage unceasing war against the Japanese aggressors.

Given the bitter relations between Chiang and the Communists, Chiang having been trying for a decade to annihilate them, it seems surprising that the CCP did not simply assassinate him. That they refrained from doing so was not clemency but a calculated risk; by allowing Chiang not merely to survive, but to remain as the recognised leader of China, the CCP had won a major propaganda victory. It had shown remarkable restraint in forgoing party advantage for the sake of the national struggle. In return, Chiang made a formal commitment to:

- cease all attempts to suppress the CCP
- recognise the CCP as a legitimate party
- lead a new United Front against the Japanese invader.

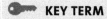

KEY TERM

Trading space to buy time Giving ground to the Japanese which would both overstretch their resources and allow the Chinese the opportunity to build up their own strength.

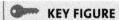

KEY FIGURE

Zhou Enlai (1898–1976)

A committed Mao loyalist since the 1920s, he was second only to Mao in his importance as a Communist revolutionary; after 1949, he became an outstanding minister and foreign statesman.

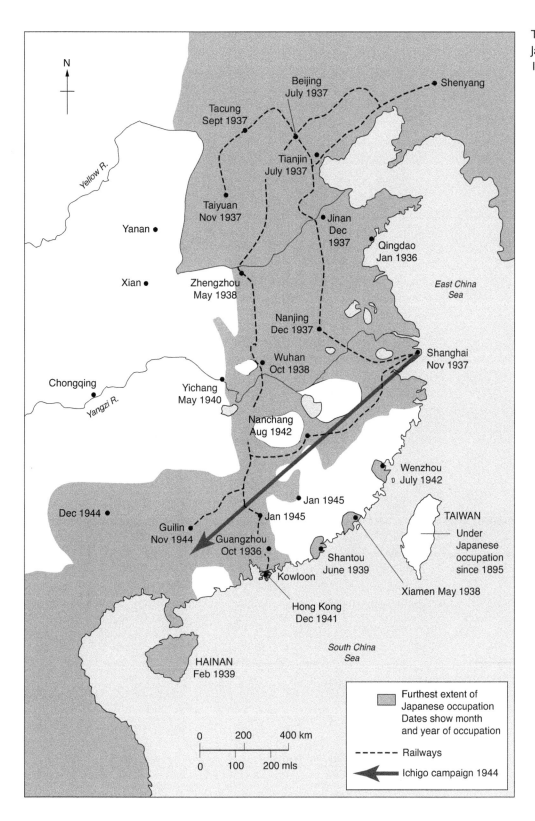

The Sino-Japanese war 1937–45.

The Communists could now claim that it was they who were the genuine nationalists whose prime motivation was their love of China as expressed in their willingness to fight under Chiang's leadership. At the same time, they had undermined the GMD's claim to be the sole representative of the nation. Chiang for his part did not feel bound by his Xian promises and frequently went back on his word by renewing his attacks on the Communists. Throughout the ensuing eight years of the Sino-Japanese war, Chiang's principal aim remained the defeat of the CCP; victory over Japan was a means to that end.

Failure of the United Front

The complex turn of events that led to the formation of a second United Front meant that from the beginning it was a marriage of convenience, never a genuine alliance. The CCP and GMD forces invariably fought as separate armies and, although they did liaise on occasion, their mutual distrust meant that they rarely acted as a combined force. Outweighed by Japanese military strength, which made them reluctant to risk large-scale battles, the Nationalist–Communist allies engaged mainly in sniping and **guerrilla warfare** tactics.

Given the inability of the United Front to mount sustained resistance it was not surprising that matters went badly for China in the early stage of the war. By 1938, Beijing, Shanghai, Guangzhou and Nanjing had all fallen to Japan, disasters which obliged the GMD government to withdraw their capital westwards along the Yangzi River to Chongqing (see the map on page 19).

The Hundred Regiments Offensive of 1940

A major exception to China's poor military showing was the Hundred Regiments Offensive of 1940. It was undertaken by Mao's Communists to convince the GMD and the Chinese people of the dedication of the CCP to the anti-Japanese war. It followed a period of relative quiet when the Japanese, having seized a large number of provinces and cities by 1938, slowed their advance and concentrated on consolidating the gains already made. In August 1940, under the overall command of **Peng Dehuai**, the Communist forces, numbering 400,000 troops in over 100 regiments, undertook a series of attacks on Japanese positions in northern and central China. For two months the Communists had considerable success. A number of Japanese garrisons were overrun and over 950 km (600 miles) of railway lines were destroyed along with extensive damage to roads, bridges and canals.

Communist defeat

Under the slogan of 'Kill all, Burn all, Loot all', Japanese forces responded with a terror campaign against the population in the areas which had supported Communists' attacks. Murder, mutilation and rape were the order of the day. Whole villages were systematically destroyed. By December 1940, the Japanese counteroffensive had regained the territory lost earlier. Over 100,000 Communists, a quarter of the force, were killed.

KEY TERM

Guerrilla warfare A hit-and-run style of fighting, avoiding pitched battles and using local knowledge of people and terrain to harass the enemy.

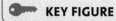

KEY FIGURE

Peng Dehuai (1898–1974)

One of the Chinese army's ablest commanders and one of the few Communists with the courage to criticise Mao openly. Mao tolerated him because of his abilities as a soldier.

Recriminations followed within the CCP. Mao dismissed Peng Dehuai, not simply for being defeated by the Japanese but for causing the CCP to lose reputation among the Chinese people. What had also angered Mao was that the Hundred Regiments Campaign had revealed to Chiang Kai-shek the true size and disposition of the **PLA**'s forces. It was certainly the case that Chiang exploited the defeat of the Communists to renew his attack on them. In a set of ambushes and surprise raids in January 1941, the Nationalist forces inflicted 4000 casualties on the retreating PLA. It was not difficult to see that Chiang regarded the Communists as a greater enemy than the Japanese. He was making a fiction of the supposed GMD–CCP alliance against the occupier.

Character of the war: Japanese brutality

The grimmest aspect of the Sino-Japanese war was the savagery with which the occupiers treated the Chinese people. Easy military successes early in the war confirmed the deeply held conviction of the Japanese that they were a **superior race**, entitled to treat those they defeated with contempt. One of the commanders of the first Japanese invasion force to arrive in China in 1937, Sakai Ryu, declared: 'The Chinese people are bacteria infesting world civilization.' Lieutenant Ryukichi of the Imperial Japanese Army remarked to a foreign correspondent, 'you and I have diametrically different views of the Chinese. You may be dealing with them as human beings, but I regard them as swine. We can do anything to such creatures.'

SOURCE D

The aftermath of a Japanese air raid on Shanghai in 1937. Although the picture appears to have been composed by the photographer, there is little doubt that what became an iconic image represented the reality of the Japanese bombardments of Chinese cities.

KEY TERMS

PLA The People's Liberation Army, formerly the Red Army.

Superior race An equivalent Japanese notion to the Nazi concept of the Germans as the master race.

What is there about the photo in Source D that suggests it was posed?

The rape of Nanjing 1937

It was the Japanese contempt for the Chinese that resulted in one of the worst atrocities in twentieth-century warfare: the rape of Nanjing. In December 1937, after spirited resistance and the refusal of its defenders to surrender, the city eventually fell to the Japanese attackers. Responding to the specific instruction of their commander, Asaka Yasuhiko, 'to kill all captives', the Japanese soldiers engaged in a sustained month-long programme of murder and terror. The details tell a fearful story:

- 300,000 Chinese people were slaughtered during the four-week period.
- The ways of killing included: shooting, bayoneting, beheading, burying alive, soaking in petrol and setting on fire, and suspending on meat hooks.
- 20,000 girls and women were serially raped regardless of their age. Many were so abused that they died from the rape itself or the mutilations that were inflicted afterwards; those who did not die were bayoneted to death.
- A Japanese private later confessed, 'We sent out coal trucks to the city streets and villages to seize a lot of women. And then each of them was allocated to fifteen to twenty soldiers for sexual intercourse and abuse.'
- Half the city was burned to ashes.

SOURCE E

? Why should the Japanese government have wished to prevent actions such as those shown in Source E from becoming known in Japan?

A souvenir photo taken by a Japanese soldier in Nanjing in December 1937, showing the burying alive of bound Chinese prisoners.

Chinese collaboration with the Japanese

As Japan gained ground in China, it sought to consolidate its military hold by enlisting Chinese leaders who were willing to co-operate in the setting up of nominally independent areas. In an effort to wreck the United Front, Japan, which saw the Communists as the major enemy, offered to recognise Chiang Kai-shek as the national spokesman for China if he would abandon his alliance with the CCP. Chiang refused. While it is true that Chiang's ultimate objective was the defeat of the Communists, he was not willing to abandon his claim to the leadership of China by throwing in his lot with the Japanese.

However, there were lesser public figures who were prepared to respond to the Japanese approaches. One such was **Wang Jingwei**, a former colleague of Chiang. Judging that China could not win the war, Wang agreed in 1940 to become the head of what the Japanese called the 'New Government of China'. From Nanjing, the captured former capital, Wang denounced Chiang and his Nationalist government as traitors to the true interests of China. Wang's rival government survived for four years until his death in 1944, but it was never able to match either the GMD at Chongqing or the CCP at Yanan as expressions of Chinese aspirations. Without the backing of the occupying forces, Wang's government was powerless.

China and Japan at war 1941–5

On 7 December 1941, Japanese air forces attacked the US naval base at Pearl Harbor in Hawaii with the aim of destroying the US Pacific fleet and forcing the Americans to settle on Japanese terms. It proved a fateful miscalculation. Rather than make peace, the Americans committed themselves to total war against Japan. The importance for China of Japan's attack on the USA in 1941 was profound. What had been a Sino-Japanese conflict now became a theatre of the much larger world war. From that time on:

- China was seen by the Allies as a chief means of defeating Japan. It was supplied with vast resources in an Allied effort to turn it into a base of operations.
- By 1945 the USA had invested over $1 billion dollars in China.
- The USA's entry gave a tremendous political, as well as military, boost to Chiang Kai-shek as China's leader.

The USA's entry into the war did not bring immediate relief to China, despite the influx after 1941 of US money and supplies. Indeed, Japanese pressure increased. Chiang and the GMD remained reluctant to face the Japanese head on. There were few pitched battles between Chinese and Japanese forces. To avoid being overwhelmed by the superior Japanese armies, the Chinese necessarily fought a guerrilla war. This could not prevent the cities and urban areas suffering severely from Japanese air strikes. It was in the GMD-held areas in central and southern China that the Japanese found the easiest targets to bomb. Chongqing,

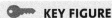

KEY FIGURE

Wang Jingwei (1883–1944)
A former left-wing GMD member, whose collaboration with the Japanese led to his being reviled by both the Nationalists and Communists.

for example, suffered prolonged periods of aerial attack that made it the most heavily bombed city in twentieth-century warfare.

Continued GMD–CCP rivalry

The friction between the supposed defenders of China worsened the situation. The term United Front had become a misnomer. By 1940, fighting between the Nationalists and Communists had broken out again. The CCP had gained control of nineteen 'liberated' areas in northern China and resisted all the efforts of the GMD to retake them. Thus, between 1940 and 1945 there were two wars going on in China: the national war of resistance against the Japanese and the continuing CCP–GMD civil war.

The war's end

In 1944, the Japanese unleashed the **Ichigo campaign** (see the map on page 19), their largest offensive undertaken in China. Chiang's armies were unable to stem the advance, which carried the Japanese deep into southern China. What eventually saved the GMD forces was not the quality of their resistance but the curtailing of Japan's war effort in China as the Japanese mainland fell under increased Allied attack from 1944 onwards. The climax came with the atomic bombing of Japan by the USA in August 1945; within a few days the Japanese had surrendered. The war's sudden ending dramatically changed the internal situation in China, leaving problems that could not be resolved except by civil war.

> **KEY TERM**
>
> **Ichigo campaign**
> A sweeping Japanese movement from April to December 1944 that brushed aside Chiang's forces.

Summary diagram: The Sino-Japanese war

Onset
- Marco Polo Bridge incident
- The pretext for the extension of the Japanese occupation
- Chinese resistance 1937–45 created the Sino-Japanese war

Japanese brutality: the outstanding feature of the war. Why?
- Tradition of deep Sino-Japanese animosity
- Japanese notion of Chinese racial inferiority
- Contempt for prisoners

The rape of Nanjing 1937
- The most graphic example of deliberate brutality towards civilians

GMD–CCP officially re-formed the United Front; uneasy alliance but produced some resistance to Japanese
- The Hundred Regiments Offensive 1940, abortive Communist attack on Japanese
- Fearsome Japanese response

Japanese assisted in their occupation by collaborators
- Wang Jingwei's Japanese-backed 'New Government of China' 1940–4

Pearl Harbor changed the character of the war
- The USA now an ally of China
- Chiang elevated to international status

5 # Mao's 'rectification of conduct' campaign 1942–4

▶ *What methods did Mao use to achieve and enforce his leadership and authority?*

For all its claims to be a movement of liberation, the brand of communism that Mao developed at Yanan was fundamentally oppressive. Discipline and obedience were required of all those living under it. In one sense this was understandable, given that the regime was engaged in a constant fight for survival against both the Japanese and the GMD. But it went deeper than that. Mao had begun to manifest a belief that was to become a dominant feature of his outlook – the notion of **revolutionary correctness**.

Mao held that, unless the party maintained a constant struggle against error, the revolution would be betrayed from within. For Mao, an obvious danger was that those responsible for running the party would become a bureaucratic, self-justifying élite. To fight this tendency, in 1942 he launched a 'rectification of conduct' campaign. Party members were to engage in public self-criticism. To assist them in their search for revolutionary truth they were obliged to study prescribed texts, among which Mao's own writings figured prominently. In Source F, Mao explained why all good party members should undertake self-criticism.

SOURCE F

From Mao's talk at Yanan, 23 May 1942, in Anne Freemantle, editor, *Mao Tse-tung: An Anthology of His Writings*, Mentor Books, New York, 1962, p. 263.

One who has a truly good intention must take the effect into consideration by summing up experiences and studying methods, or in the case of creative work, the means of expression. One who has a truly good intention must criticize with the utmost candor his own shortcomings and mistakes in work, and make up his mind to correct them. That is why the Communists have adopted the method of self-criticism.

The chief organiser of the purge was Mao's head of security, **Kang Sheng**. He was a frightening figure who dressed totally in black and rode a jet-black horse. Kang, asserting that 70 per cent of the party were infected by **revisionist** ideas, made it his task to expose and punish them. In Mao's name, Kang ordered the arrest of some 1000 CCP members, many of whom were subsequently imprisoned and tortured. Peter Vladimirov, a Russian Comintern agent, described the prevailing system of thought-control that he observed at first hand in Yanan in (see Source G, page 26).

KEY TERMS

Revolutionary correctness The idea that Chinese communism (Maoism) was a body of political, social and economic truth which all CCP members had to accept and live by.

Revisionist Reactionary, anti-party thinking. Used by Maoists, similar to 'counter-revolutionary', to describe party members regarded as not fully committed to Mao's revolution.

According to Source F, what is Mao's justification for requiring party members to undergo self-criticism?

KEY FIGURE

Kang Sheng (1898–1975)

Trained in Moscow in interrogation techniques; he became Mao's feared security and intelligence chief.

According to the writer of Source G, what has driven party activists 'psychotic'?

SOURCE G

From *La Bureaucratie au Vietnam* by Pyotr Vladimirov, quoted in Michael Lynch, *Mao*, Routledge, London, 2004, p. 121. Vladimirov was a Russian Comintern agent and here he gives a hostile account of what he witnessed while living with the Communists in Yanan in the early 1940s.

Party discipline is based on stupidly rigid forms of criticism and self-criticism. The president of each cell decides who is to be criticised and for what reason. In general it is a Communist who is attacked each time. The accused has only one right: to repent his 'errors'. If he considers himself to be innocent or appears insufficiently repentant, the attacks are renewed. The cruel method of psychological coercion that Mao calls moral purification has created a stifling atmosphere inside the Party in Yanan. A not negligible number of Party activists in the region have committed suicide, have fled or have become psychotic. Under the protocol of criticism and self-criticism, the thoughts and aspirations and actions of everyone are on full view.

Vladimirov was not exaggerating the psychological effects of rectification. Sixty Communist Party officials committed suicide rather than undergo public humiliation. Mao did relent a little in the light of such grim news and lessened the severity of the campaign, but he was in no way apologetic about the need for the rectification process itself. He curtly dismissed suggestions that individual suffering should be allowed to modify party policy. In 1942, he wrote: 'Some comrades do not understand the Party's system of democratic centralism; they do not understand that the Party's interests are above personal interests.'

Notable victims of the rectification campaign were **Wang Shiwei** and **Ding Ling**. Wang was a brilliant young Communist writer who, in 1942, published an article heavily critical of members of the CCP who lived comfortable lives in Yanan while Red Army comrades were dying in the struggle against the Japanese and the GMD. For this, he was rounded on by those party officials, who felt that they had been implicitly accused. Mao, angered by Wang Shiwei's charge that he as leader was behaving improperly with pretty young women, backed the officials and chose to attack Wang as representing the **intellectual class** he despised.

Initially, a number of other writers came to Wang's defence. One of these was the feminist Ding Ling, who had joined the CCP only to be shocked by what she regarded as the party's hypocrisy in relation to the principle of female equality. The CCP claimed to treat women as equals, but her experience was that women in the party were in practice treated as inferiors. However, when Ding made her findings public, she was brought before a party gathering and accused of insulting the CCP. She broke under the pressure, withdrew her previous criticisms and also abandoned Wang Shiwei. Left friendless, Wang was then subjected to a **show trial** at which he was accused of 'anti-party thinking'. He resisted courageously, refusing to retract what he had written. His temerity

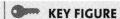

KEY FIGURE

Wang Shiwei (1906–47)
A believer in social justice, he was offended by the CCP's terror tactics.

Ding Ling (1904–86)
A prolific novelist, essayist and feminist writer.

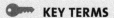

KEY TERMS

Intellectual class Those, according to Mao, who merely talked and theorised rather than acted.

Show trial A public hearing in which the accused, whose guilt is assumed, is paraded as an enemy of the people.

earned him a life sentence and eventual execution in 1947 on Mao's personal order. His body was chopped into small pieces and thrown down a well.

Wang Shiwei's disgrace had the intended effect. It terrified the CCP's officials. Between 1943 and 1944, leading party members came forward to engage in public self-criticism. It was an extraordinary spectacle. Expressing contrition for past mistakes, they pledged total loyalty to Mao Zedong and the party. Even Zhou Enlai admitted to having been dilatory in carrying out Mao's orders.

Consequences of the 'rectification of conduct' campaign

- Mao had rid himself of opposition and consolidated his position as leader.
- Mao had finally triumphed over the pro-Moscow wing of the party.
- Mao had begun to move towards **cult status** in Yanan.
- Chinese communism was now so closely identified with him personally that it had become Maoism.
- Mao was elected Chairman of the Central Committee of the CCP in 1943.
- By 1945, when the Japanese war came to an end, Mao was being regularly referred to as the **Great Helmsman**.

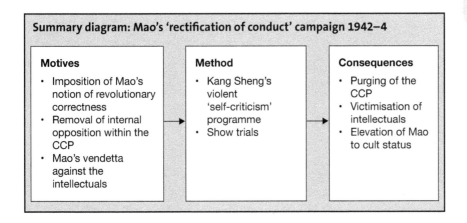

Summary diagram: Mao's 'rectification of conduct' campaign 1942–4

Motives	Method	Consequences
• Imposition of Mao's notion of revolutionary correctness • Removal of internal opposition within the CCP • Mao's vendetta against the intellectuals	• Kang Sheng's violent 'self-criticism' programme • Show trials	• Purging of the CCP • Victimisation of intellectuals • Elevation of Mao to cult status

6 The impact of the occupation

▶ *How were China's two conflicting parties affected by Japanese occupation?*

The Japanese occupation changed China's domestic politics in ways that the two contending parties, the Nationalists and the Communists, had not seen or planned for in 1937. This transformation became particularly marked after 1941 when the Sino-Japanese conflict transmuted from a regional Asian struggle into part of a world war.

KEY TERMS

Cult status A position that entitles the holder to a special veneration among the people and puts him beyond criticism.

Great Helmsman An adulatory reference to Mao's unmatchable skill in steering the ship of state.

Communist salvation

The most striking feature of the occupation was that it saved the Chinese Communists. Mao was well aware of what a close-run thing their survival had been and how much was owed to chance and to Japan. In 1972, he told the visiting Japanese prime minister, who had been expecting a frosty reception because of his country's war record in China, that, far from being ill-disposed towards Japan, he looked on it with gratitude since it had been the Japanese occupation of China that had diverted and weakened the GMD and thus inadvertently prevented the Communists from being destroyed. The presence of the Japanese spared the Communists the all-out assault that Chiang would have unleashed had he been free to do so.

The Communists were, of course, often under attack from both the Nationalists and the Japanese, but, desperate though their situation appeared at times, they not only survived in their base at Yanan, but by the end of the war in 1945 had established their control over nineteen other 'liberated' areas in northern China. The full period of the Japanese occupation from 1931 to 1945 had seen the CCP grow from a fringe political party on the verge of extinction to a force that vied with the Nationalists for authority and that was recognised by the international powers as a political movement that could not be ignored in any settlement of Chinese affairs.

Chiang and the USA

The first phase of the occupation did not go well for Chiang. The Japanese expansion seemed unstoppable and the Communists had survived. All that seemed to change in 1941. Chiang referred to 8 December 1941, the day the USA declared war on Japan, as the happiest day of his life. It is easy to see why. The Americans, anxious to use China principally as a means of defeating Japan, naturally turned to Chiang. As the leader of China, acknowledged as such even by the CCP under the Xian agreement (see page 18), he was the obvious person with whom to liaise. President Roosevelt now regarded Chiang as an important world figure.

Chiang Kai-shek proved a difficult ally after 1941. He frequently quarrelled with the American advisers and demanded that those he disagreed with be replaced. Not wishing to weaken the war effort, the USA tended to do as he asked, despite the charge made by many American observers that Chiang's perverse preoccupation with crushing the Communists was a principal cause of China's poor showing against the Japanese. A prominent critic was **General Stilwell**, the US chief of South-East Asia command.

What dismayed the Americans was that the GMD **conscript armies** too often lacked the will to fight and rarely gained the wholehearted support of the Chinese people whose protector they supposedly were. Indeed, a feature of the war was the unpopularity of the GMD armies among the Chinese peasantry,

KEY FIGURE

General Joseph ('Vinegar Joe') Stilwell (1883–1946)

His dislike of Chiang Kai-shek, whom he dismissed as 'the peanut', led him to emphasise the role of the Chinese Communists in opposing the Japanese.

KEY TERM

Conscript armies Unable to attract volunteers, the GMD became notorious for the brutality with which it rounded up peasants and forced them to become soldiers by fearsome discipline.

a product of the abusive treatment the peasants invariably received at the hands of the Nationalist troops and of the GMD government's harsh conscription policies. Reports reached US ears that the Communists were far more popular with the ordinary Chinese people and resisted the Japanese more resolutely.

The USA and the Chinese Communists

Arguably, the USA grasped the importance and strength of the Chinese Communists only after it was too late. In its eagerness to defeat Japan, the USA gave its support to Chiang and the GMD. Yet the interests of Chinese Communists and the Americans in China often coincided, the most obvious example being their joint determination to defeat Japan. Moreover, at that stage their ideological differences were not an insurmountable hurdle. During the Japanese occupation, the CCP deliberately played down its political aims; it dropped its call for a class war and emphasised that it was engaged in a national struggle against the Japanese aggressor. Mao asked the Americans to understand that his party members were 'agrarian reformers' rather than violent revolutionaries. However, any real chance of the USA switching its allegiance was stopped short by the sudden end of the war in August 1945.

The impact of the sudden ending of the war

The surrender of Japan in August 1945, directly following the nuclear devastation of Hiroshima and Nagasaki, was in one obvious sense a great Chinese victory. Japan had finally been defeated after fourteen years of struggle. But it had not come the way that Chiang had expected. For him, the war had ended too soon. His belief throughout had been that the fanatical Japanese resistance would eventually lead to two critical developments:

- The landing in China of huge US armies, which would roll up the Japanese in a large land operation.
- In the course of this, the Americans would overwhelm not only the Japanese but the Chinese Communists as well. This would leave Chiang both the victor over Japan and the master of China.

But events betrayed him. When the war abruptly ended in August 1945, the location of the Japanese within CCP-held areas in northern China meant that it was invariably Mao's forces to whom the Japanese formally surrendered. The events of August 1945 had thus destroyed Chiang Kai-shek's dream. He did not have the expected US troops at his disposal in China, which prevented him from crushing the Communists as he had planned. A further limitation on Chiang's claim to mastery of China was that **Soviet forces** had now occupied Manchuria, the USSR having declared war on Japan the day after the Nagasaki bombing.

CCP–GMD conflict over Japan's surrender

The Communists resisted the GMD's claim to the nineteen liberated areas, which during the occupation had become Communist-administered zones. Mao

KEY TERM

Soviet forces Stalin's armies had begun occupying Manchuria one day after the Nagasaki bombing.

Zedong ordered the Red Army to occupy the former Japanese-controlled regions, receive the formal surrenders of the Japanese and hold them as prisoners. Chiang's government at Chongqing, however, insisted that the Japanese should surrender only to representatives of the Nationalists. But the GMD could not enforce this demand since they had no troops in the Communist areas. Chiang, therefore, instructed the Japanese to continue to maintain order and discipline in their former regions until Nationalist forces arrived.

The Nationalists would have been unable to accomplish this had the USA not stepped in. Anxious to prevent Soviet forces in Manchuria from extending their control southwards, the Americans mounted a huge airlift of GMD forces to the liberated areas. **General MacArthur** declared that only Chiang Kai-shek's GMD had the right to receive Japan's surrender in China. The question now was whether the Communists would accept this. Although Mao condemned Chiang and the GMD as 'fascists', he announced that he was willing to make the necessary concession. Mao explained why to his followers: 'Without these concessions, we will not be able to shatter the GMD's plot for civil war, nor take the political initiative, nor gain the sympathy of the rest of the world ... nor gain legal status for our party.'

Mao knew that the recent **Soviet–GMD friendship treaty** meant that he was unlikely to receive support from the USSR should he openly challenge Chiang's US-backed claims over the surrender issue. Despite Mao Zedong's caution at this stage, it would soon become clear that the net result of the Sino-Japanese war had been to leave the Communists in a position of strength from which, within five years, they were able to take control of the whole of China. The Japanese war had served as the great catalyst in Chinese politics.

Final breakdown of GMD–CCP alliance

Even before the defeat of Japan, the Americans hoped that the two rival parties in China could be brought together into some form of power sharing. Patrick Hurley, the US ambassador, sponsored a number of meetings between the CCP and the GMD. Intermittent talks between the two parties were held in 1944–5. Mao declared himself willing to consider a compromise. However, in March 1945, Chiang broke off negotiations, announcing that he had no intention of sharing power with the Communists.

Again through American auspices, further talks were held in Chongqing in August 1945, following the Japanese surrender. Mao Zedong and Chiang Kai-shek met face to face for the first time in twenty years. They even drank toasts to each other. But this was for show; there was no mutual respect, nor could there be in the light of their long animosity. The truth was they were preparing for civil war with each other. President Truman, however, still believed that a compromise could be achieved. He sent the USA's most distinguished soldier and diplomat, **George Marshall**, to try to broker a lasting agreement.

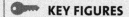

KEY FIGURES

General Douglas MacArthur (1880–1964)

The Allied commander-in-chief in the Far East.

George Marshall (1880–1959)

US Army chief of staff during the Second World War and Roosevelt's chief military adviser.

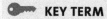

KEY TERM

Soviet–GMD friendship treaty Chiang's August 1945 agreement to allow Soviet forces into Manchuria in return for the USSR's recognition of his party as the only legitimate authority in China.

Marshall spent some months attempting to resurrect the GMD–CCP talks but by March 1946 he had to admit that a compromise settlement was impossible. There were two complementary fears that prevented agreement between Chiang and Mao:

- The GMD's concern that the Communists, while willing publicly to recognise Chiang Kai-shek as the legitimate leader of China, were not willing to co-operate in practice and were planning to overthrow him.
- The Communists' profound doubt, based on past experience, that the Nationalist regime would honour its promise to allow them to retain the liberated areas that they now held. It was their fear over this that led the Communists to walk out of the talks.

Put simply, neither side trusted the other. Even as they talked they were seizing territory and preparing for the conflict they knew was coming. Initial skirmishes had already occurred before the civil war broke out in earnest in June 1946. It was to last for three years.

Summary diagram: The impact of the occupation

Communist salvation
- GMD weakened
- CCP internationally recognised

Chiang and the USA
- Acknowledged as China's leader
- Hated by some Americans
- US recognised CCP's growing popularity

Impact of the sudden ending of the war
- Chiang in wrong location
- CCP took Japanese surrender
- Soviet forces in Manchuria

Final breakdown of GMD–CCP alliance
- US efforts at mediation failed
- Both parties prepared for civil war
- Lack of trust

Chapter summary

Originally united in their revolutionary aims, the CCP and the GMD drew apart. This was less a matter of their conflicting ideas than of the characters of their leaders. Chiang and Mao were driven personalities, each convinced of the correctness of his own position. Both attempted to stamp their authority on their respective parties, Chiang with less success than Mao, who emerged from the war as master of the CCP, having crushed opposition within the party in a violent 'rectification of conduct' campaign. The second GMD–CCP United Front against Japan was continually riven and weakened by mutual suspicion, arising largely from Chiang's abiding desire to exterminate the Communists. By an extraordinary irony it was the presence of the Japanese that saved the CCP since it diverted the Nationalists from their destructive campaigns.

The United Front had already broken down irrevocably by the time of the war's sudden ending in 1945. By then, the parties' response to the Japanese occupation had revealed that their deep divisions over China's future development could not be reconciled. Although smaller in number and in control of fewer Chinese regions than the GMD, the Communists in 1945 were better positioned strategically to win the civil war that soon broke out.

Refresher questions

Use these questions to remind yourself of the key material covered in this chapter.

1 In what sense was Mao a dialectician?

2 Why was Mao at Yanan opposed by the 'Twenty-eight Bolsheviks'?

3 How did the CCP exercise its control in the liberated areas?

4 How did the GMD government deal with the issue of the foreign presence in China?

5 What principles inspired the New Life Movement?

6 What factors undermined the New Life Movement?

7 What difficulties prevented Chiang Kai-shek from fully achieving his political aims?

8 How successful had Chiang's Nationalist government been in the period 1936–45?

9 Why were some Chinese people willing to co-operate with the Japanese occupiers?

10 How did the entry of the USA into the war change the character of the Sino-Japanese conflict?

11 How did Chiang's expectations change after December 1941?

12 What did the behaviour of the Japanese in Nanjing reveal about their attitude towards the Chinese?

13 Why did Chiang's Nationalists decline in popularity during the war?

14 Why did the USA support the GMD rather than the CCP between 1941 and 1945?

15 In what ways did the sudden ending of the war in August 1945 act as a catalyst in Chinese politics?

Question practice

ESSAY QUESTIONS

1 'The entry of the USA into the Pacific war in 1941 strengthened the CCP and undermined the GMD.' Explain why you agree or disagree with this view.

2 How far did Mao Zedong use the rectification campaign at Yanan to consolidate his authority over the CCP?

3 'The Japanese occupation of 1937 to 1945 fundamentally altered the Chinese political situation.' Assess the validity of this view.

SOURCE ANALYSIS QUESTIONS

1 With reference to Sources 1 and 2 and your understanding of the historical context, which of these sources is more valuable in explaining why Mao asserted his authority over the CCP at Yanan?

2 With reference to Sources 1, 2 and 3, and your understanding of the historical context, assess the value of these sources to a historian studying the ways in which Mao and the Communists controlled Yanan and the liberated areas.

SOURCE 1

From Edgar Snow, *Red Star Over China*, Penguin, 1972, p. 220, first published in 1937. Snow was an American admirer of Mao and lived with the Communists in Yanan. In his book, Snow described what he witnessed.

While theoretically the soviet was a 'workers and peasants' government, in actual practice the whole constituency was overwhelmingly peasant in character. Various committees were established under each of the district soviets. An all-powerful revolutionary committee was elected in a mass meeting shortly after the occupation of a district by the Red Army. Under the district soviet, and appointed by it, were committees for education, co-operatives, military training, political training, land, public health, partisan training, revolutionary defence, enlargement of the Red Army, agrarian mutual aid, Red Army land tilling, and others.

The work of all these organizations and their various committees was co-ordinated by the Central Soviet Government, the Communist Party, and the Red Army. The aim of soviet organization obviously was to make every man, woman, or child a member of something, with definite work assigned to him to perform.

SOURCE 2

From Wang Shi-wei, *New Left Review*, July–August 1975. In 'Wild Lilies', 1942, the writer, Wang, initially a committed supporter of Mao, became disillusioned with what he regarded as the growth of privilege in Yanan. It was published in English in 1975.

Young people have come here to be in the revolution, and they are committed to self-sacrifice. They have not come to seek the satisfactions of food and sex or the pleasures of life.

Some say there is no system of hierarchy and privilege in Yanan. This is not true. It exists. Others say, yes, there is but it is justified. This requires us to think with our heads.

I am no egalitarian. But I do not think it is necessary or justified to have multiple grades in food and clothing. If, while the sick can't even have a sip of noodle soup some quite healthy big shots are indulging in extremely unnecessary and unjustified perks, the lower ranks will be alienated.

SOURCE 3

From *La Bureaucratie au Vietnam* by Pyotr Vladimirov, quoted in Michael Lynch, *Mao*, Routledge, London, 2005, p. 121. Vladimirov was a Russian Comintern agent and here he gives a hostile account of what he witnessed while living with the Communists in Yanan in the early 1940s.

Party discipline is based on stupidly rigid forms of criticism and self-criticism. The president of each cell decides who is to be criticised and for what reason. In general it is a Communist who is attacked each time. The accused has only one right: to repent his 'errors'. If he considers himself to be innocent or appears insufficiently repentant, the attacks are renewed. The cruel method of psychological coercion that Mao calls moral purification has created a stifling atmosphere inside the Party in Yanan. A not negligible number of Party activists in the region have committed suicide, have fled or have become psychotic. Under the protocol of criticism and self-criticism, the thoughts and aspirations and actions of everyone are on full view.

CHAPTER 2

Communist victory and the consolidation of Mao's rule 1946–53

Using its own strengths and exploiting the GMD's weaknesses, Mao's CCP proved victorious in the civil war. As leader of the newly established People's Republic of China (PRC), Mao imposed his will on both party and people by rigorous means. Domestic problems were matched by foreign-affairs issues as the new nation sought to stabilise itself in the face of international hostility.

These developments are the material of the following themes:

★ Reasons for the Communist victory in 1949

★ The establishment of Communist power 1949–52

★ Mass campaigns and repression

★ The PRC's international position and regional issues

Key dates

1946–9	The civil war	**1950**	Sino-Soviet treaty signed
1949		**1950–3**	Korean War
October	Mao declared the creation of the PRC	**1951**	'Anti-movements' launched
December	Chiang Kai-shek fled to Taiwan	**1952**	Political parties other than the CCP banned
1950	Tibet invaded by PLA		

1 Reasons for the Communist victory in 1949

▶ *Why did the Communists win and the Nationalists lose the civil war?*

The war in outline

The civil war began with the Nationalists' attempt in 1946 to seize Manchuria, the region where the CCP was at its strongest. Chiang was hoping for a swift victory, for which he had good reason. But despite having overwhelming resources on his side, he was unable to break the Communists, who, having survived the attempt to dislodge them from Manchuria, then seized the initiative. Pushing out from its northern bases, the PLA built up a momentum which led to its eventual domination of central and southern China. By October 1949, Mao Zedong was in a position to claim total victory and to declare the birth of a new Communist nation, the People's Republic of China (PRC). Accepting defeat, Chiang Kai-shek transferred his remaining forces to the island of Taiwan, where he began the construction of a separate Nationalist state.

The Nationalists under Chiang Kai-shek entered the civil war with many more troops and greater resources than the Communists. The 5 million troops of the **NRA** outnumbered those of the PLA by over four to one. Chiang also received millions of dollars' worth of military equipment from the USA. But Chiang failed to exploit his side's initial advantages, and it was the poor showing of the GMD militarily, politically and economically that gave eventual victory to his opponents.

Nationalist (GMD) weaknesses

Internal divisions

After some seemingly impressive successes in the first year of the war, the Nationalists were unable to achieve a single major victory between 1947 and 1949. Faced by growing desertions, and betrayed by moles among the higher ranks of the officers, who passed information to the Communists, Chiang could never wholly rely on his supposed supporters, a problem that rarely troubled Mao Zedong. Splits occurred in the GMD ranks; rival factions opposed to Chiang, such as the **Left GMD and the Democratic League** came into being. Against this background, it became progressively more difficult for Chiang's Nationalists to sustain their war effort. Chiang himself in his post-war reflections acknowledged that Nationalist morale had been 'cripplingly low' and that his 'high-level officers began as complacent and ended as defeatist'.

Unpopularity

Unable to sustain a genuinely popular following among the people, Chiang increasingly resorted to coercion as the war went on. Property was seized, money expropriated and enlistment enforced. Protesters were arrested in large numbers and summary executions became commonplace. In August 1948, Shanghai witnessed particularly bloody scenes, including street-corner beheadings and shootings by government troops. Such atrocities alienated the Nationalists' diminishing band of supporters and dismayed their foreign sympathisers, most significantly the Americans.

KEY TERMS

NRA National Revolutionary Army of the Guomindang (GMD).

Left GMD and the Democratic League Made up of breakaway Nationalists who despaired of Chiang's leadership and the GMD's policies. They wanted a compromise settlement with the CCP.

Strategic errors

Military historians emphasise that Chiang's basic military failing was his eagerness to establish a grip on northern China, the area where the Nationalists were at their least influential. In a reversal of the 'trading space to buy time' strategy he had followed against the Japanese, he rushed his armies into Manchuria in the hope of a quick victory over the Communists. In doing so he sacrificed the advantage that his greater resources initially gave him. Chiang also inadvertently made things worse by appointing commanders according to their personal loyalty to him rather than their military skills.

Losing 'the struggle for the hearts of the people'

The PLA were not chivalrous knights, but the Communists did prove adept at winning what Mao called 'the struggle for the hearts of the people'. Against the Nationalist government's corruption and dependence on US aid, Mao claimed an understanding of, and sympathy with, the masses of the Chinese peasantry. By a striking irony the CCP were better positioned to fulfil the Three People's Principles (see page 11) than the Nationalists.

For balance, it should be mentioned that, while there were idealists who willingly backed the Communists, the popularity of the CCP among the peasants is largely explained by the licence the party gave them to seize the property of their hated landlords. The CCP's land policy was as much expedient as it was idealistic. In areas where it paid to be moderate in order to win the support of the local gentry, the CCP was quite prepared to recognise landowners' rights. However, in areas where there was no such gain to be made, the peasants were encouraged to seize the land and publicly degrade its former owners. Chiang's failing was that he could not turn all this to his advantage since his own regime was equally repressive.

The GMD's political failings

Although wars are ultimately decided on the battlefield, political and economic factors are also profoundly important. The GMD's major political weakness was that its record in government was one of incompetence and self-seeking. Its attempts at reform were unimpressive in the eyes of contemporaries. The Communists made capital out of this by portraying themselves as essentially different; their initial willingness to co-operate with the GMD, despite its murderous attitude towards them, suggested a high degree of selflessness.

The GMD's failure to win the localities

One of Chiang's major political errors was his failure to gain the support of the localities. All Chinese leaders since imperial days had found it difficult to maintain their authority in the regions; China was so large and communications were so slow. The customary way of solving the problem was to do a deal with those who held power in the regions. Unofficial agreements were made that the central government would not interfere with the local power structure provided the local leaders recognised the ultimate authority of the Chinese government. The rules were seldom written down but the understanding provided a workable system.

Chiang Kai-shek made the mistake of disregarding this convention. After 1945, he gave too little thought to the **local power structures**. He simply tried to impose GMD rule by dismissing the officials already there and replacing them with Nationalist appointees, who were invariably ignorant of the prevailing political and social conditions. It was a short-sighted policy that alienated the local communities from the GMD.

Limited base of the GMD's support

There was a fundamental flaw in the composition of the GMD that undermined its claim to be a party of the people. Relying for the bulk of its funding on the bankers and commercial interests of urban China, the GMD became a party that represented, not the masses, but a social and political élite who had little interest in the impoverished peasants and workers. This tainted Chiang's party and government, which became associated in the public mind with aloofness and **nepotism**. Mao was swift to mock Chiang's assertion, as expressed in the New Life Movement he had founded, that the GMD was a moral force in Chinese society (see page 14). *China's Destiny*, a book that Chiang had published in 1943 in which he appealed to all Chinese to abandon selfish thoughts and work for the good of the nation, was presented to the people as an inspirational text for all to follow. But it was impossible for most people to reconcile the book's lofty injunctions with the reality of how the GMD actually behaved in government.

The GMD's economic failings

Arguably, what finally undermined the Nationalist government was not war or politics but economics. The military and political success of the Communists under Mao Zedong obviously played an essential role in preparing the way for their takeover in 1949, but it is arguable that the single most powerful reason for the failure of the GMD government was **inflation**. In 1941, the chronic but relatively mild rise in prices that China had experienced throughout the republican period began to climb uncontrollably (see Table 2.1).

The soaring inflation had been caused initially by the Japanese occupation of China's most productive provinces after 1937. After 1945, the costs of maintaining an army of 5 million troops accounted for nearly 80 per cent of the government's expenditure. To meet its revenue needs, the government resorted to heavy taxation of individuals and companies. It also borrowed heavily from abroad and greatly increased the issue of paper currency. But these measures had disastrous effects: the rate of inflation reached astronomical heights and by 1949 China's monetary system had collapsed. Financial failure demoralised the people and discredited the GMD government.

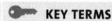

KEY TERMS

Local power structures Officials, businessmen, lawyers and financiers, who administered the regions during Japan's occupation and expected to continue after the GMD's return to power in 1945.

Nepotism Giving position and special favours to cronies and family members.

Inflation A fall in the value and purchasing power of money.

Table 2.1 Inflation in China 1937–48

Year	Total nominal value of notes in circulation (in millions of Chinese dollars)	Price index (100 in 1937)
1937	2,060	100
1938	2,740	176
1939	4,770	323
1940	8,440	724
1941	15,810	1,980
1942	35,100	6,620
1943	75,400	22,800
1944	189,500	75,500
1945	1,031,900	249,100
1946	3,726,100	627,000
1947	33,188,500	10,340,000
1948	374,762,200	287,700,000

> **KEY TERM**
>
> **Price index** The cost of a selected set of basic goods at a given date against which the cost at any other time is then calculated.

The NRA's conscription methods

A policy that proved especially damaging to the Nationalists in terms of public relations was their practice of conscription. Increasingly desperate for manpower as the war continued, but unable to raise enough volunteers, Chiang's government authorised the rounding up of peasants by armed recruitment

SOURCE A

Roped peasants are marched away barefoot after being rounded up by an NRA conscription squad.

> **?** What effect were scenes such as the one shown in Source A likely to have on the attitude towards the GMD among ordinary Chinese people?

squads. Once enlisted, the troops were treated with contempt by their officers. The president of the Chinese Red Cross described the barbarity suffered by the Nationalist conscripts. 'They were tied to one another to prevent their escaping, were savagely beaten if they upset their officers, and were starved of food. Under cruel treatment like this, many of them died before they could even be sent to the front.'

Chiang's explanation for the defeat of the GMD

It is instructive that in the final months of the war, Chiang Kai-shek himself listed five basic reasons why his forces had lost to the Communists:

- The GMD's military commanders had lacked skill and judgement and fought 'muddle-headed battles'.
- The rank-and-file soldiers lacked training and were incompetently led.
- GMD morale was low, a result of the complacency among the high-level officers, many of whom were concerned solely with their own self-interest.
- The GMD was unable to inspire its forces in the field because as an organisation it lacked discipline and effective propaganda, attributes in which Mao and the Communists excelled.
- The GMD failed to make effective use of the arms and resources with which they were provided by the USA. Too often the weapons fell into Communist hands.

Communist strengths

Mao's opportunism

The Communists' overthrow of the GMD in 1949 was a great military success but it was also a triumph of propaganda and public relations. Later accounts written by his supporters described Mao as having followed a carefully planned path to victory. They suggested that Mao, disregarding the half-hearted support of the Soviet Union and the meddling of the USA, had confidently followed his own judgement. By enlightened policies in the countryside, he had formed an unbreakable bond with the Chinese people and led them in a great social revolution against Chiang and the Nationalists.

This narrative became the official CCP version of what had happened. However, what modern historians, including many Chinese writers, suggest is that the critical factor in Mao's success was not his long-term planning but his opportunism. When the civil war was renewed in 1946, Mao's most optimistic hope was that the CCP would be able to retain the bases it had acquired by the end of the Japanese struggle. He did not foresee that within three years his Communist forces would have taken the whole of China. It was the Nationalists who made that possible by throwing away their initial superiority.

Mao's dominance of the CCP and PLA

What is difficult to dispute in the Communist legend is that without Mao Zedong's power and ability as a leader, the CCP would not have won the war. His self-belief and conviction of his own correctness inspired the PLA's commanders and men. Mao possessed the strength of will that wins political and military struggles. It had expressed itself in the ruthlessness with which he had suppressed opposition within his own party in the rectification programme of the early 1940s (see page 25). Indeed, it was his absolute domination of the party that enabled him to have the final word in the organising of the PLA's campaigns during the civil war. It was that control which allowed him to overcome the doubts of many of his commanders and redirect strategy at critical moments in the civil war.

Mao's leadership

Historians now suggest that of all the factors accounting for the CCP's ultimate victory Mao's military leadership was the most significant. It was under him that the Communist forces who were essentially rural guerrilla fighters in 1945 had, by 1949, become an effective modern army.

Mao's outplaying of Stalin

There is sense in which Mao's victory in the civil war also marked a personal victory over Stalin. Since the 1920s, the Soviet leader had refused to believe that the Chinese Communists could achieve a genuine revolution. The low estimation in which Moscow held Mao and the CCP was revealed in August 1945 when the Soviet Union formally signed a friendship treaty with Chiang's Nationalist government (see page 30), ending 'all outstanding grievances' between China and the USSR. A British newspaper, *The Observer*, commented on the significance of the Soviet Union's abandoning of the Chinese Communists: 'The cynic may be inclined to regard Russia's part in the conclusion of the treaty with China as a sacrifice of the Yanan regime for the sake of greater prestige and influence in Chungking and hence over all China.'

Subsequent events confirmed the accuracy of *The Observer*'s assessment. The USSR was manoeuvring itself into a position from which it could seize Chinese territory. Soviet armies occupied Manchuria between August 1945 and May 1946 and did not withdraw until they had stripped the region of its economic resources.

During the civil war, Stalin made occasional gestures of goodwill towards Mao Zedong and continued to send his representatives to CCP gatherings, but, even when the PLA began to drive the Nationalists from their bases, Stalin could not bring himself to change tack. As late as 1949, the year in which the PLA forced the GMD off the Chinese mainland, the USSR persisted in recognising Chiang Kai-shek as China's leader. Stalin believed throughout this period that the

USA would not tolerate a Communist victory in China. Anxious not to provoke further US intervention in the Far East, he urged Mao to come to terms with the Nationalists, even if this meant accepting a China divided between the CCP in the north and the GMD in the south.

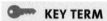

According to Mao in Source B, what was the disagreement between him and Stalin in 1949?

KEY TERM

South and North dynasties A reference to the partition of China during the civil wars of the fifth and sixth centuries AD.

SOURCE B

Mao speaking at Beijing University in 1957; here he explains why, in 1949 he had rejected Stalin's suggestion that the Chinese Communists should settle for the partitioning of China between themselves and Nationalists. From Harrison Salisbury, *The New Emperors Mao and Deng: A Biography*, HarperCollins, 1992, p. 15.

*Even in 1949 when we were about to cross the Yangtze River, someone [Stalin] still wanted to prevent us. According to him we should under no circumstances cross the Yangtze. If we did so America would send troops to China and become directly involved in China's Civil War and the **South and North dynasties** would reappear in China. I did not listen to what they said. We crossed the Yangtze, America did not send troops and there were no South and North dynasties.*

Later I met that person who intended to prevent us from crossing the Yangtze. His first words in conversation were: 'the victor bears no blame.' I had not listened to him. As a result he not only did not blame me. On the contrary he recognized me as the victor. It is very important that one should analyse and solve problems on one's own and always seek truth from facts.

Importance of Mao's success

That both the USA and the Soviet Union continued to support the GMD until almost the last moment vindicated Mao Zedong's long-held belief that salvation for China was possible only from within China itself. Mao read the unfolding of events as a justification for the independent Marxist line that he had taken since the mid-1920s. By 1949, he was more than ever convinced that, for China, the only path was the Chinese path. Given the different national, cultural and ideological standpoints from which they started, there had never been a real likelihood that Mao Zedong and Stalin would come to share a common purpose and vision. Mao's success in 1949 owed little to Stalin and the Soviet Union. Indeed, it is arguable that had Mao heeded Stalin's advice there would have been no Communist victory in the Chinese civil war.

Summary diagram: Reasons for the Communist victory in 1949

Military
- Chiang's flawed strategy in attempting to seize northern China before his forces were ready
- Overextension of supply lines damaged NRA effectiveness
- Inability to hold the countryside
- Ineffective generalship
- Rivalry among the commanders
- Lack of loyalty among NRA commanders at the highest level
- Constant desertions
- Betrayal from within by pro-Communist moles and informants
- Low morale caused by the brutal way NRA troops were treated
- Misuse of US aid, much of which fell into Communist hands

Political
- Restricted power base of the GMD
- The GMD's financial dependence on the banking interests
- Chiang never in total control of the GMD
- The failure to fulfil the Three People's Principles
- Corruption in government
- Savage conscription methods alienated the people
- Overwhelmed by hyperinflation
- Failed to win over the localities
- Resorted to coercion to maintain control

The establishment of Communist power 1949–52

▶ *How did Mao seek to consolidate Communist authority in the newly established PRC?*

Initial steps

On taking power in 1949, Mao did not immediately rush to reform China. His initial moves were cautious. The property of those Nationalists who had fled with Chiang Kai-shek to Taiwan was seized and the banks and the **public utilities** were taken under state control. All foreign assets, except for those of the USSR, were also taken over. But the new regime was prepared to offer compensation to those former owners who declared their willingness to work in the new China. Mao announced that the PRC was ready to use the resources of the **national capitalists** to begin the reconstruction of Communist China.

Mao was also aware that, although the Chinese **middle classes** were a relatively small part of a population overwhelmingly made up of peasants, their importance was greater than their numbers. It was they who provided the officials, the civil servants and the industrial managers. Those who had not fled with the defeated GMD were invited to stay in their positions and become loyal servants of the new government. Most accepted the offer and to these were added a significant number of **expatriate Chinese** who returned in a spirit of idealism, eager to serve the new regime.

 KEY TERMS

Public utilities Gas, electricity and the transport system.

National capitalists Those who had run China before 1949.

Middle classes Broadly made up of professionally qualified people.

Expatriate Chinese Chinese nationals living abroad.

All did not go well for them. They were promised that if they pledged themselves to the new China they would not suffer for their past behaviour. For a short period this undertaking was honoured, but once they had served their purpose by providing the young PRC with the necessary continuity of administration the officials were turned on as **class enemies**.

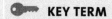

KEY TERM

Class enemies
Reactionaries who refused to accept the new Communist China.

The structure of the PRC

For administrative purposes, the country was divided into six regions (see the map on page 45), each governed by a bureau of four major officials:

- chairman
- party secretary
- military commander
- political commissar.

Since the last two posts were filled by officers of the PLA, this effectively left China under military control, a situation which Mao Zedong considered offered the best means of stabilising China and maintaining the rule of the CCP. The overarching governmental power resided in the Central People's Government Council. This was composed of 56 leading party members, the majority of whom were veterans of the Yanan years. Six of these served as vice-chairmen under Mao who, as chairman of the council, was the unchallengeable figure in government.

CCP rule in the PRC under Mao

It should be noted that despite the coercive society that Mao's China was in practice, in theory it was one of the freest in the world. The CCP claimed that all power rested with the people and that the party officials and the government acted as servants of the nation. Figure 2.1 on page 46 shows a model of how the government supposedly operated. It was the workers and peasants who exercised authority through the various connected and overlapping bodies.

The Chinese Communists made much of the claim that elections for party officials and administrators were held in the villages, localities and regions and that the members of the National People's Congress, which was the body formally responsible for deciding national policy, were themselves elected as the people's choice. What was not emphasised was that only one party could stand for election, all others being outlawed, and that even those who stood as independents had to acknowledge publicly that the CCP had an absolute right to rule. An additional factor was that party officials oversaw all the elections, which meant that there was little real chance of anyone critical of Mao or the government ever being successful.

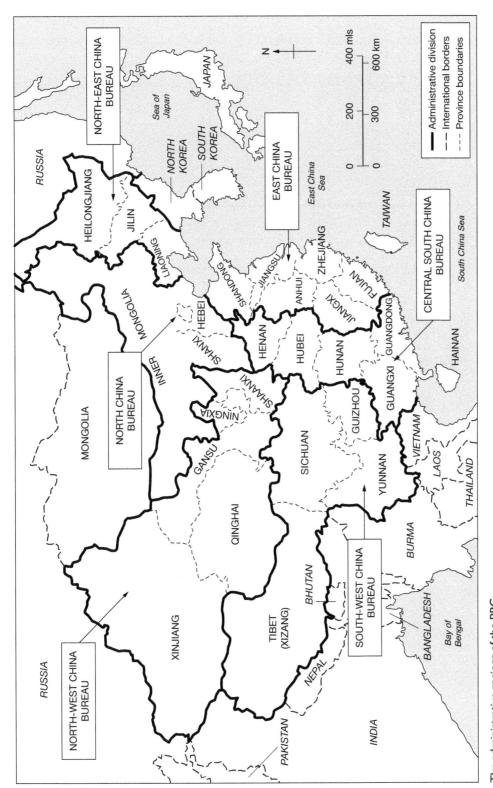

The administrative regions of the PRC.

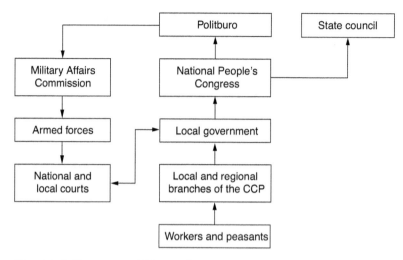

Figure 2.1 The pattern of Chinese Communist Party rule.

The Politburo

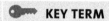
Despite appearances, the reality was that the Communist Party, not the people, ruled in the PRC. Moreover, the party in this context did not mean all the members of the CCP. In effect, government was carried out by the **Politburo**. The National People's Congress simply rubber-stamped the decisions made by the Politburo; its job was to applaud the party's leaders when they made their appearances on the platform. There was never a genuine case of the Congress's reversing party policy on any issue that mattered.

Mao's authority over the Politburo

The Politburo, in turn, was under the authority of Mao Zedong. This did not mean that he initiated every detail of policy; sometimes he chose not to attend Politburo meetings. Nevertheless, nothing could be done of which he disapproved. He was the ultimate authority. What adds to the oddity of Mao's position is that his power did not rest on any formal position that he held. It is true that he was chairman of the party but the title did not confer power on him; rather it was recognition of the power that he already wielded. That was why he was able on occasion to withdraw from the political frontline and subsequently return with his power undiminished. An example of this occurred at the time of the famine in the early 1960s, when he effectively left government in the hands of **Liu Shaoqi** and **Deng Xiaoping** and later returned to take up the reins again (see page 101).

Mao and democratic centralism

Western observers were sometimes puzzled by the Chinese situation in which a party, dedicated to the notion of the rule of the masses, allowed itself to be controlled by one man, Mao Zedong. Part of the answer lies in the concept of

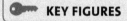

democratic centralism. This idea had first been formulated by **Lenin** in Russia. The argument, which Mao took up and applied to his own interpretation of revolution in China, was that true democracy in the Communist Party lay in the obedience of the members to the authority and instructions of the leaders. The justification for this was that while, as representatives of the workers, all Communists were genuine revolutionaries, only the leaders were sufficiently educated in the science of revolution to understand what needed to be done.

In practice, democratic centralism meant the Chinese Communists doing what Mao told them to do. One of the ironies of this was that in spite of the power he wielded, Mao became increasingly paranoid. The more authority he gained, the more he feared that opposition to him was growing. It is a feature of his personality that explains why he was so ready to launch anti-campaigns and purges against those he suspected irrationally of plotting to overthrow him.

Military control

In a series of three **'reunification' campaigns**, three separate PLA armies were despatched to impose control:

- One army was sent into Tibet in October 1950.
- A second went into Xinjiang.
- A third went into the southern province of Guangdong.

KEY FIGURE

Lenin (1870–1924)
The chief interpreter of Marx and the man who had led the Communists to power in the 1917 Russian Revolution.

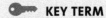

KEY TERM

'Reunification' campaigns
The CCP's euphemism for forcibly bringing the invaded provinces into line.

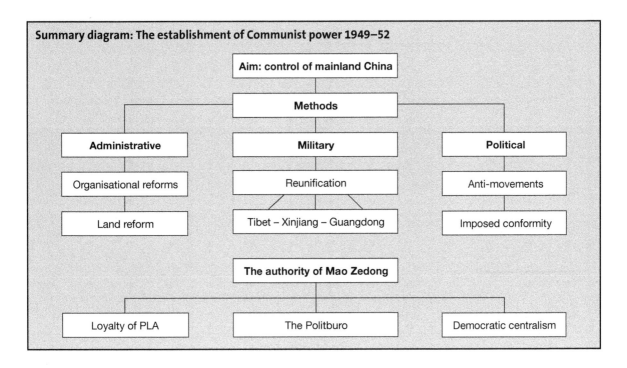

Summary diagram: The establishment of Communist power 1949–52

```
                    Aim: control of mainland China

                            Methods

   Administrative           Military            Political

Organisational reforms     Reunification      Anti-movements

    Land reform      Tibet – Xinjiang – Guangdong   Imposed conformity


                The authority of Mao Zedong

   Loyalty of PLA         The Politburo      Democratic centralism
```

Mass campaigns and repression

▶ *What methods did Mao employ to enforce his authority on the CCP?*

▶ *What forms did repression take in Mao's China?*

The 'anti-movements'

Having tightened its military grip over China, Mao's government turned its attention to extending its political control. In 1951, Mao announced the beginning of the three 'anti-movements', the targets being:

- waste
- corruption
- inefficiency.

This was expanded in 1952 into the five 'anti-movements', which were intended to stimulate the economy by attacking:

- industrial sabotage
- tax evasion
- bribery
- fraud
- theft of government property.

The identification of particular targets was not in itself important. The object was to provide as wide a justification as possible to attack class enemies. The concept of class enemies was basic to the social and political strategies of the Communists in government. Invoking the traditional Chinese duty of respecting authority, Mao and the CCP leaders began campaigns against anyone in public life who opposed official policy. An atmosphere of fear and uncertainty was systematically created by the 'anti-movements', launched against those who were regarded by the CCP as socially or politically suspect. The Chinese people were encouraged to expose all those who had co-operated with the former GMD government. It was enough for individuals to be charged by their neighbours with having belonged to the privileged classes for them to be publicly denounced and to have their property seized. Their pleas of loyalty to Mao's new China were ignored.

Mao defined the main aim of the 'anti-movements' as the destruction of the remnants of 'the bureaucratic capitalist class', who were engaged in reactionary or counter-revolutionary activities. In 1952, he justified his tough line in a widely broadcast public statement in which he defined the **bourgeoisie** as outcasts against whom 'the people's army, the people's police and the people's courts' would be mercilessly used. The vengeful atmosphere was intensified by China's involvement in the Korean War of 1950–3 (see page 54). This struggle placed great demands on the young PRC and made those who were less than

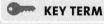 **KEY TERM**

Bourgeoisie Middle-class capitalists; exploiters of the workers.

wholehearted in supporting it open to the charge that they were imperilling the nation's existence.

Purges of party members

Purges were also carried out within the CCP. Members who did not slavishly follow official CCP policy were liable to be condemned as 'rightists' who were opposed to the progress of the PRC. Purges were alternated with periods when party members were encouraged to criticise current policies and air their grievances. Those who were rash enough to do so were then attacked as 'rightists'. The apparent liberalising was invariably followed by the imposition of even tougher restrictions on freedom of expression. Such purges were to become a recurrent feature of Chinese politics until Mao's death in 1976.

The PRC as a one-party state

On the pretext of defending the people from their enemies, Mao and the CCP began to resort to terror as a basic method of control. It soon became clear that China was to become a one-party state. At the time of the Communist success in 1949 there had been over ten separate political parties in China. These included the Left GMD and the Democratic Leagues. By 1952 they had disappeared, destroyed in a set of repressive moves which denied the right of any party to exist other than the CCP.

Mass terror

The political purges were accompanied by a series of mass campaigns aimed at extending the CCP's authority over the people of China. A concerted attack was launched against 'anti-socials, counter-revolutionaries and imperialists', catch-all terms that were used to condemn anyone who showed signs of disapproving of the Communist regime.

Particular CCP severity was evident in the early 1950s in Shanghai and Guangzhou, cities which had been notorious for their underworld gangs and **triads** in the years of Nationalist rule. Having used the local knowledge of the former gangsters to consolidate its hold on the city, the CCP turned on them in a violent bloodletting. Of the 130,000 'bandits and criminals' rounded up by the authorities in Guangzhou, over half were executed. A similar process led to a death toll of 28,000 in Shanghai.

Enforcing mass conformity

To maintain its control, the CCP turned China into a nation of informers. Local party officials created a system in which:

- neighbour spied on neighbour
- workers snooped on their mates
- children reported on their parents

KEY TERMS

Purges In theory, the purifying of the party by removing corrupt elements; in practice, a method for silencing opponents and critics.

Triads Chinese secret societies, usually criminal, involved in drugs, gambling and prostitution.

- each street or tenement block had officially appointed 'watchers' who kept the local CCP informed on anyone or anything suspicious
- community associations, which were set up with the declared aim of providing mutual help, became a major means of exerting control and conformity.

Such developments had the effect of forcibly politicising the nation. Individuals or families who declined to become involved were immediately labelled as class enemies. Indeed, 'labelling' became the chief means of enforcing conformity. Those people who had a middle-class or non-revolutionary background knew that this would be enough to condemn them. To prove the sincerity of their acceptance of the new proletarian China, they became especially eager to denounce others as 'bourgeois elements' and 'imperialist lackeys'. In the People's Republic there was to be no toleration of independent thinking, let alone dissent.

As part of the CCP's coercion of China, youth organisations were either closed down or taken over by party **cadres**. Religion was selected for special attack (see page 119); China was being structured as a society of informers in which conformity was maintained by exploiting the traditional fear Chinese people had of being publicly exposed as political or social deviants.

Registration

A notable method by which the party imposed its will was the system which required individuals to register themselves. There were three main types:

- the *danwei* – a permit without which an individual could not hold a job
- the *hukou* – a certificate which entitled a family to obtain accommodation
- the *dangan* – a dossier held by local party officials containing the personal details and record of every individual.

Of the three, the *dangan* was the most intrusive. A veritable army of party clerks spent its working hours collecting and collating material on everyone in the population. Hundreds of millions of records were kept. The *dangans* became the chief means by which the authorities maintained political and social control over the Chinese people. A person's right to employment, housing or a pension, or indeed to freedom, depended on the contents of his or her dossier.

The attack on the middle class

Mao's aim in pressing these policies on the people was nothing less than the destruction of a whole class – China's bourgeoisie. Having used this class to help see the PRC through its teething troubles, he was then ready to obliterate it. He regarded it as an essential step in the creation of China as a fully Marxist state in which only one class would exist – the **proletariat**.

Mao insisted that proletarian revolution could be achieved only through the use of violence. While it was possible to take a softer line with the peasants since

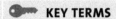

KEY TERMS

Cadres Dedicated CCP workers whose special task was to spy and report on fellow CCP members and the public.

Proletariat The revolutionary workers and peasants.

they had been the powerless exploited class, the exploiting bourgeois class had to be broken by force. He contended that no ruling class ever gives up power willingly; it has to be torn from them. And even then, the dispossessed class will attempt to fight back; that is why there are always reactionaries. The task of Communist China was, therefore, to show no mercy in annihilating the bourgeoisie that was still attempting to undermine the new China. Mao spelled this out with great clarity when addressing a gathering of the party leaders in 1955, as described in Source C.

SOURCE C

From *Selected Works of Mao Tse-tung*, quoted in Merle Goldman, editor, *An Intellectual History of Modern China*, Cambridge University Press, 2002, p. 419.

After the agrarian revolution, when the peasants had come over entirely to our side, it was possible for us to start the movements against the Three Antis and Five Antis. Agricultural co-operation will enable us to consolidate our alliance with the peasants on the basis of proletarian socialism and not of bourgeois democracy. This will isolate the bourgeoisie once and for all and facilitate the final elimination of capitalism. On this matter we are quite heartless. On this matter, Marxism is indeed cruel and has little mercy, for it is determined to exterminate imperialism, feudalism, capitalism and small production to boot. Some of our comrades are too kind, they are not tough enough; in other words, they are not truly Marxist. Our aim is to exterminate capitalism, obliterate it from the face of the earth and make it a thing of the past.

According to Mao in Source C, why is it essential that the bourgeoisie be shown no mercy?

The repression imposed on the nation at this stage has to be understood in relation to two developments that dominated the early years of the PRC: the Korean War (1950–3) and Mao's first Five-Year Plan (1952–6). The Korean struggle (see page 54) and the drive for industrialisation (see page 66) placed huge additional burdens on the young Communist republic and these were used to justify the extension of state control. There was also a third personal factor: the centralisation of power under Mao was an expression of his fear of rivals.

Mao's fear of rivals

Mao never forgot the lessons learned in the CCP power struggles in Jiangxi and Yanan. Notwithstanding the apparent harmony that the CCP leaders publicly displayed, tensions and rivalries were never far below the surface. The godlike status that Mao achieved among the Chinese people after 1949 did not make him more trustful of his colleagues. Indeed, his suspicions increased to the point of paranoia.

A characteristic of Mao that many biographers have stressed is that the more powerful he grew, the more detached he became from his political and governmental associates. Such was the awe in which he was increasingly held that his colleagues did not find it easy to converse or to exchange ideas with him and it is doubtful that they ever gave him their honest opinions. While it

KEY TERM

'Going to the people'
Mao's practice of periodically travelling through parts of China, supposedly to listen to what the people had to say.

is true that Mao made a point in the 1950s of **'going to the people'**, his travels within China were largely stage-managed affairs. His claim that such journeys brought him in touch with the real feelings of the people is unconvincing; those peasants and workers who were selected for the privilege of speaking to him were coached into telling him only what he wanted to hear. The result, according to some observers, was that this remoteness from reality created irrationality in him. Desire for power mixed with paranoia made him not the saviour but the oppressor of his people.

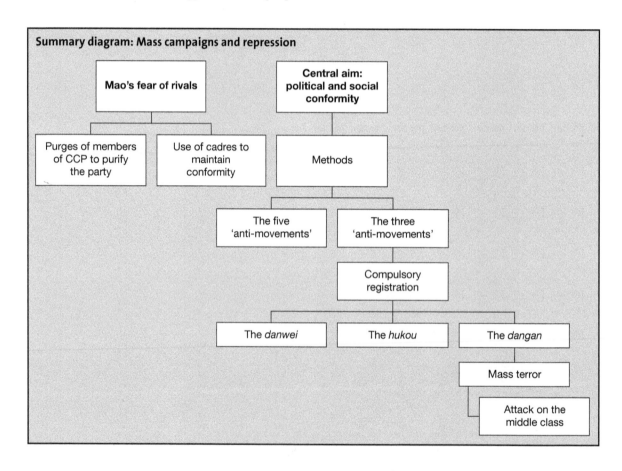

Summary diagram: Mass campaigns and repression

The PRC's international position and regional issues

> ▶ *What issues in regional and foreign affairs did Mao face after the formation of the PRC?*

The PRC's 'reunification' campaigns

Mao's determination not to allow the Communist victory in 1949 to become an opportunity for regional independence to assert itself was very evident in the way he enforced PRC control over China's outlying areas.

Tibet

A PLA army was sent into Tibet in October 1950. The stated justification for the invasion was that the region had historically always belonged to China. The claim was an assertion, not a statement of fact. The Tibetans were markedly different in race, culture and religion from the Chinese and had always regarded themselves as a separate people. This was evident from the spirited resistance the PLA met when it invaded; a hastily assembled force of 60,000 Tibetans fought determinedly to preserve their land and culture.

However, the struggle was hopeless. Without a trained army and possessing only outdated weapons, the Tibetans had no chance of matching the occupying PLA. Within six months open resistance had been suppressed. The PLA then imposed a regime of terror aimed at wiping out all traces of separate Tibetan identity, a process that was to drag on over many decades and bring immense suffering to the people of Tibet (see page 80).

Xinjiang and Guangdong

Similar PLA harshness was shown in Xinjiang. This distant western province, which bordered Soviet-controlled Outer Mongolia, had a large Muslim population. The CCP feared that it would either declare its independence from China or fall into Soviet hands. By 1951, within a year of their arrival, PLA detachments had imposed Communist authority over the region. Strict controls were imposed on religious worship in an attempt to undermine the sense of local identity. At the same time, a third PLA army brought the Guangdong province, in southern China, under PRC dominance.

Taiwan

In 1949, following the Communist takeover of the mainland, the GMD had fled to Taiwan, where it proceeded to build an alternative Chinese republic. Mao's attitude towards Taiwan was very simple. The island, he said, was now illegally occupied by Chiang and the Nationalists; it was not a separate state but merely a breakaway province of mainland China. Mao's initial intention after taking power in 1949 was to extend the civil war by immediately invading Taiwan and reclaiming it. He was prevented from doing so by Cold War considerations.

In the USA, the hardening of the Cold War had produced a pro-Taiwan lobby in **Congress**, which argued strongly that the Nationalists, whatever their failings, were an Asian bastion against the spread of international communism and could not, therefore, be deserted. This view prevailed with the result that until 1971, the USA ignored political reality and pretended that Chiang's tiny island regime in Taiwan was the true Chinese nation, entitled to be a member of the United Nations (UN) and take its seat as a permanent member of the **UN Security Council**. Although the USA did not formally commit itself to the military defence of Taiwan, Mao could not risk that occurring. He maintained the right to send his forces to take Taiwan at any time but, with the PRC's forces heavily involved in the Korean War, he held back from carrying out the threat.

The Korean War 1950–3

Geographically, the Korean peninsula hung like an appendix on mainland China. Between 1910 and 1945, it had been occupied by Japan. With the defeat of Japan in 1945, Korea was partitioned along the 38th parallel, with the USA taking responsibility for protecting the area to the south of that line, while the Soviet Union did the same in the north. In 1950, the North Koreans crossed the parallel with the aim of imposing their Communist control over the whole peninsula.

The US **State Department** believed that the incursion had been initiated by Mao in collusion with Stalin. It was assumed that the North Korean invasion of the South was the first joint venture of the new Communist bloc formed by Mao's China and the USSR. However, it is now known that although Mao eventually backed North Korea, he did not initiate the invasion. Korea seems hardly to have been discussed at the meetings between Stalin and Mao in Moscow in 1950 (see page 59). China's military plans were exclusively concerned with Taiwan, Xinjiang and Tibet. Indeed, apart from those areas, the PRC had recently made the decision to cut back on military expenditure and redirect its resources into the rectification campaigns within China.

Stalin's motives

What commentators now suggest is that Stalin had colluded with **Kim Il Sung**, the North Korean leader, in organising the venture and that he called on the Chinese to give support only after the fighting had started. Stalin was playing Cold War politics. Having been convinced by Kim that North Korea was capable of sustaining a major war effort against the Americans, Stalin anticipated that the USA would be sucked into a conflict in Asia which it could not win. As he saw it, the great advantage was that war in Korea entailed no risk to the USSR since Soviet forces would not be directly involved.

Stalin calculated that, if the North Koreans could bring the whole of Korea under Communist control, the USA would have been humiliated and the Soviet Union would have acquired a very powerful position in the Far East at very little cost to itself. There was also the consideration that if Mao's PRC could be pushed into the war, it would distract the newly fledged nation from thinking of challenging the USSR's leadership of international communism or causing trouble over disputed Sino-Soviet border territory. Stalin did not, of course, reveal his true motive to the Chinese. Writing officially to Mao in 1950, Stalin implied strongly that the USSR would enter the war and stressed that the PRC could not risk waiting.

SOURCE D

From Stalin's letter to Mao, 1950, quoted in Robert Service, *Stalin: A Biography*, Macmillan, 2004, p. 556.

*I had to reckon with the fact that, despite its lack of preparedness, the United States may still pull itself into a big war for reasons of prestige; consequently China would be dragged into the war and the USSR which is bound to China by the pact of mutual assistance, would be dragged into the war as well. Should we be afraid of this? In my opinion we should not since together we will be stronger than the United States and Great Britain. If war is inevitable, let it happen now and not in a few years when Japanese militarism will be restored as a US ally and when the United States and Japan will have a beach head on the Asian continent ready in the form of **Syngman Rhee**'s Korea.*

According to Stalin in Source D, why ought the PRC to enter the war immediately?

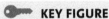

KEY FIGURE

Syngman Rhee (1875–1965)

US-backed, anti-Communist president of South Korea from 1948 to 1960.

Mao's reaction

Since he had not been a party to the plan devised by Stalin and Kim Il Sung, Mao was at first hesitant to commit China formally to the Korean struggle. But once he realised the affair was a ***fait accompli*** he felt obliged to enter. Korea was too close geographically for China to remain detached, and at this early stage in its development the PRC invariably followed the Soviet lead in international affairs. This was not because the PRC wanted to, but because it had to, its lack of resources making it heavily dependent on the USSR, the only possible supplier. As Jung Chang in her biography of Mao puts it: 'Chinese soldiers would fight the Americans for Stalin in exchange for Soviet technology and equipment.'

Yet, whatever gains he might have been hoping for, Mao still had difficulty in persuading his military that he had made the right decision. Leading commanders argued that the PRC's primary task was to crush its internal enemies and that it did not have the resources to fight in Korea. Mao's counterargument was that once US troops had entered Korea it would be impossible for China to stay out; if the Americans were to take Korea they would possess a stepping stone to China itself.

KEY TERM

Fait accompli Something done in such a way that it cannot be changed.

China's entry into the war

The Western view of the Korean crisis was that it was the fault of the North Koreans in crossing the 38th parallel and attacking the South. The PRC counter-claimed that the South Koreans had committed the initial aggression. When US forces under the UN flag landed in Korea in June 1950, China's foreign minister, Zhou Enlai, condemned it as an imperialist invasion. Organised mass demonstrations took place in China's cities. The principal slogan was 'North Korea's friends are our friends. North Korea's enemy is our enemy. North Korea's defence is our defence.'

Zhou warned that China would be forced to intervene if US troops pushed into North Korea. In fact, thousands of PLA soldiers were already fighting alongside the North Koreans as 'volunteers'. In October 1950, US forces crossed northwards over the 38th parallel. China promptly declared itself to be fully engaged in the war. It was to be a three-year struggle before ending in stalemate in 1953.

KEY TERM

Panmunjong truce The agreement ending the Korean War. It decided little since the two sides simply agreed to recognise the division of Korea at the 38th parallel.

Consequences of the war for the PRC

- The **Panmunjong truce**, which ended the fighting in 1953, left Korea still divided and with no prospect of a Communist takeover of the South.
- Chinese deaths numbered around a million, a third of the total PRC forces involved.
- The USA pledged itself to the defence of Taiwan and to the continued support of Nationalist China's membership of the UN, a position that was maintained until 1971. This effectively ruled out any possibility of the PRC's reclaiming Taiwan by force.
- The war was a huge drain on the young PRC's economy. Industrial resources earmarked for domestic growth had to be diverted into the war effort. Mao remarked that China had to pay down to the last bullet for the Soviet supplies it received during the conflict.

These were obviously damaging consequences, but the war did have some positive results for Mao:

- Mao's call for national unity in the war effort provided a justification for the increasing political and social repression imposed by the government.
- The three-year experience of war hardened China's resolve to stand alone in a hostile world.
- Mao could proudly claim that Chinese comrades had shed their blood in the cause of international Communism.
- The PRC for three years had matched the USA in combat and remained undefeated.

The PRC and the USSR

The PRC was formed in 1949 after the Cold War had begun to take shape. The prospect, therefore, was that as a Communist state it would naturally line up with the USSR against the USA and the capitalist world. Stalin calculated that China, as a newly formed Marxist state in a hostile capitalist world, would look to the USSR, the first great Communist nation, for guidance and protection. However, events were to show that Mao Zedong and China were far from regarding themselves as mere creatures of Stalin and the USSR. The consequence was that tension rather than harmony was the predominant feature of Sino-Soviet relations after 1949.

While it was the case that at the beginning the PRC 'leaned to one side', Mao's term for its alliance with the Soviet Union, things were never as simple as that. Mao and Stalin had a strained relationship. This went back before 1949 to the period of the civil war, when it was apparent that Stalin had little faith in Mao's Communists and doubted they would survive. That was why he had given only partial help to the CCP, which he did not fully support until after it had defeated the GMD. Stalin's disdain was something Mao never forgot.

The main factors making for rivalry rather than friendship between the PRC and the USSR were as follows:

- territorial disputes
- ideological differences
- national rivalry
- Mao and Stalin: a clash of personalities.

Territorial disputes

At the end of the Pacific war in 1945, Manchuria, which had been occupied by the Japanese, was returned to China but only after the withdrawing Soviet forces had stripped the region of its industrial resources, depriving China of over $2 billion worth of plant and machinery. Even after the PRC had been established in 1949, border disputes continued to sour Sino-Soviet relations for decades.

Ideological differences

For Mao, Marxism provided a programme for achieving revolution in China, but it was essential that the Chinese revolutionaries interpret that programme in their own terms. His approach was essentially nationalist; revolutionaries outside China could not dictate to the Chinese revolutionaries how they should conduct themselves (see page 4). Such a **Sino-centric** view of Marxism and revolution was bound to cause friction between Communist China and the Soviet Union, which regarded itself as the only true interpreter of Marxism–Leninism. Sino-Soviet relations after 1949 often descended into a battle over who represented the true faith, the Soviet Union or Maoist China.

 **KEY TERM**

Sino-centric Having Chinese interests at the centre of things with all other considerations secondary.

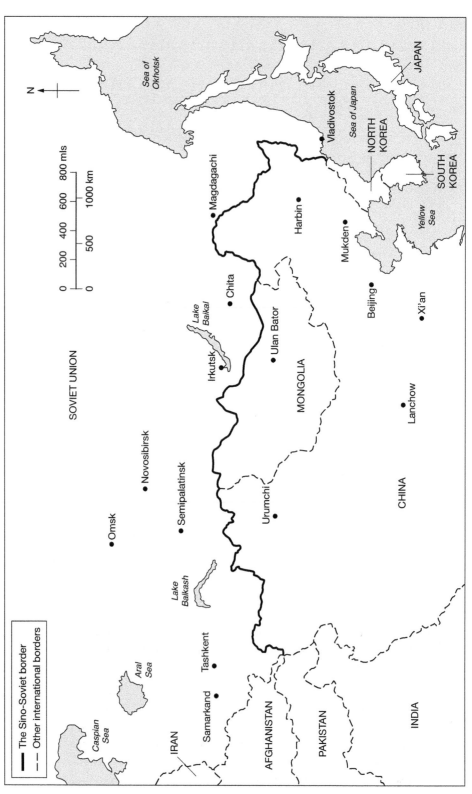

The Sino-Soviet border.

National rivalry

Mao judged that what the Soviet leader wanted was a disunited and divided China that would leave the USSR as the dominant force in Asia. This was why Mao found it hard to accept the USSR, despite its revolutionary pedigree, as the true voice of international Marxism. He came increasingly to believe that what motivated the Soviet Union was not Communism but national self-interest. Nevertheless, in the early years of its existence, the PRC's economic needs meant that Mao could not afford to antagonise the USSR since that was the only country from whom he could draw economic support.

Mao and Stalin: a clash of personalities

It was to negotiate such support that Mao paid an official visit to the USSR in 1950. His experience there confirmed his doubts concerning Stalin's attitude. Mao was offended by the superior air adopted by the Russians and by Stalin's dismissive treatment of the Chinese delegation. His hosts had made no arrangements to entertain him beyond the formal round of official meetings and banquets. Mao felt slighted. Biographers suggest that the two leaders disliked each other as people; their personalities conflicted because they were so similar in type. Once Mao had negotiated the treaty, which was the sole purpose of his visit, he left as quickly as possible.

The Sino-Soviet treaty 1950

It soon became apparent that Mao's mistrust of Stalin was well founded. The Chinese realised soon after the treaty had been signed that the Soviet Union was intent on exploiting the agreement in its own favour. This was in spite of Mao's initial belief that the hard-won treaty had obliged the USSR to provide China with expertise and aid at low cost. Its wording, which spoke of 'friendship and equality' and 'economic and cultural co-operation', had appeared to promise much. But Stalin had struck a hard bargain. Under the terms of the treaty:

- The $300 million Soviet advance was a loan, not a gift; the PRC had to undertake to repay the full amount plus interest.
- The upkeep of the 10,000 Soviet economic and military advisers who went to China had to be paid for fully by the Chinese.
- China had to give the bulk of its bullion reserves to the Soviet Union.

Nikita Khrushchev admitted that the treaty had been 'an insult to the Chinese people. For centuries the French, English and Americans had been exploiting China, and now the Soviet Union was moving in.'

Mao's realisation that China had been exploited put the barely formed Sino-Soviet partnership under great stress. The tension was felt as early as the Korean War, which began in 1950 (see page 54). Mao remarked that China had to pay heavily for the Soviet supplies it received during that conflict (see page 56). There were also suggestions that Stalin deliberately prevented an early armistice being reached in Korea in order to exhaust the Chinese.

 KEY FIGURE

Nikita Khrushchev (1894–1971)

Emerged from the power struggle that followed Stalin's death to become the Soviet leader between 1956 and 1964.

Angered though he was by what amounted to Soviet exploitation, Mao tolerated it because he judged that for the time being there was no alternative. In his address of 30 January 1962 (see Source E), he explained the predicament the PRC had faced in its early years.

SOURCE E

Extract from Mao's address, 30 January 1962; here he explains why in the early years of the PRC its economic inexperience meant that it had to follow the Soviet way of doing things. From Stuart Schram, editor, *Mao Tse-tung Unrehearsed: Talks and Letters, 1956–71*, Penguin, 1974, p. 140.

The situation was such that, since we had no experience in economic construction, we had no alternative but to copy the Soviet Union. In the field of heavy industry especially, we copied almost everything from the Soviet Union. At that time it was absolutely necessary to act thus, but at the same time it was a weakness – a lack of creativity and lack of ability to stand on our own feet. Naturally this could not be our long-term strategy. From 1958 we decided to make self-reliance our major policy: and striving for foreign aid a secondary aim. We adopted the general line of 'going all out and aiming high to achieve greater, faster, better and more economical results in building socialism.' In the same year the people's communes were also established, and the slogan of a 'Great Leap Forward' was issued.

According to Mao in Source E, why had the PRC initially copied the Soviet Union's industrial methods?

Mao had judged that the new China could not survive without the USSR's economic assistance. The reality was that the PRC's isolation in a capitalist world left it unable to obtain adequate resources and expertise from anywhere else. Mao was resolved to gain economic independence, but until that was achieved (see page 68) he could not afford to break the link with the Soviet Union. Mao later reflected on the reasons for the strains in the PRC's relations with Stalin's Soviet Union (see Source F).

SOURCE F

From Stuart Schram, editor, *Mao Tse-tung Unrehearsed: Talks and Letters, 1956–71*, Penguin, 1974, p. 191.

*In fact its roots lie deep in the past, in things which happened very long ago. They did not permit China to make revolution: that was in 1945. Stalin wanted to prevent China from making a revolution, saying that we should not have a civil war and should co-operate with Chiang Kai-shek, otherwise the Chinese nation would perish. But we did not do what he said. After the victory of the revolution he next suspected China of being a **Yugoslavia**, and that I would become a second Tito. Later when I went to Moscow to sign the Sino-Soviet Treaty of Alliance and Mutual Assistance [1950], we had to go through another struggle. He was not willing to sign a treaty. After two months of negotiations he at last signed. When did Stalin begin to have confidence in us? It was the time of the Resist America, Aid Korea campaign, from the winter of 1950. He then came to believe that we were not Tito, not Yugoslavia.*

According to Mao in Source F, why were the PRC and the USSR not on good terms?

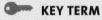 **KEY TERM**

Yugoslavia Under its leader Marshal Tito, it was the one Communist country in Eastern Europe that successfully resisted all efforts by the USSR to control it.

The PRC and the USA

For a generation after 1949 relations between the PRC and the USA were tense and bitter. The PRC mounted a continuous propaganda campaign against 'American imperialism', which included the ritual daily chanting by China's schoolchildren of, 'Death to the American imperialists and all their running dogs.' The reasons for such animosity are not hard to locate. The victory in 1949 of Mao's CCP in the Chinese civil war showed that the USA had been wrong to swallow its doubts about Chiang and commit itself to the support of the Nationalists. The USA's recrimination over its misjudgement seemed to strengthen its suspicion of the PRC's intentions. The USA's sensitivity over the **'loss of China'** in 1949 led the Americans to assume that the Communist invasion of South Korea was the first joint venture of the new Communist bloc formed by Mao's Communist China and the USSR.

The USA's protection of Taiwan

Despite the disillusion many US officials felt about their pro-Chiang, anti-Mao stance before 1949, the USA maintained diplomatic and financial support for Chiang Kai-shek's Nationalist Taiwan, continuing until 1971 to recognise it as the only legitimate China. This was not because of any great belief in Chiang but because Cold War divisions proscribed any form of US policy other than to back anti-Communist regimes no matter how undemocratic they might be. Mao saw this as proof of the inherent corruption of US capitalism.

The USA's refusal to recognise the PRC

In Mao's eyes, the Americans compounded their offence of supporting Taiwan by refusing to grant diplomatic recognition to the PRC. For the USA to maintain the fiction that Chiang and the routed Nationalists skulking on an offshore island represented the Chinese nation was deeply insulting to the PRC and its huge population. Mao condemned the USA's sponsorship of Taiwan's membership of the UN, which thereby denied that right to the PRC, as an act of folly that the USA and its capitalist lackeys would come to regret.

CIA involvement in Tibet

There was evidence that **CIA** agents tried, albeit unavailingly, to assist the Tibetans in their 1950 rising against the PLA (see page 53). Although this work was never on as large a scale as the PRC propagandists claimed, it was enough for Mao to charge the US imperialists with interference in the affairs of the PRC as a sovereign state.

The conflict in Korea

Whatever the merits of the PRC's case for entering the Korean War, the outcome was three years of struggle with the USA as the main enemy fighting under the UN flag. The bitterness of the fighting and the high death toll on the Chinese

KEY TERMS

'Loss of China' The US State Department's term for US failure to prevent the victory of Mao's Communists in China in 1949.

CIA Central Intelligence Agency, the USA's espionage and counter-espionage organisation.

side deepened Sino-American hostility to the point where Mao defined the US endeavour as a preliminary to an assault on the PRC itself.

From the time of the Korean War onwards, Mao was convinced that the USA was planning a destructive attack on China. Mao calculated that when the West was ready it would move to obliterate Chinese communism. This was not simple paranoia. As a Marxist, Mao held that the laws of the dialectic determined that at some point there would be a final great struggle between capitalists and proletarians. Given this premise, it was not entirely fanciful for Mao to think that the capitalist USA harboured destructive intentions towards the PRC.

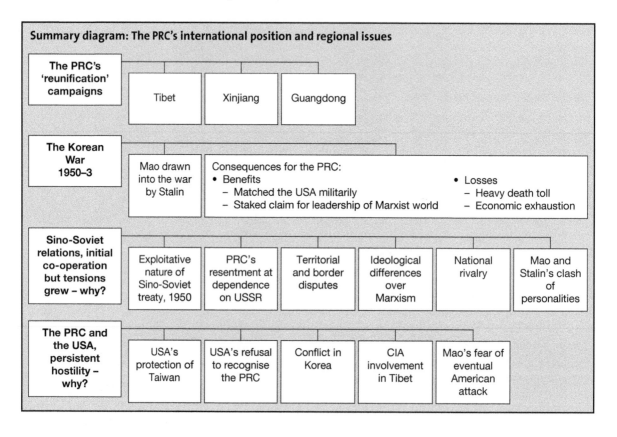

Summary diagram: The PRC's international position and regional issues

Chapter summary

By exploiting Chiang's strategic and political mistakes, Mao's CCP overcame its initial disadvantages in manpower and resources to outmanoeuvre the Nationalists. Playing on Chiang's blundering public relations, Mao pointed out the corruption of the GMD government that undermined its claim to the moral leadership of China. The NRA's poor leadership and lack of morale handed the initiative to the Red Army who, over four years, pushed south into China, eventually forcing Chiang to flee with the remnant of his forces to Taiwan.

A triumphant Mao declared the creation of the PRC in 1949 and proceeded by unflinching terror to build a conformist, obedient society. Using party purges and 'anti-campaigns' against the people, he stifled criticism as he set out economic policy. He refused to allow independence movements to flourish, and sent PLA troops to suppress resistance in the troublesome provinces. With Communist China now part of the Cold War and fighting in Korea, Mao found himself on difficult terms with both capitalist USA and communist USSR. Dependent on Soviet economic aid, he accepted treaty terms that were much to the PRC's detriment. By 1953 the PRC had survived its first years but its future was still insecure.

Refresher questions

Use these questions to remind yourself of the key material covered in this chapter.

1 Why were the Nationalists unable to win the civil war?

2 Why was Chiang unable to gain the support of the Chinese regions?

3 Why was the NRA so brutal in its treatment of its own troops?

4 Why were the Communists ultimately successful in the civil war?

5 Why was the Soviet Union so reluctant to support the CCP during the civil war?

6 How did Mao impose himself on the people of China?

7 How was Communist authority imposed over mainland China?

8 What methods did Mao's government use to extend its political and social control?

9 How did Mao maintain his authority over the CCP?

10 How did democratic centralism operate under Mao?

11 Why was Mao so determined to destroy the middle class?

12 What were Mao's reasons for committing China to the Korean War?

13 What lay at the root of the mutual suspicion between Mao and Stalin?

14 Why were Sino-American relations so hostile in the early years of the PRC?

Question practice

ESSAY QUESTIONS

1 'It was not the Communists' strengths but the Nationalists' weaknesses that enabled Mao to win the civil war of 1945–9.' Explain why you agree or disagree with this view.

2 How far did Mao's 'anti-campaigns' of the early 1950s achieve their objectives?

3 'The Soviet Union was a greater threat to the survival of the People's Republic of China in its early years (1949–62) than the USA.' Assess the validity of this view.

4 'Taiwan was a key factor in Sino-American relations in the period 1949–72.' How far do you agree with this statement?

SOURCE ANALYSIS QUESTIONS

1 With reference to Sources B (**page 42**) and E (**page 60**) and your understanding of the historical context, which of these two sources is more valuable in explaining why the Soviet Union had a strong influence on the PRC over the period 1949–53?

2 With reference to Sources B (**page 42**), E (**page 60**), and F (**page 60**), and your understanding of the historical context, assess the value of these sources to a historian studying Sino-Soviet relations over the period 1949–53.

3 Why is Source B (**page 42**) valuable to the historian studying Sino-Soviet relations over the period 1949–53? Explain your answer using the source, the information given about it and your own knowledge of the historical context.

4 How much weight do you give to the evidence in Source E (**page 60**) as an explanation of Mao's attitude towards the Soviet Union in the early years of the PRC? Explain your answer, using the source, the information given about it and your own knowledge of the historical context.

5 How far could the historian make use of Sources B (**page 42**) and E (**page 60**) together to investigate relations between Mao and Stalin in the period 1949–53? Explain your answer using the sources, the information given about it and your own knowledge of the historical context.

CHAPTER 3

The transition to socialism 1952–62

Mao knew that the PRC had to develop its economy in order to survive. To this end he extended his revolutionary ideas into the restructuring of agriculture and industry. Mao's policies had disastrous social consequences and aroused opposition; his response was to intensify coercion. On the international front, Mao had to determine what China's relations with the outside world were to be in the aftermath of the Korean War.

This chapter covers these themes under the following headings:

★ Economic developments: industry

★ Economic developments: agriculture

★ Political developments 1952–62

★ China's international relations 1953–62

The key debate on *page 88* of this chapter asks the question: What were Mao's motives in launching the Hundred Flowers campaign?

Key dates

1952–6	First Five-Year Plan	1959	Lushan conference
1954	Fall of Gao Gang and Rao Shushi		Tibetan rising
1957	Hundred Flowers campaign	1962	Sino-Indian War
1958–62	Great Leap Forward		Cuban Missile Crisis
	China's great famine		Liu Shaoqi and Deng Xiaoping appointed to tackle famine
1959	Soviet advisers withdrawn from PRC		

1 Economic developments: industry

▶ *What were Mao's objectives in his reforming of China's industry?*

Mao believed that the modernisation of the economy was essential to the PRC's survival as a nation. His early attempts at economic reform carried the stamp of Soviet influence. Initially dependent on Soviet assistance and impressed by the apparent success of **Stalin's Five-Year Plans** in the USSR, Mao wanted the PRC to build on the same model. In 1952 China's first Five-Year Plan was

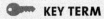
KEY TERM

Stalin's Five-Year Plans
In the USSR, between 1929 and 1953, Stalin had revolutionised the Soviet economy by a series of government-directed plans.

introduced. Its aim was to develop the state-directed growth of **heavy industry**. A partial basis for this already existed. During their period of government in the 1930s and 1940s, the GMD under Chiang Kai-shek had established a National Resources Committee (NRC), which had taken control of industrial investment policy. A large number of NRC managers and over 200,000 of its workforce had stayed on in China after 1949. In addition, a significant population shift had begun with the coming to power of the CCP. Between 1949 and 1957 migration from the countryside to the towns nearly doubled the urban population from 57 million to 100 million.

The result was that, as the PRC began its economic reforms, it already had available a large potential workforce and considerable industrial expertise. However, the new government's first notable success was scored unaided. In its first two years it brought under control the galloping inflation from which China had suffered during the final years of the GMD. From a rate of 1000 per cent in 1949, inflation had dropped to a manageable fifteen per cent by 1951. This was largely achieved by:

- slashing public expenditure
- raising tax rates on urban dwellers
- replacing the old Chinese dollar with a new currency, known as the renminbi or **yuan**.

The first Five-Year Plan 1952–6

Under the plan, the areas targeted for increased production were coal, steel and petrochemicals. Attention was also to be given to the development of a Chinese automobile industry. As a morale boost, a number of spectacular civil-engineering projects were undertaken. An outstanding example was the construction of a vast road and rail bridge across the Yangzi River at Nanjing. The degree of success achieved by the plan can be gauged from Table 3.1.

Table 3.1 Statistics of the first Five-Year Plan 1952–6

Output	1952 output targets	1957 output achieved
Gross industrial output (yuan, millions)	53,560	65,020
Particular areas of production		
Coal (millions of tonnes)	113	115
Oil (millions of tonnes)	2,012	1,458
Steel (millions of tonnes)	4.12	5.35
Electric power (billions of kilowatts)	15.9	19.34
Hydroelectric turbines (kilowatts)	79,000	74,900
Machine tools (units)	12,720	28,000
Locomotives (units)	200	167
Freight cars (units)	8,500	7,300
Merchant ships (tonnes)	179,000	54,000
Trucks (units)	4,000	7,500
Bicycles (units)	550,000	1,174,000
Manufactured chemicals (millions of tonnes)	1,580	2,087

Care has to be taken with these statistics. As in the USSR under Stalin, so in the PRC under Mao, there was a tendency for officials to massage the figures relating to economic performance. All those in the spiral of command, from CCP officials and industrial managers down to foremen and workers, were anxious to appear to be fulfilling their targets. The presence of party cadres checking on production targets meant that in many areas of industry there was what amounted to an organised conspiracy to adjust the figures so that they appeared as impressive as possible.

The Plan's success

The statistics in Table 3.2, which have been filtered through Western analyses, do indicate a considerable degree of success for the plan, this at a time when the Korean War required China to finance a major war effort.

Table 3.2 PRC expenditure (as percentages of national budget)

	1950	1952	1957
Economic development	25.5	45.4	51.4
Education and culture	11.1	13.6	16.0
Defence	41.5	26.0	19.0
Government administration	19.3	10.3	7.8
Miscellaneous	2.6	4.7	5.8
Total (yuan, millions)	6,810	16,790	29,020

China's economic growth rate of nearly nine per cent between 1953 and 1957 compared favourably with that of the USSR in the 1930s. In the circumstances of the 1950s it was natural that China should measure itself against the yardstick of the Soviet Union's industrial performance and seek to match its success.

The second Five-Year Plan: the Great Leap Forward

The Great Leap Forward was the term Mao used to describe the second Five-Year Plan of 1958–62. His aim was to turn the PRC into a modern industrial state in the shortest possible time. He believed that by revolutionising China's agriculture and industry the PRC could build an economy that would catch up with those of the major nations and then overtake them.

Mao had led the Chinese peasants to victory in 1949. Yet he was convinced that China's future as a great power actually depended not on the peasants and agriculture but on the workers and industry. It was industrialisation that mattered. He held that history had reached the stage where China, having lagged behind the rest of the advanced industrialised world, would now surpass it purely through the dedicated efforts of the Chinese people, led by their inspired Communist government. That was why he used the word 'leap'. China would bypass the stages through which the advanced nations had gone, and go straight from being a rural, agricultural economy to becoming an urban, industrial one.

As Mao described it, the leap would allow China 'to overtake all capitalist countries in a fairly short time, and become one of the richest, most advanced and powerful countries in the world'. In 1957, while attending a gathering of international Communist leaders in Moscow, the Soviet capital, he said, 'the East wind will prevail over the West wind, because we are powerful and strong. You just cannot decide things with the quantity of steel and iron; rather, first and foremost, things are determined by people's hearts and minds.'

It was not by chance that Mao made his announcement while in Moscow. He admired the Soviet Union for what it had achieved economically. However, he did not enjoy his visits to Moscow and he regretted that the PRC had been so dependent on the Soviet Union since 1949. He was determined to match the USSR's economic achievement but without slavishly following Soviet methods. By 1957, he felt that the PRC was strong enough to begin ending its earlier economic dependence on the USSR (see page 60).

(see page 60)

> **KEY TERM**
>
> **Lift-off** Increasing output and production at such a pace as to turn China into a modern industrial power.

Mass effort

Mao resolved to achieve industrial **lift-off** for China by harnessing what he regarded as the nation's greatest resource – its massive population. Mao's conviction was that the Chinese people could achieve two great advances:

- First, the collectivised peasants, working in their communes, would produce a surplus of food that could be sold abroad to raise money for the expansion of Chinese industry.
- Second, the workers would create, literally with their own hands, a modern industrial economy, powerful enough to compete with the Soviet Union and the capitalist West.

Mao assumed that simply by an effort of will the output achieved under the first Five-Year Plan could be vastly increased. The emphasis was on heavy industry and large projects. Mao, like Stalin, was greatly impressed by the grand project. Size mattered. It was the scale of a construction rather than its economic value which appealed to him. He was convinced that by sheer manpower China could solve all the problems of industrial development.

It is certainly true that prodigious feats were achieved by manual labour alone during the Great Leap Forward. Mechanical diggers were shunned in favour of the earth being moved by the hands of the workers. Giant span bridges, canals and dams were constructed. These were lauded by the CCP as the visible proof of China's resurgence under Communism. It became a common sight across China to see thousands of workers, men, women and children, dressed in identical blue uniforms and toiling with only the most rudimentary of tools. The government's propaganda newsreels of the day showed them all gaily smiling and singing as they went about their joyful task of reconstructing China. This was in addition to thousands of prisoners forced to work under the gaze of armed guards. A fitting description was that Mao Zedong had become 'the emperor of the blue ants'.

Although the second Five-Year Plan was introduced in 1958 in a blaze of propaganda, there was a sense in which the plan was not a plan at all. It was true that targets and quotas were constantly set and reset, but these were not based on sound economic analysis. Rather, they were plucked from the air on a whim. They were acts of faith in Communist China's ability to produce, not on a hard-headed assessment of what was realistically possible. That is why the projected figures were changed so frequently. They were usually revised upwards by officials in order to assure Mao that they were responding to his call for a mass collective effort. A finance minister admitted how disorganised the whole thing was when he said in 1958, 'At present the central authorities are compiling targets for the second Five-Year Plan, but have not been able to catch up with the swift changes in practical conditions that require upward revision of the targets almost every day.'

'General Steel'

Chinese planners liked to speak figuratively of two great soldiers who would lead the nation to economic victory: 'General Grain' and 'General Steel'. They claimed that just as General Grain was triumphing in the battle to increase China's food supplies (see page 75), so, similarly, General Steel would win the struggle to turn China into a successful industrial economy.

The backyard furnaces

Mao had a simple belief that by producing masses of steel China would somehow solve all its economic problems. The outstanding expression of this was his insistence on the construction of **backyard furnaces**. China would draw its supplies of iron and steel not only from large foundries and mills but also from small family kilns.

KEY TERM

Backyard furnaces
Primitive smelting devices that every family was encouraged to build on its premises.

Here was a communal activity in which all of China's people could participate, conscious that by their own efforts they were helping to build the new society. Everybody, peasants as well as workers, young children and old people, could be involved. Enthusiasm, not skill, was the basic requirement. People would develop successful techniques as they went along. It would be a glorious example of 'learning by doing'. At Mao's command, the Chinese rushed to build their little furnaces. It became a national movement. The sky at night was reddened by the flames of millions of kilns. In daytime, large areas of China were covered by a pall of smoke that sometimes obscured the noonday sun.

Foreigners in China were amazed by the scale and intensity of the people's response. Roderick MacFarquar, a celebrated writer on Chinese affairs who was then living in Beijing, described the 'seething, clattering frenzy' that had overtaken China. 'People carried baskets of ore, people stoked, people goaded buffalo carts, people tipped cauldrons of white-hot metal, people stood on rickety ladders and peered into furnaces, people wheeled barrows of crude steel.'

SOURCE A

Backyard furnaces: scenes such as these were widespread across China.

? Why were so many people so willing to join in the production of steel in the localised way as shown in Source A?

🔑 **KEY TERM**

Zhongnanhai The building compound off Tiananmen Square, the historic centrepiece of Beijing, which housed the government offices and ministers' residences.

? How does the report in Source B convey the enthusiasm of the people's response to the call for collective effort?

Even ministers and their families joined in. In **Zhongnanhai**, hundreds of tiny furnaces were to be found, each one turning out its quota of homemade steel. Excited officials reported back to Beijing on how eagerly and successfully the people of China were answering Mao's call for steel.

SOURCE B

From an official report from Shaoyang, quoted in Pei-kai Cheng and Michael Lestz, editors, *The Search for Modern China: A Documentary Collection*, W.W. Norton, 1999, p. 404. A local CCP official gives an account in 1958 of how the people in Hunan province responded to Mao's call for mass effort to industrialise China.

Iron smelting and steel making in Shaoyang, Hunan Province, are rapidly developing on a mass scale. In a short period in the autumn of 1958, 12,378 local blast furnaces were built in this area. The strength of the masses is tremendous. All the problems of funds, raw materials, equipment, fuel, and geological survey of resources, which seemed hard to solve in the past, disappeared before the resourcefulness of the people. In honor of the anniversary of the Communist Party (July 1), 67,000 people in Hsinhua County worked for three days and nights on end and built 1,025 blast furnaces. Many people hearing the news came from as far as 100 li [64 km, 40 miles] away to join in the work, carrying timber and bamboo and their food and clothes. In Szetu Township, 53 couples came to put their names down offering to help in industrial production. Within a few days this county collected a fund of more than 1.6 million yuan. To solve the housing problem, the people of Tienping Township, in one morning, spontaneously vacated more than 500 rooms. The contributions from the masses became a mighty torrent, and the blast furnaces were set up very quickly.

Weakness of the campaign

The people may have been eager but they were hardly successful. Goodwill did not necessarily produce good steel. The only steel suitable for industrial use came from the large foundries. The homemade variety was worthless. Most of it was not steel in any recognisable sense. Smelted from such domestic oddments as pots, pans and bicycles, 'the people's steel' ended up as large, hard, unusable blobs. The authorities knew this, but they went on pretending. The steel continued to be regularly gathered from beaming peasants by beaming collectors, who drove it away and dumped it in deep pits which were then covered over. The fate of the worthless steel could be taken as symbolising the Great Leap Forward itself – lots of energy, noise and endeavour but little substance.

State-owned enterprises

An important feature of the Great Leap Forward was the creation of state-owned enterprises (SOEs). This was an attempt to bring industry under total government direction. Existing firms and companies could no longer operate as private, profit-making concerns. Instead, they would work for the state as designated SOEs. The workers could no longer bargain with employers over rates of pay and conditions. Prices, output targets and wages were to be fixed by the state.

In theory, the SOEs fulfilled the Communist notion of centrally controlled industry. But, in practice, they performed less well than anticipated. This was because they were basically inefficient, largely as a result of their abandoning any idea of incentives. Under the new system, the SOEs were given state subsidies and the workers received guaranteed wages. This destroyed any motive for the managers or the workers to show initiative. It did not matter whether an SOE was efficiently managed, since any surplus it earned went straight to the state. Similarly, no matter how conscientious or idle a worker was, he or she still received the same pay.

In performance terms, the system was stultifying; it destroyed any sense of endeavour. However, for the workers, the positive side of the system was that they had an **iron rice bowl**, the Chinese term for a secure job for life. Moreover, the SOEs also provided the workers with accommodation and medical and educational benefits for their families.

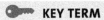 **KEY TERM**

Iron rice bowl The system that provided a worker with a guaranteed job and wage.

Production under the second Five-Year Plan

As Table 3.3 on page 72 shows, there were some apparently impressive increases in output.

The picture is one of an initial expansion up to 1960 and then a serious falling away in production in the early 1960s. What needs to be stressed here is that, although some of the figures may seem impressive, they relate only to the production of materials. They do not reveal how the materials were then used.

Table 3.3 Production from 1957 to 1964, covering the second Five-Year Plan of 1958–62

Industrial production	1957	1958	1959	1960	1961	1962	1963	1964
Coal (millions of tonnes)	131	230	290	270	180	180	190	200
Steel (millions of tonnes)	5.4	8	10	13	8	8	9	10
Oil (millions of tonnes)	1.5	2.3	3.7	4.5	4.5	5.3	5.9	7
Chemical fertilisers (millions of tonnes)	0.8	1.4	2.0	2.5	1.4	2.1	3.0	3.6
Cotton cloth (billions of metres)	5.0	5.7	7.5	6.0	3.0	3.0	3.5	4.0

KEY TERMS

Manufactured goods
Sellable products made from raw materials.

Quality control The monitoring of industrial production to maintain set standards.

The fact is there was no integrated plan for turning what had been produced into **manufactured goods**. A crippling weakness was that China lacked the following essentials:

- technical skills
- managerial know-how
- efficiently run factories and plants
- an adequate transport system.

Without these essentials, China could not build the modern economy that Mao had promised would overtake the world in a great leap. The failure is evident in Table 3.4. Instead of growing under the Great Leap Forward, the output of industrially produced goods actually fell.

Table 3.4 Production of manufactured goods 1959–62

To an index of 100	1959	1960	1961	1962
Light industrial	100	91.2	78.4	70.0
Heavy industrial	100	90.0	66.4	44.2

The limitations of the Great Leap Forward

Many of the communal endeavours that took place under the plan thrilled the Chinese and impressed foreigners, but the plan as a whole did not reach its objective of laying the basis of a modern industrial economy. Among the explanations for this were:

- The quality of finished products fell short of China's industrial needs.
- Political interference made the plan impossible to manage purely as an economic enterprise.
- Officials issued demands and threats but few detailed instructions as to how things were actually to be done.
- Despite the setting up of SOEs, so much was left to local initiative that China never operated an integrated national plan.
- The result was that effective organisation and **quality control** became difficult to achieve.
- In 1959 the USSR withdrew technical assistance, which resulted in the closure of half the 300 industrial plants that the Soviets had sponsored in China.

SOURCE C

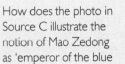

How does the photo in Source C illustrate the notion of Mao Zedong as 'emperor of the blue ants'?

Workers constructing a dam in 1958.

Mao's limitations as an economic planner

Mao's belief was that **applied communism** would always produce an effective system of production. However, what passed for planning was really only a set of politically inspired slogans. The reports of the party conferences called to discuss the progress of the Great Leap Forward describe the delegates shouting slogans and counter-slogans at each other instead of addressing the real economic problems.

 KEY TERM

Applied communism
Planning according to Marxist principles involving state direction of the economy and the ending of private ownership.

Yet Mao would not accept that his policies were at fault. He interpreted the lack of economic achievement not as a failure of planning, but as the result of sabotage by bourgeois elements and backsliders. His invariable reaction to the news of failure was to deny the bad results and then, when they could no longer be disputed, to search for the culprits responsible for administering the policies wrongly, either through incompetence or deliberate sabotage.

There is no doubting the ambition of Mao's economic policies; he aimed to place the PRC on a par with the world's major industrial powers. But ambition was not enough. His economic strategy proved to be misconceived. He did not understand the industrial process and mistakenly believed that simply by a massive deployment of manpower China could achieve advanced industrialisation. In no sense was Mao qualified as an economic planner. He admitted as much: 'I only understand social sciences but not natural sciences.' His experience as a political in-fighter and military strategist had not prepared him for the task of shaping the economy of a vast nation. His approach was necessarily a series of intuitive leaps. The result was calamitous. His five-year plans wasted rather than exploited China's vast natural and human resources.

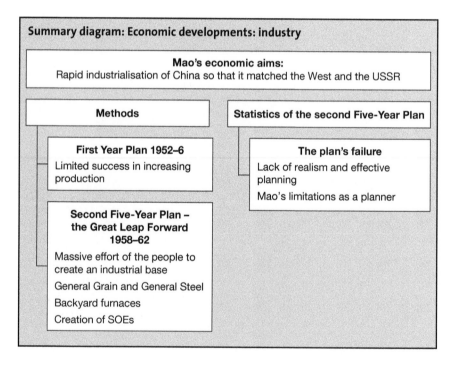

Summary diagram: Economic developments: industry

Mao's economic aims:
Rapid industrialisation of China so that it matched the West and the USSR

Methods

Statistics of the second Five-Year Plan

First Year Plan 1952–6
Limited success in increasing production

The plan's failure
Lack of realism and effective planning
Mao's limitations as a planner

Second Five-Year Plan – the Great Leap Forward 1958–62
Massive effort of the people to create an industrial base
General Grain and General Steel
Backyard furnaces
Creation of SOEs

Economic developments: agriculture

▶ *Why did Mao introduce collectivisation and with what consequences?*

Mao's attitude towards the peasants

The agricultural policy that Mao adopted has to be seen as a complement to his industrialisation plans, which had priority over all other considerations. By the mid-1950s, the organisers of the first Five-Year Plan had become aware that China had a severe labour shortage; those employed in industry were still only a minority of the Chinese working population. The industrial workforce would have to be greatly increased if targets were to be met. It was also the case that, although the peasants were undoubtedly producing more food, this was not finding its way to the urban workers. The common view among the economic planners was that this was the fault of the peasants: they were indulging themselves by overeating and by having larger families, which meant more mouths had to be fed.

Mao often became impatient with what he regarded as peasant obstinacy. In 1953 he urged his officials: 'Educate peasants to eat less. The State should try its hardest to prevent peasants eating too much.' One of the extraordinary things about Mao was that, although he was himself a peasant and had led a great peasant revolution, he had a very low opinion of the class from which he came. In 1959, he declared to a group of ministers: 'Peasants are hiding food and are very bad. There is no Communist spirit in them! Peasants are after all peasants. That's the only way they can behave.'

Collectivisation

China's initial land reforms of the early 1950s had been introduced in the excitement accompanying the 1949 formation of the PRC. The land had been seized from the landlords and given to the peasants. Yet, even at that time, the peasants had been urged to pool their resources by joining in farm **collectives**. This was the principle that was now forcibly extended. Between 1956 and 1958 the government directed that the existing 750,000 collectives be amalgamated into a number of large **communes**. In 1958, Mao made this collectivisation process an essential part of the Great Leap Forward:

- The 750,000 collectives were merged into 26,000 communes.
- The communes collectively contained 120 million households (an average household having five members).

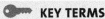 **KEY TERMS**

Collectives Areas where the peasants farmed communally rather than for themselves individually.

Communes Organised regions where collectives were grouped together.

- The whole system was under the direct control of the central government; farming methods, the sale and distribution of produce, and the setting of prices were to be dictated from above.
- Private farming was ended.
- The peasants needed internal passports to pass from one commune to another.

Mao maintained that collectivisation, far from being forced on the peasants, was a direct response to their wishes. In the summer of 1958 the CCP's Central Committee declared in Mao's name that 'the people have taken to organizing themselves along military lines leading toward a happier collective life and further fostering ideas of collectivism among the peasant masses'. Official newspapers carried the same message as can be seen in Source D.

SOURCE D

According to Source D, what evidence is there that the commune movement was spontaneously started by the peasants?

From an editorial, 'Hold High the Red Flag of People's Communes', quoted in Pei-kai Cheng and Michal Lestz, editors, *The Search for Modern China: A Documentary Collection*, W.W. Norton, 1999, p. 412. The editorial of 3 September 1958 in *The People's Daily*, the CCP's official newspaper, claims that collectivisation was a spontaneous movement of the Chinese people.

This movement has been spontaneously started by the mass of peasants on the basis of great socialist consciousness. When a small number of people's communes were first established, their sources at once inspired many of the agricultural producers' co-operatives to follow suit. The movement gradually gained momentum. Now, with the encouragement and guidance given by the Central Committee of the Communist Party and Chairman Mao Zedong, it is making even greater strides forward. Dazibao [big-character posters] are appearing everywhere in the countryside, and a great number of applications have been made for the establishment of people's communities. Virtually all the peasants in Hunan and Liaoning provinces are now members of people's communes and the movement is in high tide in the provinces of Hebei, Heilong-jiang, and Anhui. Meanwhile, preparations are being made in northwestern China, the Yangtse valley and provinces south of the Yangtse River to establish people's communes after the autumn harvest.

The CCP's claim was a misrepresentation. Collectivisation had been imposed on the Chinese peasantry as part of a massive social experiment in which the wishes of the peasants themselves were simply ignored. This disregard for the ordinary people of China was to have disastrous consequences.

China's great famine 1958–62

The collectivisation programme that began in 1958 entailed a vast social transformation which resulted in a famine of unprecedented severity. The disruption caused by the ending of private farming was a major cause of hunger since it discouraged the individual peasant from producing food beyond his or her own immediate needs. But equally significant was Mao's belief that Chinese **agronomists** had made a series of discoveries about crop growing that would revolutionise food production.

Lysenkoism

Chinese scientists were tragically influenced by the theories of **Trofim Lysenko**, a Soviet quack, who claimed to have developed techniques that resulted in crops like rice and wheat yielding up to sixteen times more food than under traditional methods. It was later realised and admitted that Lysenko was a fraud whose 'super-crop' theories were wholly worthless. But so strong was the influence of the USSR in the early years of the PRC that Chinese agricultural researchers were taught that Lysenko was infallible. A Beijing doctor recorded: 'We were told that the Soviets had discovered and invented everything; we had to change textbooks and rename things in Lysenko's honour.' Mao made Lysenkoism official policy in 1958 when he personally drafted an eight-point agricultural 'constitution' based on the theories of crop growth advanced by Lysenko and his Chinese disciples, which farmers were forced to follow. The eight headings were:

- use new breeds and seeds
- plant closely
- plough deeply
- increase fertilisation
- use new farm tools
- improve field management
- control pests
- increase irrigation.

Taken separately, these instructions might have had some value. But the demand that all the instructions be applied universally, regardless of the type of crop or of the soil and climate of the region, destroyed whatever benefits they might have brought if applied intelligently. Across China crops withered in the field.

'Sparrowcide'

The most vivid example of the tragic results that followed from unthinking application was in regard to pest control. The whole Chinese people were called on to end the menace of sparrows and other wild birds which ate crop seeds. So, at prescribed times, the Chinese came out from their houses and with any implement they could lay their hands on made as much noise as possible. Clanging plates, metal pots and pans, they kept up a continuous din that prevented the birds from landing, so that they eventually dropped exhausted from the sky. The thousands of dead birds were then publicly displayed as trophies. Villages and regions competed with each other over who could kill the most birds.

KEY TERM

Agronomists Agricultural scientists.

KEY FIGURE

Trofim Lysenko (1898–1976)

A pseudo-scientist regarded by Stalin as a model exponent of 'socialist science'.

The outcome was catastrophic. With no birds now to thin their numbers, insects and small creatures gorged themselves on the grains and plants. The larger birds that would have fed off the smaller ones were no longer around to prey on rats and their kind. Vermin multiplied and destroyed stocks of grain. The absurdity of the enterprise became only too evident in the hunger that followed.

Starvation

The bewildered local peasant communities, whose way of life had already been dislocated by collectivisation, had no means of preventing the famine that followed. They became defeatist in the face of impending doom. Those peasants who tried to ignore the new regulations and carry on with their old ways of farming were rounded up and imprisoned as 'rightists'. The bare statistics of the famine are shown in Table 3.5.

Table 3.5 China's agricultural output 1952–62

Year	Grain production (millions of tonnes)	Meat production (millions of tonnes)
1952	163.9	3.4
1953	166.8	3.8
1954	169.5	3.9
1955	183.9	3.3
1956	192.8	3.4
1957	195.1	4.0
1958	200.0	4.3
1959	170.0	2.6
1960	143.5	1.3
1961	147.5	1.2
1962	160.0	1.9

The figures show a marked reduction in food production from 1958 onwards, the years of the famine. Although the decline does not look especially dramatic, it has to be emphasised that the figures refer to China overall; the food shortages were much more severe in the famine provinces of central China. Nearly every province in China was affected by the famine, but the greatest suffering occurred in central China. Of the 50 million who died throughout China, the worst death toll was in a great arc of misery that swept through China's rural provinces from Shandong in the east to Tibet in the west:

- Shandong: 7.5 million
- Anhui: 8 million
- Henan: 7.8 million
- Sichuan: 9 million
- Qinghai: 1 million
- Tibet: 1 million.

Hebei and Xinjiang were other areas that experienced terrible suffering. Parents sold their children, and husbands their wives, for food. Women prostituted themselves to obtain food for their families, and there were many instances

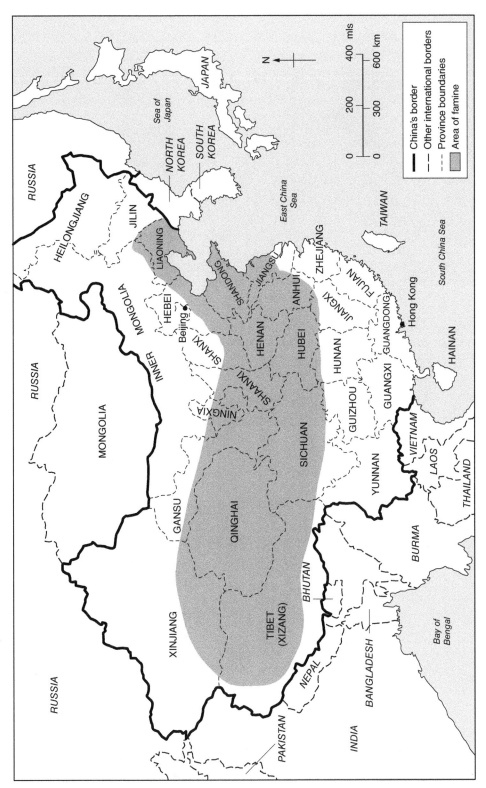

The areas in China worst hit by the famine. How does the map help to explain why the famine might be referred to as an 'arc of misery'?

of peasants offering themselves as slaves to anyone who would supply them with food. Source E describes the cannibalism that occurred in a number of provinces.

What insight does Source E give into the way the authorities responded to the famine in parts of China?

SOURCE E

From Jasper Becker, *Hungry Ghosts*, John Murray, 1996, p. 218. A CCP local newspaper in Liaoning in 1959 reports an example of cannibalism in the province and describes the stern measures taken by the authorities to prevent further cases.

A peasant woman, unable to stand the incessant crying for food of her two-year-old daughter, and thinking perhaps to end her suffering, had strangled her. She had given the girl's body to her husband, asking him to bury it. Instead, out of his mind with hunger, he put the body in the cooking pot with what little food they had foraged. He had forced his wife to eat a bowl of the resulting stew. His wife, in a fit of remorse, had reported her husband's crime to the authorities. Although there was no law against cannibalism in the criminal code of the People's Republic, the Ministry of Public Security treated such cases, which were all too common, with the utmost severity. Both husband and wife were arrested and summarily executed.

A conspiracy of silence

What deepened the tragedy was that government advisers were well aware of the facts. They knew that people were dying by the million, but they dared not speak out. Indeed, the reverse happened; cadres and officials reported back to Beijing that production targets were being met and that the Great Leap Forward was on course. Sir Percy Craddock, British Ambassador in China in the 1960s, described how provincial leaders 'cooked the books', pretending their region had witnessed immense increases when in reality the people were starving. To impress Mao and suggest abundant growth, it was known for crops to be lifted from the fields and massed together alongside the railway track along which Mao's special train travelled. After Mao had passed through, the crops were returned to their original fields.

The famine in Tibet

Relative to the size of its population, Tibet was the province that suffered most during the famine. A quarter of its 4 million people were wiped out. This figure becomes even more appalling when it is realised that the death toll was intended. The famine in Tibet was a man-made disaster. Since 1950, when the PLA had imposed 'reunification' on Tibet, Chinese occupiers had engaged in the systematic destruction of the cultural, social and religious identity of the country. Despite the pressure it came under, the Tibetan resistance survived as an underground movement to re-emerge in 1959 to lead a national rising against the Chinese occupation. The Chinese authorities responded by sending in PLA units to suppress the demonstrations. What gave the Tibetan rising in 1959 a

SOURCE F

Why has the photo in Source F been described as notorious?

One of the most notorious propaganda photos of the time purported to show children playing on crop leaves that grew so thickly in the field that the youngsters did not fall through.

SOURCE G

Despite evidence such as the photo in Source G, why did so many people inside and outside China find it hard to believe that there was a great famine in China?

Starving refugees from the famine begging for food in Hong Kong in 1962. It was from Hong Kong, to which thousands of rural Chinese tried to flee, that news of the famine came to Western attention.

terrible twist was that it coincided with the development of famine across China. In one of its most ruthless acts, the PRC chose deliberately to extend the famine to Tibet.

Traditional Tibetan farming had two main forms: the growing of barley and oats by farmers and the rearing of yaks and sheep by nomadic herders. For centuries this had been sufficient to meet Tibet's needs. However, the Chinese occupiers demanded that 'the communal and socialist farming techniques created by Chairman Mao' now be adopted in Tibet. The farmers were forbidden to grow barley, which provided the staple Tibetan diet, and instructed to sow wheat and maize instead. Since neither crop was suited to the local soil or climate, the order led to the destruction of Tibet's arable food production. This assault on the traditional methods of the crop farmers was matched by the destruction of the ways of life of Tibet's **khampas**, who were forbidden any longer to roam the pasture lands with their yak herds. Instead, they were told that they were not nomads now but farmers and were forced to live with their herds in communes. The result was the emaciation of the animals and the starvation of the Tibetans.

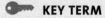

KEY TERM

Khampas The nomadic herdsmen of Tibet.

? What evidence does Source H provide that the famine in Tibet was not simply a natural disaster but a deliberate act of genocide?

SOURCE H

From Jasper Becker, *Hungry Ghosts*, John Murray, 1996, p. 169. A Tibetan eyewitness gives her account in 1961 of the treatment to which her people were subjected by the Chinese authorities during the famine.

Every day five or six people would be found dead in the morning. The bodies of the children and old people were always swollen with hunger. Since most men had been arrested, about 60 per cent of the adult population were women. We could collect grasses from the fields, boil them and force this mixture down our throats. If you didn't, then you would die. Although we were dizzy and faint, we still had to keep working and then we would try and pick up grain or grass to eat. But you had to keep an eye out for the guards. If they caught you, then they would grab you by the throat and choke you to make you spit out the grass seeds. They would body-search all of us when we returned from working in the fields. There were also special teams which searched people's homes for grain, digging up the floors, breaking open walls and looking through the fodder for the horses. The searches went on all through the famine. If they discovered any food, even a few grains, the guilty person would have a big wooden sign hung on him and then he would be paraded round, beaten and spat on.

Mao's responsibility for the famine in China

So devastating was the famine in Tibet and the other provinces that eventually Mao came to accept that it was happening. But his reaction was characteristic. He refused to acknowledge that the disaster was a result of his policies of collectivisation and applied Socialist science. Instead of taking the blame on himself, Mao put the famine down to three factors:

- the hoarding of grain by the peasants
- the mistakes by local officials
- the exceptionally bad weather of the years 1958–61.

There was no truth in the first of Mao's explanations, some in the second, and a little in the third. But poor weather does not explain the famine. The starvation of the Tibetan people was not a misfortune of nature; it was a direct and fatal consequence of Mao's decisions.

Summary diagram: Economic developments: agriculture

<table>
<tr><td colspan="2" align="center">The reform of agriculture</td></tr>
<tr><td>Aim</td><td>Methods</td></tr>
<tr><td>To provide a basis for industrialisation</td><td>Collectivisation of the peasants</td></tr>
<tr><td>To revolutionise food production</td><td>Abolition of private ownership</td></tr>
</table>

<table>
<tr><td colspan="2" align="center">China's great famine 1958–62</td></tr>
<tr><td>Impact</td><td>Causes</td></tr>
<tr><td>Worst effects in rural China in an 'arc of misery'</td><td>Collectivisation</td></tr>
<tr><td>Social disruption</td><td>Lysenkoism</td></tr>
<tr><td>Disease</td><td>Bad weather</td></tr>
<tr><td>Cannibalism</td><td>Deliberate policy</td></tr>
<tr><td>Death</td><td></td></tr>
</table>

<table>
<tr><td colspan="2" align="center">Why was the famine so severe?</td></tr>
<tr><td>Disorientation of the peasants</td><td>A conspiracy of silence</td></tr>
<tr><td>Refusal of officials to admit scale of hunger</td><td>Mao's refusal to face facts</td></tr>
<tr><td></td><td>Deliberate genocide in Tibet</td></tr>
</table>

 # Political developments 1952–62

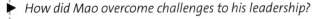
▶ *How did Mao overcome challenges to his leadership?*

The repression already imposed on the nation was intensified by Mao after he began his sweeping economic changes. His justification for extending the anti-campaigns and increasing the purges was that the fate of the nation was in the balance. Unless the PRC modernised it could not survive. In the face of such danger, it would be a betrayal of the revolutionary cause to tolerate internal dissension and criticism. Those who could not accept the need for rapid economic change were no better than counter-revolutionaries.

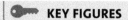
The Gao Gang and Rao Shushi affair 1954

Mao claimed that many officials were only half-hearted in their efforts to promote industrialisation. He identified two major culprits: **Gao Gang** and **Rao Shushi**. Mao asserted in 1954 that these two leading party officials, rather than working to advance China's industrialisation, had misused their authority to establish 'independent kingdoms'. Mao's charges resulted in the Central Council's dismissing both men from their positions. Gao Gang killed himself, an act described by Deng Xiaoping, who had been highly active in hounding him, as 'the ultimate treason'.

Mao's fears for his leadership

The high party status and reputation that Gao and Rao had enjoyed made their sudden fall all the more remarkable. It was clear evidence of the increasing centralisation of power in the party and government and of Mao's refusal to tolerate potential rivals. Despite his apparently close working relations with colleagues, his political sense, based on his experience of overcoming internal party opposition in the 1930s and 1940s, told him that no one was to be fully trusted. His suspicion that his industrialisation programme might be used as a pretext to challenge his leadership was aroused by a CCP congress in November 1956, during which members, while applauding him lustily, passed a formal resolution confirming that the government of the PRC was a collective not an individual affair. In itself, this was not especially threatening to Mao since the fiction had always been that, despite the reality of Mao's dominance, the PRC had been founded in 1949 on the principle of collective leadership.

More troubling to Mao was the congress's acceptance of a proposal put forward by **Peng Dehuai**, that it should omit the standard reference to Mao Zedong's thought as the inspiration of the party and nation. Mao took the proposal badly. He felt that this showed there were elements in the party willing to challenge his authority. To counter this, he resorted to what proved to be an ambiguous line of policy.

The Hundred Flowers campaign 1957

In 1956 Mao informed his government and party colleagues that it would now be an appropriate time to allow greater freedom of expression to those who might wish to comment constructively on how well Communist China was achieving its aim of turning the nation into a proletarian state.

In a widely reported speech on 'Contradictions', given to leading party workers early in 1957, Mao stated his satisfaction with the economic advances made under the first Five-Year Plan, but went on to complain of the heavy-handedness with which some CCP officials were applying national and local policies. He hinted that the time might have come to allow intellectuals a greater say in debate. This was an unusual shift since Mao had an abiding distaste for intellectuals. But he had been sufficiently tolerant in 1956 not to back a campaign against Hu Feng, a writer who had challenged the notion that Marxist–Leninist values were the only criteria for judging artistic merit. Hu's argument had brought bitter denunciations from among the upper ranks of the CCP. However, Mao joined Zhou Enlai in suggesting that China had made such progress under the first Five-Year Plan that it could afford to be lenient towards Hu, who was simply confused and mistaken.

Another possibility was that Mao was influenced by events in the USSR. In 1956 the new Soviet leader, Nikita Khrushchev, shook the Communist world by launching an extraordinary attack on the reputation of Joseph Stalin, who had died three years earlier. In a programme of de-Stalinisation, Khrushchev denounced his predecessor for his **cult of personality** (see page 90). Mao could see how easily this charge could be made against himself in China. His apparent encouragement of criticism from within the party was, perhaps, a way of preventing a comparison being made between him and Stalin.

Mao invites criticism

Early in 1957 Mao urged Communist Party officials to be prepared to undergo criticism from the people. With the slogan, 'Let a hundred flowers bloom, let a hundred schools of thought contend', he called on critics within the party to state openly where they thought the government and the CCP had gone wrong.

Once they had overcome their initial fear that they might be thought of as being anti-party, members rushed to respond by pointing out the mistakes that had been made. Individuals and policies were complained against on the grounds of corruption, inefficiency and lack of realism. Leading figures in government, education and the arts were heavily censured for their failures. Things even went so far as to include mild criticism of Mao himself.

Mao's U-turn

Whatever the uncertainties about Mao's reasons for the Hundred Flower campaign, there was no doubting his response to its consequences. Taken aback by the flood of criticism that came forth, he immediately called a halt to the campaign. Everything now went into reverse; it became a time not of freedom of expression but of fierce repression. The Hundred Flowers campaign was abandoned and replaced by an **anti-rightist movement**. Those who had been foremost in responding to Mao's call to let 'a hundred schools of thought contend' were now forced to retract their statements. University staff and schoolteachers, research scientists, economists, writers and artists were rounded on. Mao described the campaign against them as 'squeezing the pus out of an abscess'.

The party was purged of those members who had been too free with their objections to government and party orders. Those who had co-operated by helping the 100 schools of thought contend were now made to confess their 'evil thoughts' and purge themselves through 're-education' in remote labour camps.

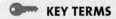 **KEY TERMS**

Cult of personality
A reference to the unlimited power that Stalin had taken into his own hands at the expense of the party.

Anti-rightist movement
An extension of the earlier anti-campaigns; having no precise definition, rightist could refer to anyone suspected.

Some were to languish in such places for twenty years. Estimates of the number of victims vary between half and three-quarters of a million party members. What had begun as a call for free thought had ended as a programme of thought control.

Even high-ranking members were vulnerable. Zhou Enlai, despite being one of Mao's most loyal supporters, was obliged to make a humiliating self-criticism: in front of a large party gathering, Zhou admitted to having been too slow in putting Mao's industrialisation plans into action. In ordering Zhou to make this statement, which was simply untrue, Mao was showing that nobody in the party or government, no matter how prominent his position, was beyond investigation and criticism. All the members of the CCP and the government understood the message; if someone as respected as Zhou Enlai could be treated in this way, then nobody was safe. The only way to avoid suspicion, therefore, was to conform absolutely to Mao's wishes.

Despite his reassertion of power, Mao was concerned that the famine which began in 1958 might become an occasion for a renewed political challenge to his leadership. To prevent this, he made a subtle move. In April 1959, he formally confirmed that he was giving up the position of state chairman. This was intended to wrong-foot possible challengers by his appearing to accept a reduction in his power. But that was not the case; the position of state chairman was a purely honorary title. It did not confer power, only recognised it. He remained head of the Communist Party and the 'Great Helmsman'. He accompanied the announcement by declaring that 'speaking out should involve no penalty; party members are entitled to their own opinions'. As had been his intention, the party feared that this was another Hundred Flowers campaign, a luring of opponents into the open before removing them. The test of whether they would take the risk came at the Lushan conference in the summer of 1959.

The Lushan conference 1959

Officially this party gathering had been summoned in order to consider the progress of the Great Leap Forward, but all the delegates knew that it had been convened by the party desperate to find ways to limit the spreading hunger. The question was whether the members would face reality and speak the truth. The answer soon came – they would not. The refusal of those at the top to tell the truth was one of the great betrayals of the Chinese people. Nor can it be said that they were denied the opportunity. One of the first speakers was Peng Dehuai, who fearlessly recounted what he had witnessed on his journey through his own native province of Anhui: 'I saw my people lying dead and dying in the fields and by the roadside.' Here was the moment for the others to back him by confirming the truth of what he had described. But none did.

Unwilling to offend Mao, the delegates persisted in their sycophancy towards him by denouncing Peng as a troublemaker and dismissing his eyewitness account as a fabrication. They then proceeded to make speeches noting the advances made under the Great Leap Forward and praising Mao for his inspired leadership. Zhou Enlai was so dismayed by the tone of the conference and so ashamed of his own silence that he stopped attending the sessions. Full of remorse, he hid away in his hotel room and drank himself into a stupor.

Mao's suppression of criticism

In an angry speech, Mao ridiculed Peng Dehuai and told the slavishly applauding delegates that he was prepared to use the PLA against any in the party who tried 'to lead the peasants to overthrow the government'. The delegates took this as Mao's way of saying that the supposed famine was really a fiction created by those reactionary peasants who were resisting collectivisation. What Mao had done was to declare that to talk of famine was tantamount to treason against him and the party. It was an unscrupulous move on his part but a clever one, and it worked. Faced with Mao's fierce determination, the party members, with the memories of the Hundred Flowers campaign fresh in their minds, dropped all thought of serious opposition. The tragedy was that since Mao had declared, in effect, that the famine did not exist, it followed that little could be done in an official, organised way to relieve it. Hence the miseries of the ordinary Chinese were intensified.

Martial law imposed

The members of the CCP may have been prepared to hide the truth but many of the ordinary people became so desperate that in a number of provinces demonstrations against the authorities began to spread; one of the key demands of the protesters was that the communes be done away with. By 1962, Liu Shaoqi was so worried that he spoke of a civil war breaking out in China. He ordered preparations to be made to impose **martial law** and asked the PLA to stand by to suppress rebellion. Two factors prevented the crisis reaching the level Liu feared:

- The famine was at its worst in rural China, where the people lacked the knowledge and skills to mount an effective anti-government rising.
- The policies that Liu himself and Deng Xiaoping introduced in 1962 began to ease the famine (see page 101).

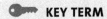 **KEY TERM**

Martial law The placing of the civilian population under military authority and discipline.

Mao withdraws

After his Lushan victory, Mao tended to withdraw from the political frontline. The evidence suggests that he felt that, while his policies had not led to open opposition, his reputation within the party had been damaged. Nevertheless, his ultimate authority remained intact. His withdrawal was a tactical move that absolved him from personal culpability for policy failures. The reality was that Mao's god-like status within the party rendered his control absolute, regardless of any formal title he held. As the party acknowledged, he could resume his full authority whenever he chose.

Summary diagram: Political developments 1952–62

Gao Gang and Rao Shushi crushed in 1954 for opposing industrialisation programme	
Mao saw this as a threat to his leadership	Launched Hundred Flowers campaign 1957: • a genuine desire for debate *or* • a reaction to de-Stalinisation *or* • a flushing out of opponents?

Mao's U-turn 1957–8	
Anti-rightist movement	Mao feared opposition over famine, but: • Lushan conference confirmed Mao's authority • Mao temporarily withdrew to avoid taint over famine • Mao's power undiminished

4 Key debate

▶ *What were Mao's motives in launching the Hundred Flowers campaign?*

Many historians have discussed the question of why Mao introduced the Hundred Flowers campaign. They are interested in this particular theme because it relates to the essential question of how Mao governed China.

Was it a trick?

Some writers, most notably Jung Chang in her 2005 biography of Mao, argue that the speed with which he reversed his policy was proof that from the beginning the campaign had been a trick on his part. She suggests that, far from being intended as a liberalising measure, it was a deliberate manoeuvre by Mao to bring his critics into the open so that they could be easily exposed, identified and removed.

EXTRACT I

From Jung Chang and Jon Halliday, *Mao: The Unknown Story*, Jonathan Cape, 2005, p. 435.

Few guessed that Mao was setting a trap, and that he was inviting people to speak out so that he could use what they said as an excuse to victimise them. Mao's targets were intellectuals and the educated, the people most likely to speak up.

How far do Extracts 1–4 concur or differ in their interpretation of Mao's motives for introducing the Hundred Flowers campaign in 1957?

As Jung Chang sees it, the Hundred Flowers campaign was part of the movement towards a controlled society in which all expression of opinion had to meet the criteria of political correctness as defined by Mao. The way in which 'the anti-rightist' campaign purged the government and party of his critics was of a scale and ruthlessness that anticipated the upheavals of the Cultural Revolution a decade later (see page 128). This is a strongly put case. However, there are other viewpoints.

Was Mao genuinely seeking criticism?

Lee Feigon, a US scholar, in a revisionist argument published in 2002, contends that Mao had been genuine in his original appeal for ideas to be expressed. This was not to say that Mao was being tolerant. His intention was to undermine the bureaucrats in the government who, in the short time that the PRC had been in existence, had come to have too big an influence in the running of affairs.

EXTRACT 2

From Lee Feigon, *Mao: A Reinterpretation*, Ivan R. Dee, 2002, p. 112.

By giving scientists and engineers the freedom to express their ideas, Mao sought to prevent party bureaucrats from interfering with technical decisions. He wanted intellectuals to expose and attack corruption and bureaucracy. He also wanted peasants, students and workers to speak out and even demonstrate to prevent government bureaucrats from running roughshod over their rights.

Was the campaign part of a structured process?

Interpreting the motives behind the campaign as sinister, Yves Chevrier, a French scholar, suggests that the Hundred Flowers campaign was a stage in an unfolding process by which Mao set out to reassert his authority and destroy all vestiges of opposition.

EXTRACT 3

From Yves Chevrier, *Mao and the Chinese Revolution*, Interlink Books, 2004, p. 123.

The 100 Flowers turned out to be the eye of the cyclone that would bring the Great Leap, itself a precursor of the Cultural Revolution. This moment of open debate when contradictions were openly discussed for the first time in years, was like a carnivorous flower, ready to close upon its prey. It enabled Mao's political comeback within the party leadership.

Was the campaign simply a muddle?

Jonathan Spence, widely acknowledged by his fellow historians as an outstanding authority on Mao's China, dismisses the idea that the Hundred

Flowers campaign was a ruse by Mao to bring his enemies into the open. Spence sees the affair as the confused result of contradictory thinking among the CCP leaders.

EXTRACT 4

From Jonathan Spence, *The Search for Modern China*, W.W. Norton, 1990, p. 574.

It was rather, a muddled and inconclusive movement that grew out of conflicting attitudes within the CCP leadership. At its core was an argument about the pace and development that was best for China, a debate about the nature of the First Five-year Plan and the promise for further growth. From that debate and the political tensions that accompanied it sprang the Great Leap Forward.

5 China's international relations 1953–62

▶ *Why, under Mao, were China's relations strained with both the USA and the USSR?*

Mao's China and the USSR

Since Stalin's uncompromising manner had been a major factor in causing disharmony between Moscow and Beijing, it was reasonable to expect that after the Soviet leader's death in 1953 relations would ease. This appeared to happen at first; something of a Sino-Soviet honeymoon period intervened in the mid-1950s. The new Soviet leaders were willing to provide China with further loans and technology. But even as better relations developed, events undermined the possibility of a genuine partnership.

In February 1956, Nikita Khrushchev staggered the Communist world by launching a detailed attack on Stalin for his 'crimes against the party'. A particular charge that rang alarm bells in China was that Stalin had put himself above the party by engaging in a 'cult of personality' (see page 85). While Mao had had profound differences with Stalin, he was deeply disturbed by the ferocity of this assault on Stalin's record. He read the denunciation of the cult of personality as an intended criticism of his own style of leadership in China.

Mao was also disturbed by the political developments that occurred in the **Eastern bloc** in the wake of the de-Stalinisation programme. Greater freedom appeared to be offered to the **Soviet satellites** to criticise their Communist governments and to question their subordination to the USSR. This had not been Khrushchev's intention, as he was quick to demonstrate by ordering the

KEY TERMS

Eastern bloc The USSR and the central European countries it dominated.

Soviet satellites The various countries that had fallen under Soviet control between 1945 and 1948 and now made up the Eastern bloc.

suppression of an anti-Soviet rising in Hungary in November. But for Mao the Hungarian rising and those that had also occurred in Poland and East Germany were the direct result of the Soviet Union's relaxation of its ideological grip. Mao was angered by the failure of the post-Stalin leadership to control what he regarded as the reactionary forces within the Communist bloc.

Mao was equally offended by the Soviet Union's adoption of a policy of *détente* towards the West. Moscow now seemed to accept that there were alternative ways of achieving revolution in the modern world other than by armed struggle. Khrushchev had by the late 1950s concluded that, in a world of nuclear **superpowers**, the Marxist–Leninist notion of a final violent conflict between the international proletariat and the forces of capitalism was no longer acceptable. He said that had comrade Lenin lived in a nuclear age he would have adjusted his views.

This was rejected by Mao as heresy. He believed that the final struggle was unavoidable and that it was the duty of all revolutionaries not only to prepare for it but also to hasten its coming. For Mao, Khrushchev's policy of *détente* was clear evidence that Soviet Communism had taken the revisionist path.

Mao's second visit to the USSR 1957

Disturbed by the disquiet in the Marxist camp, Khrushchev in 1957 convened a conference in Moscow of the world's Communist parties. His broad aim was to repair the differences between the USSR and the other Marxist countries. At the meeting, Mao was still prepared to recognise the USSR's unique place in Communist history. He also approved a Sino-Soviet declaration that expressed China's readiness to co-operate. But at the same time he let it be known that he regarded Moscow's approach to the West as too accommodating. He called on the Soviet Union to abandon **revisionism**, and return to the true Marxist–Leninist path. Rather than making concessions to capitalism, it was the Soviet Union's revolutionary duty to fight the international class war. This could not be done by extending peaceful overtures to class enemies, the imperialist Western nations.

What prompted Mao's words was his suspicion that the Soviet Union was following a policy of *détente* with the West in order to leave China internationally isolated. Mao's chief spokesman at the Moscow meeting was Deng Xiaoping, who excelled himself in putting over the Chinese version of international revolution. Deng argued powerfully that the proletarian world revolution was achievable only through armed struggle; capitalism had to be overcome by force. In a tense series of exchanges he got the better of the leading Soviet political theorists and won the admiration, if not the open support, of many of the other delegates. The Russian hosts were embarrassed and angered by Deng's performance.

 **KEY TERMS**

Détente Easing of tensions between the Soviet Union and the Western powers.

Superpowers Nations that possessed advanced nuclear weapons.

Revisionism Betraying original revolutionary ideas and values.

Mao and Khrushchev

Despite Mao's strong words about the Soviet Union, Khrushchev made another attempt to improve relations with the PRC. In 1958, following the mishandling by the Soviet ambassador in China of negotiations regarding a joint Sino-Soviet naval programme, Khrushchev flew to Beijing to meet Mao again. He came to assure Mao that the ambassador had given the wrong impression by suggesting that China's navy must be brought under Soviet control.

Mao, however, was not disposed to listen. In a tit-for-tat for what he regarded as the poor treatment he had endured during his visits to Moscow (see page 59), Mao deliberately set out to make Khrushchev uncomfortable. He arranged for the Soviet delegation to be put up at a hotel without air-conditioning; the Russians sweltered in Beijing's fierce summer heat and were plagued by mosquitoes.

SOURCE I

> Why might the happy smiles shown in the photo in Source I be regarded as misleading?

Mao and Khrushchev together in China in 1958.

In one notorious incident Mao insisted that a round of talks take place in his private swimming pool. Mao was a regular swimmer; Khrushchev hated the water. Nonetheless, to humour his host Khrushchev agreed. In a pair of baggy shorts and squeezed into a barely buoyant rubber ring, the rotund Soviet leader desperately floundered and splashed while interpreters raced round the pool's edge trying to make sense of his gurgled replies to Mao's questions. The talks were not a success.

PRC accuses the USSR of chauvinism

The failure of the Moscow talks was not simply the result of the swimming-pool farce. Deng Xiaoping was again let loose to savage the Soviet delegation as he had in Moscow. He attacked the USSR for its 'great nation, great party **chauvinism**', in acting as if it was the only true interpreter of Marxist theory. Deng repeated Mao's accusation that the technical advisers sent to China by Moscow were in fact Soviet spies. He accused the Soviet Union of betraying the international Communist movement. It has been suggested that it was Mao's remembrance of Deng Xiaoping's brilliant onslaught on the USSR that saved Deng from harsher treatment at the time of his disgrace in the Cultural Revolution in 1966 (see page 133).

The Taiwan issue

In 1958 the simmering Taiwan issue provided another test of the genuineness of Sino-Soviet sympathies. Without consulting Moscow, Mao ordered Chinese forces to make ready for full-scale assault on the Nationalist-held island (see page 96). The USA responded by preparing for war with mainland China. In the event, Mao held back from a direct attack on Taiwan. It is doubtful that he really intended to attack but the reason he gave for not doing so was that the USSR had declined to offer China even moral support.

Khrushchev countered by saying that he was unwilling to put the USSR at risk by recklessly 'testing the stability of the capitalist system'. He denounced Mao and the Chinese as **Trotskyists** who had lost all sense of political reality. The resulting deterioration in relations led the Soviet Union in 1959 to withdraw its economic advisers from China and to cancel its commercial contracts there.

Soviet reaction to China's Great Leap Forward

Sino-Soviet relations were not helped by Moscow's response to China's Great Leap Forward. In 1959, Mao was enraged by the news that the Soviet Union had dismissed as a total blunder his attempt to revolutionise the Chinese economy. He was particularly angered by rumours that one of his own chiefs-of-staff, Marshal Peng Dehuai, had passed on to Moscow details of the widespread starvation that the 'great leap' had caused (see page 67).

Sino-Soviet rivalry over Albania

China had condemned de-Stalinisation for the encouragement it had given to counter-revolution in the Eastern-bloc countries. Yet, when the Chinese leaders saw the chance to embarrass the Soviet Union by supporting the socialist countries hostile to the USSR, they took it. In retaliation for what Mao saw as the Soviet Union's attempt to undermine China's standing among the Communist nations, the PRC gave support to those countries which defied the USSR. An especially clear example was **Albania**.

KEY TERMS

Chauvinism Exaggerated and aggressive belief in the value of one's own ideas and attitudes.

Trotskyists Followers of Stalin's great rival, Leon Trotsky, who believed in the necessity of world revolution at any cost.

Albania Run by an oppressive neo-Stalinist regime, it was the only Communist state in Europe to recognise China rather than the USSR as leader of the international revolutionary movement.

In 1961, the Soviet Union, angered by the Albanian government's refusal to accept dictation from Moscow, withdrew its financial aid. The PRC immediately stepped in to supply Albania with money and technical assistance. It did not matter that the country was a minor player on the socialist stage. It was enough for the Chinese that it was on bad terms with the USSR.

China's walkout from the 1961 Moscow conference

It was the Albanian question that brought matters to a head and led to the severing of diplomatic relations between the Soviet Union and the PRC. The occasion was Zhou Enlai's walkout from the 1961 Moscow Congress of the Communist Party of the Soviet Union, to which China had been invited as an observer. Khrushchev's speech at the congress, abusing the Albanian Communist leaders for their backward Stalinist ways, was interpreted by the Chinese as a deliberately intended attack on themselves. Having expected such an onslaught, Zhou and the Chinese delegation quit the hall in accordance with a rehearsed plan. This dramatic gesture was the climax to a decade of Sino-Soviet recrimination. The collapse of diplomatic relations encouraged the Soviet and Chinese leaders to be still more offensive in their personal references to each other. Khrushchev abused Mao as an 'Asian Hitler' and 'a living corpse'. Mao responded by dismissing his Soviet adversary as 'a redundant old boot' that ought to be thrown into a corner.

One result of this flurry of insults was the sharpening of the disputes between the USSR and China along their common border. Mao angrily asserted that the refusal of the USSR to return the Chinese territories that Russia had acquired by the **unequal treaties** of the nineteenth century made it as guilty of imperialism as the original tsarist land grabbers. Beijing's news agency spoke of the 'anti-Chinese atrocities of the new Russian tsars'.

The Sino-India War 1962

The Chinese were especially incensed by the USSR's attitude during the **Sino-Indian War** that broke out in 1962. The Soviet Union was formally neutral but it provided India with fighter-planes and its moral support was all on India's side. Mao regarded the offer by the Soviet Union to act as mediator between the PRC and India as hypocrisy. He rejected it as yet another Soviet attempt to undermine China's international standing.

The Cuban Missile Crisis 1962

A dramatic Cold War episode in 1962 provided China with the opportunity to ridicule the Soviet Union's claim to the leadership of world revolution. In October of that year, the USSR exploited its influence over **Communist Cuba** to install rockets and nuclear warheads on the island. Since Cuba stood only 145 km (90 miles) off the coast of the USA, President Kennedy demanded the withdrawal of the weapons. After a tense stand-off Khrushchev complied. The two superpowers then made a compromise settlement in which the USSR

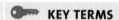
KEY TERMS

Unequal treaties The one-sided agreements imposed by the European powers on imperial China.

Sino-Indian War In 1962, a long-running territorial dispute, compounded by India's granting sanctuary to the Dalai Lama, led to an outbreak of fighting on the Tibetan border.

Communist Cuba In 1959, revolutionary forces had taken power on the island; their leader, Fidel Castro, later declared himself a Communist.

agreed to withdraw all its weapons and installations in Cuba in return for the USA's promise never to invade the island and to withdraw its own nuclear weapons from Turkey.

China scorned Moscow for its original 'adventurism' in siting detectable nuclear warheads in Cuba and for its subsequent 'capitulationism' in abjectly bowing to the US threat to retaliate. Was this, Mao asked contemptuously, the way to inspire the world's struggling masses in their fight against US imperialism?

Sino-Soviet ideological disagreements

The broad response in the West to the ending of the Cuban Missile Crisis was to congratulate both Kennedy and Khrushchev for their statesmanship in drawing back from the brink of war. Khrushchev was praised for putting his policy of coexistence with the West into practical effect. That was not how Mao saw it. Mao condemned coexistence as collusion with the imperialist enemies. Mao also censured Khrushchev for his attempt to modernise Soviet agriculture and industry by a policy of decentralised planning and wage incentives. He dismissed this as a return to capitalism. Mao called on Communists in all other countries to reject the USSR's lead and develop their own form of true Marxism along Chinese lines.

The vital concept for Mao was that of 'continuing revolution'. Fierce ideological battles over this notion had been fought earlier within the Soviet Union. Trotsky, Stalin's arch opponent in the 1920s and 1930s, had made 'continuing' or 'permanent' revolution the essence of Marxism–Leninism. For Trotsky, revolution was not an event but a continuing process that guaranteed the ultimate victory of the international proletariat. Revolutions that did not constantly renew themselves would fall prey to reaction. Mao Zedong's own definition of continuing revolution corresponded to Trotsky's. Mao wrote: 'Our revolutions are like battles. After a victory, we must at once put forward a new task. In this way, cadres and the masses will forever be filled with revolutionary fervour.'

Rivalry over the leadership of international Communism

The dispute between the USSR and China over the meaning of revolution raised the demanding question as to which nation was the real leader of the Communist world. Was it the USSR, direct heir of the great 1917 Revolution, or Mao's China, whose peasant-based revolution in 1949 offered an inspiring model for all oppressed peoples?

In strict Marxist theory, true proletarian revolution could occur only in an urban, industrial society. According to Soviet political scientists, China, being a preponderantly rural peasant society, could not be a fully developed Communist state. They asserted that Mao had distorted Marxism to make it fit the Chinese context. The CCP's theorists retorted that the Soviet Union was betraying the cause of world revolution by pursuing a suicidal policy of *détente* with the West. It was a Sino-Soviet dispute that would outlive Mao.

The PRC and the USA

There is a sense in which one would expect hostility to be a consistent feature of Sino-American relations. After all, they represented opposite ends of the political spectrum: the USA with its thriving capitalist system was a natural enemy of the PRC, which was ideologically committed to the destruction of capitalism within its own borders and worldwide. Mao's political instinct was to back all revolutionary movements wherever they occurred in the world, which was why from the earliest days of the PRC its agents were to be found in Latin America bidding to replace the Soviet Union as promoters of Communist revolution.

Initially, the USA held that the USSR and China were acting as a joint Communist bloc and it took some time for the reality of the deep Sino-Soviet fissure to be appreciated by the Americans. In the meantime, US perception of a joint Sino-Soviet conspiracy created an atmosphere in which Chinese Reds were feared as much in the USA as US imperialists were in China. One product of this was **McCarthyism**, which played its part in deepening Sino-American animosity.

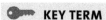

KEY TERM

McCarthyism Senator Joe McCarthy headed a Congressional Committee seeking to expose crypto-Communists supposedly working in the USA. Relying on flimsy evidence, the Committee was responsible for creating a Red Scare in the 1950s.

However, the key diplomatic issue over which hostility was expressed was Taiwan. So long as Chiang Kai-shek and Mao were adamant in their refusal to recognise the claim of the other to dominion over the island, there could be no peaceful settlement. Adding to Mao's frustration was the USA's backing of Chiang's Nationalist China as a member of the UN, in denial of the PRC's place (see page 54). Mao continued throughout the 1950s to rattle the sabre over Taiwan, ordering troop movements and manoeuvres that seemed to be a prelude to invasion, though it is doubtful that he would have risked this without an unambiguous assurance of Soviet support, something which he never received. Nevertheless, he felt justified in taking an aggressive stance in the light of US actions, which included:

- supplying Chiang's illegal regime with finance and resources
- persuading the UN to impose a trade embargo on the PRC
- using the US Seventh Fleet to patrol the straits between Taiwan and the Communist mainland
- signing the mutual security pact in 1954 in which the USA pledged to support the GMD government and to defend Taiwan against attack from outside
- installing sophisticated weaponry on Taiwan, including missiles capable of carrying a nuclear warhead.

In 1958 Mao made his most aggressive move yet when he instructed PLA shore batteries to shell the Nationalist-held islands of Quemoy and Matsu. The strength of the shelling suggested that a Communist Chinese assault on Taiwan was imminent. US vessels were also threatened in the Taiwan straits. The USA prepared for war. But no attack came from the mainland. Communist China was not in a position to invade Taiwan. Mao judged that his forces did not possess the necessary air power and landing craft to mount a successful invasion of the well-defended island.

The nuclear issue

Sino-American relations were further strained by the nuclear issue. This was understandable, given that the USA was a nuclear power and that the PRC would not develop its own atomic bomb until 1964 (see page 111). Yet in public, whatever his private fears may have been, Mao showed his apparent disdain for the USA's nuclear weapons, referring to them as **paper tigers**. Source J gives Mao's explanation as to why the PRC was unafraid of them.

KEY TERM

Paper tigers A dismissive term Mao often applied to anyone or anything whose power was more apparent than real.

According to Mao in Source J, why is the PRC not fearful of the USA's nuclear weapons?

SOURCE J

From an article by Mao Zedong, 28 January 1955, quoted in Pei-kai Cheng and Michael Lestz, editors, *The Search for Modern China*, W.W. Norton, 1999, p. 382.

Today, the danger of a world war and the threats to China come mainly from the warmongers in the United States. They have occupied our Taiwan and the Taiwan Straits and are contemplating an atomic war. We have two principles: first we don't want war; second we will strike back resolutely if anyone invades us. This is what we teach the members of the Communist Party and the whole nation. The Chinese people are not to be cowed by US blackmail. Our country has a population of 600 million and an area of 9,600,000 square kilometres. The United States cannot annihilate the Chinese nation with its small stack of atom bombs [nuclear weapons]. Even if the US atom bombs were so powerful that, when dropped on China, they would make a hole right through the earth, or even blow it up, that would hardly mean anything to the universe as a whole.

We have an expression, millet plus rifles. In the case of the United States, it is planes plus the A-bomb [atom bomb]. However, if the United States with its planes plus the A-bomb is to launch a war of aggression against China, then China with its millet plus rifles is sure to emerge the victor.

This may have been bravado; nevertheless it was an attitude that Mao sustained until the PRC itself became a superpower in the 1960s.

Summary diagram: China's international relations 1953–62

Mao's China and the Soviet Union

Mao disturbed by: De-Stalinisation
Détente
Revisionism

Mao felt personally slighted by his treatment in Moscow	PRC incensed by the USSR's siding with India during the Sino-Indian War in 1962
Deng attacked USSR's 'great nation, great party chauvinism'	Mao mocked USSR for its caving in to the USA over the Cuban Missile Crisis in 1962
Mao angered by Soviet mockery of China's Great Leap Forward	Sino-Soviet ideological disagreements
PRC delegation walked out of 1961 Moscow conference over Albanian question	Sino-Soviet rivalry over the leadership of international communism

The PRC and the USA

Ideological differences: capitalism vs communism

Mao's anger at USA's recognition and support of Taiwan

Nuclear issue: Mao's dismissal of US atomic bombs as paper tigers

Chapter summary

Determined to build the PRC's economy to the level where it matched the USSR and the Western powers, Mao embarked on a series of Five-Year Plans. The first, which had begun in 1952, had some major successes, but, since it was dependent on Soviet finance and technical assistance, it could not fully meet Mao's expectation. This gave rise to political disquiet, which Mao endeavoured to quash by means of a new form of purge, the Hundred Flowers campaign.

In a revolutionary economic move, Mao tried in the second Five-Year Plan to launch the Great Leap Forward, a programme for achieving industrial growth by relying entirely on Chinese resources. To this end, he collectivised the peasantry, calculating that this would produce surplus food for sale abroad to raise the necessary capital for industrial investment. Not only did this objective fail, but the upheaval caused by collectivisation produced a widespread destructive famine. Mao's problems were not eased by further deterioration in his relations with the Soviet Union over the issue of coexistence with the West and with the USA over the simmering Taiwan problem. At home, Mao, while not acknowledging culpability for the famine, judged it expedient to withdraw temporarily from the political scene.

Refresher questions

Use these questions to remind yourself of the key material covered in this chapter.

1 How far did the first Five-Year Plan achieve its objectives?

2 What did the case of Gao Gang and Rao Shushi indicate about the nature of Mao's terror campaigns?

3 What was Mao's motive in launching the Hundred Flowers campaign?

4 What was the government's aim in introducing state-owned enterprises?

5 What factors prevented the Great Leap Forward from reaching its full targets?

6 What was the aim of collectivisation?

7 What was Mao's adoption of Lysenkoism intended to achieve?

8 How far was China's great famine a man-made disaster?

9 Why was the famine particularly severe in Tibet?

10 What was the significance of the 1959 Lushan conference?

11 Why was Mao disturbed by the Soviet policy of de-Stalinisation?

12 Why was Mao opposed to the Soviet Union's pursuit of coexistence with the West?

13 How did the question of Taiwan further divide the PRC and the Soviet Union?

14 What lay at the root of Sino-American hostility in this period?

 Question practice

ESSAY QUESTIONS

1 'The Great Leap Forward was a spontaneous response of the Chinese people to Mao's call for collective effort.' Explain why you agree or disagree with this view.

2 'The Hundred Flowers campaign was simply a purge with a different title.' Assess the validity of this view.

3 'China's great famine of 1958–62 was not a natural disaster but a man-made one.' How far do you agree with this statement?

4 To what extent was Mao Zedong personally responsible for the tensions in Sino-Soviet relations between 1953 and 1962?

SOURCE ANALYSIS QUESTIONS

1 With reference to Sources E (**page 80**) and H (**page 82**) and your understanding of the historical context, which of these two sources is more valuable in explaining why China's Great Famine of 1958–62 was so severe?

2 With reference to Sources D (**page 76**), E (**page 80**) and H (**page 82**), and your understanding of the historical context, assess the value of these sources to a historian studying the impact on the Chinese people of Mao's Great Leap Forward in China (1958–62).

3 How much weight do you give the evidence of Source D (**page 76**) as a description of the peasants' response to the introduction of collectivisation? Explain your answer using the source, the information given about it and your own knowledge of the historical context.

4 How far could the historian make use of Sources B (**page 70**) and D (**page 76**) together to investigate the response of the Chinese people to the introduction of the Great Leap Forward? Explain your answer, using the sources, the information given about them and your own knowledge of the historical context.

CHAPTER 4

Reform and control 1962–6

During Mao's temporary detachment from frontline politics, a power struggle developed within the CCP over the policies to be followed after the failure of the Great Leap Forward. Oddly, it was while Mao was away that his personality cult reached its most intense yet. This chapter examines these themes and also surveys the social changes that had occurred in China under Mao by 1966 and how the development of a Chinese nuclear weapon affected its relations with the outside world. The material is covered under the following headings:

★ The power struggle 1962–6

★ The cult of Mao

★ Social change by 1966

★ Sino-Soviet relations: the nuclear issue

Key dates

1958	CCP condemnation of the family as the basic social unit
1962	Mao temporarily withdrew from public life
1963	Mao's Little Red Book became a standard Chinese text
	The Diary of Lei Feng published
	Formation of Socialist Education Movement
	Birth Control Bureau established
1964	Test nuclear bomb exploded by Chinese
1965	*The Dismissal of Hai Rai from Office*
	Creation of the Central Cultural Revolution Group
1949–66	Number of women workers quadrupled
	Literacy rate rose from 20 to 70 per cent
	Start of the authorities' campaign against religion
	New marriage law

The power struggle 1962–6

▶ *What issues underlay the power struggle of the years 1962–6?*

Land policy under Liu and Deng

The years 1962–6 appeared on the surface to be relatively quiet. The turmoil of the Great Leap Forward and the horrors of the famine, if not yet over, were past their worst. But this was deceptive. Politics was not placid; a power struggle was being fought. On temporarily withdrawing from direct government, Mao charged Liu Shaoqi and Deng Xiaoping with the task of bringing an end to the rural crisis and restoring adequate food supplies. In tackling the problem, Liu and Deng enlisted the aid of **Chen Yun**. Together, the three men concluded that the only workable solution to the food crisis was to allow private farming and markets to operate again; this would provide the peasant farmers with an incentive to produce surplus stocks.

The reforms that Liu and his colleagues introduced along these lines were an unspoken admission that the commune system had been a failure. What Liu had raised was the central issue of where the PRC was heading and what form socialism should take in the aftermath of the Great Leap Forward and the famine it had created. In the language of the PRC, Liu's approach was deemed to represent the political right. Unsurprisingly, Mao became uneasy with the methods adopted by Liu and Deng. Their restoration of private ownership of the land undermined the **collectivist principle** on which he had set such store as a Communist revolutionary. He had some grounds for being uneasy; in the early 1960s in the provinces of Gansu and Qinghai, supporters of Liu and Deng took over the local government and began to reverse the collectivisation programme.

There was also personal pique involved, Mao complaining that Deng and Liu treated him like 'a dead man at his own funeral'. Mao never lost his fear that his colleagues, even those who professed the greatest personal loyalty, were ready to remove him from power if the opportunity came. Mao came to convince himself that Liu and Deng were using their position to mount a challenge.

The political divisions: pragmatists and ideologues

For ease of understanding, it is possible to portray the political divide of these years in a visual form in terms of the left–right political spectrum. Figure 4.1 on page 102 indicates the main groupings in the power struggle that followed Mao's withdrawal for the political centre ground. It should be emphasised that because of the nature of Maoist politics, which were seldom open and in which opinions were often expressed obliquely, the diagram is a simplification. A visual representation cannot capture the shifts and overlaps that occurred.

 **KEY FIGURE**

Chen Yun (1905–95)
Regarded as the CCP's leading economist.

 **KEY TERM**

Collectivist principle
The Marxist notion that social advance can be achieved only by the proletarian class acting together as a body and not allowing individuals to follow their own interests.

Ideologues CCP hard liners who believed in pushing Mao's revolutionary politics to the extreme and suppressing all opposition.

Pragmatists CCP members who believed that policies should be adjusted according to circumstances rather than being slavishly followed for ideological reasons.

Nevertheless, the diagram may be useful in depicting the general lines dividing the conflicting elements. In broad definition, the left, the **ideologues**, wanted the maintenance of stringent controls and enforcement; the right wanted a relaxation of controls and encouragement rather than coercion. The centre, an ill-defined group, also to be thought of as **pragmatists**, thought that the coercion could be intermixed with a lighter touch depending on particular circumstances.

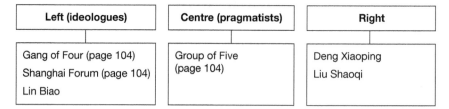

Left (ideologues)	Centre (pragmatists)	Right
Gang of Four (page 104) Shanghai Forum (page 104) Lin Biao	Group of Five (page 104)	Deng Xiaoping Liu Shaoqi

Figure 4.1 The contenders for power 1962–6.

Economic and political issues

At the heart of the divide was the question of economics. How was China to continue to develop its industry? Although it was known that Mao had accepted that the Great Leap Forward had not achieved its intended results, hard liners on the left insisted that the harsh methods with which it had been implemented must not be abandoned. Indeed, there were those prepared to argue that strict control of peasants and workers in accordance with Maoist principles had to be maintained even if this meant slower economic growth. Clearly this related to a basic political attitude that went beyond economics. For hard liners, the needs of revolution took precedence over all other considerations. Collectivism and political conformity were not methods for achieving revolution; they were a definition of the revolution, which for hard liners was synonymous with Maoism. Even when, as now, Mao was apparently not directing policies, he remained the reference point.

The Socialist Education Movement

One particular development that revealed the nature of the divide within the CCP was the creation in 1963 of the Socialist Education Movement (SEM). Despite its title, the movement was more concerned with politics than with education. It became, in fact, a dispute between Mao's concept of Communist planning which was essentially a restatement of the collectivist ideas that had inspired the Great Leap Forward and Liu Shaoqi's plan for liberalising agriculture by restoring some element of private farming.

The SEM had begun, with Mao's backing, as another anti-campaign, presented as the 'four clean-ups'. Under the pretence of being sent to learn from the peasants, government officials and party cadres were despatched to the countryside, tasked with exposing the 'reactionary elements' who had prevented the Great Leap Forward from being fully successful. However, the exposure revealed the opposite of what was intended. Liu Shaoqi, greatly aided by his wife **Wang Guangmei**, had already gone to live among the peasants to gain first-hand knowledge. What Liu and Wang discovered was not lack of effort by ordinary peasants but corruption and collusion between local party bosses and the officials sent to implement the reforms of the Great Leap Forward. 'Cadres in basic level organisations who have made mistakes are usually connected with certain cadres of higher level organisations and are instigated, supported and protected by them.'

This revelation confirmed Mao's suspicions but also angered him in that it had been Liu who had made the discoveries. In spite of his supposed retirement into the background, Mao was still prepared to intervene when he chose. Though he would later use Liu's information to attack the party bureaucracy, he summoned Liu for a personal meeting during which he berated him for using the work of the SEM to undermine the party workers, while ignoring 'peasant capitalists'. 'Though you repeat day after day that there must be democracy, there is no democracy; though you ask others to be democratic, you are not democratic yourselves.' Mao extended his criticism to include Liu's colleague Deng Xiaoping, whom he dubbed 'placid' for showing insufficient trust in the masses.

Mao's attitude towards the corruption exposure was a confused one, which is understandable given that he was supposed to have taken a back seat and that he was jealous of Liu and Deng over their impressive economic policies. How successful those policies were was evident from the figures:

- The PRC's budget deficit of 8 billion yuan in 1960 had been turned into a surplus of 1 million yuan by 1962.
- By 1965, agricultural production had been restored to the levels of 1957 before the Great Leap Forward.
- Industrial growth reached 20 per cent by 1965.
- A tenfold increase in oil production ended the PRC's reliance on Soviet supplies.

Despite these achievements, the left of the party prepared to attack what they regarded as Liu's and Den's abandonment of 'proletarian values'. Mao's publicised admonishing of Liu and Deng helped to polarise the situation by giving the left the pretext for being more open and aggressive in their criticism of Liu's 'rightism'. The power struggle intensified.

The Wu Han affair

The central importance of literary and cultural works in the mounting political power struggle was especially evident in the furore that developed over a play, *The Dismissal of Hai Rui from Office*, written by **Wu Han**. This work, performed between 1961 and 1965, was set in the days of the Song dynasty (960–1279AD) and told the story of Hai Rui, a court official, who was demoted and punished after bravely defying the orders of a cruel emperor.

KEY FIGURES

Wang Guangmei (1921–2006)

Worked earlier for a CCP–GMD reconciliation and was eager to gain an understanding of ordinary people; her talents excited the jealousy of Mao's wife, Jiang Qing.

Wu Han (1909–69)

A playwright, considered by the Maoists to be a spokesman for the reactionary elements in the CCP.

Since Wu Han belonged to a group of writers thought to be critical of Mao Zedong, it was possible to interpret his play as an intended reference to Mao's previous dismissal of Peng Dehuai for opposing the Great Leap Forward and stating the truth at Lushan about the famine (see page 86). It thus provided **Lin Biao** with a pretext for moving against the anti-Maoist elements in the Communist Party. Beginning in 1965, a series of attacks were made on Wu, charging him with blackening Mao's good name and undermining China's Communist revolution. A broken man, Wu Han killed himself two years later.

Divisions in the CCP

The Wu Han affair deepened the divisions that had begun to develop within the CCP and between the CCP and PLA. It was at this stage that Mao's wife, Jiang Qing, a former bit-part film actress in Shanghai, began to play a prominent role. As the Chairman's spouse she had an influence that was dangerous to challenge. A fierce hard-liner, Jiang denounced the 'reactionaries and revisionists' on the right of the party. She also aimed to undermine the **Group of Five**, whose essential objective was to act as peacemakers in order to prevent party splits widening. Notwithstanding their declared loyalty to Mao, the Group of Five were condemned by Jiang for their moderation at a time when utter ruthlessness was the only proper response.

The Shanghai Forum and the Gang of Four

Jiang Qing was the dominant figure in the **Shanghai Forum**, a set of Maoists who represented the most hard-line element in the CCP. The forum itself was dominated by a group of particularly uncompromising individuals, known as the **Gang of Four**. The Gang was the extreme wing of an extreme movement. The three men in the group, Zhang Chunqiao, Yao Wenyuan and Wang Honwen (see page 106), who were feared for their ruthlessness, had risen to prominence in the Shanghai section of the CCP and had become members of the Politburo.

Jiang urged that steps be immediately taken to remove Liu Shaoqi and Deng Xiaoping from their positions in the CCP. She further demanded that Chinese culture should be cleansed of those writers and artists whose attitude betrayed their lack of commitment to Mao's revolution. The severity of her approach so pleased Lin Biao that he asked her to take charge of the PLA's cultural policy.

Character of the Gang of Four

The Gang of Four was involved in the Cultural Revolution throughout its course, but a fact worth emphasising is that Jiang and her three associates were never a formal, organised bloc. Indeed, there were times when Mao told them to stop acting as if they were. What gave the Gang of Four apparent coherence was the extremity of their views; as hard liners they fought a continuous battle against those in the Politburo whom they regarded as lacking a full commitment to uncompromising Maoist socialism. For the Gang of Four, the path to socialism

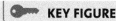

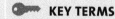

Jiang Qing

1914   Born in Shandong province

1937   Joined the Communists in Yanan

1938   Married Mao Zedong

1962–76   Led the Gang of Four

1966–76   Controlled the arts during the Cultural
             Revolution

1976   Arrested after defeat of the Gang of Four

1981   Put on trial and condemned

1991   Died

Early career

A film actress in Shanghai until the 1930s, Jiang abandoned her first husband to join the Communists in Yanan. There, she set her cap at Mao, who was so taken with her that he gave up his wife and married Jiang in 1938. They stayed together in a stormy relationship until his death. Initially, Mao restricted Jiang's involvement in politics, but from 1959 onwards, finding her aggressive public style a very useful weapon against his opponents, he encouraged her to play a much bigger part in public affairs.

Political role

An unforgiving woman who bore grudges, and was ferocious in attacking those she believed were deviating from Mao's brand of communism, Jiang was deeply involved in the in-fighting that preceded the Cultural Revolution, using her links with the Shanghai Forum to become a dominant force. During the revolution she played a key role as Mao's enforcer in attempting to reshape the whole of Chinese culture. 'I was Mao's dog. Whoever he told me to bite, I bit.'

Significance

Terrifying figure though she was, she was dependent on Mao for the power she wielded. This came to an end after Mao's death when she failed to lead the Gang of Four to victory in the power struggle that followed. She was arrested and subjected to a show trial in 1978. Refusing to acknowledge any past political crimes, she was sentenced to death, a penalty that was subsequently reduced to life imprisonment. Jiang died in mysterious circumstances in prison in 1991, the authorities claiming that she had committed suicide.

that the party was following was too slow. They wanted the ferocity of the assault on class enemies to be constantly maintained. That, they held, was what 'permanent revolution' meant. They pushed Mao's intolerance towards revisionists and class enemies to its ultimate extreme, which was why they were offended by the moderate approach of Zhou Enlai and Deng Xiaoping, which they scorned as tantamount to revisionism.

Asserting that the thoughts of Chairman Mao represented a 'new development of the Marxist–Leninist world outlook', the Shanghai Forum identified the **counter-revolutionaries** who must be struggled against and destroyed, as explained in Source A.

 KEY TERM

Counter-revolutionaries
Used by hard-line Maoists to describe those in the party who favoured more moderate policies.

SOURCE A

From a statement of the Shanghai Forum, September 1965, in *Selected Works of Mao Tse-tung*, Foreign Languages Press, 1975, vol. IV, p. 179.

China is under the dictatorship of a sinister anti-Party and anti-Socialist line which is diametrically opposed to Chairman Mao's thought. This sinister line is a combination of bourgeois ideas on literature and art, modern revisionist ideas on literature and art and what is known as the literature and art of the 1930s.

What do the writers of Source A understand by the term 'anti-Socialist line'?

Jiang Qing's associates in the Gang of Four

Zhang Chunqiao (1917–2005)

An ultra-leftist, Zhang became notorious in the 1930s as a ruthless political infighter who had clawed his way to the top of the CCP in Shanghai. At Yanan he acted as a propagandist for Mao Zedong. On the PRC's creation in 1949, Zhang returned to Shanghai, where he continued his fierce rivalry with party opponents. It was from his Shanghai base that in 1965 Zhang rounded on those who had tried to restrict his influence, condemning them as revisionists who must be removed in order to safeguard the purity of Mao's socialist revolution. This need for a party purge became the justification for Mao's launching of the Cultural Revolution. Zhang joined with Jiang, Wang and Yao in terrorising officials regarded as 'capitalist roaders'. Mao's death in 1976, however, revealed how dependent the Gang of Four had been on him for its authority. Attempting to seize power, it lacked military support and was outmanoeuvred by those it had previously persecuted. Arrested in 1976, Zhang remained mute throughout his 1981 show trial. His original death sentence having been reduced, he remained in prison until he died.

Wang Hongwen (1935–1992)

Wang made his mark as a trade union leader in Shanghai and earned a fearsome reputation for the viciousness with which he dealt with opponents. He teamed up with Zhang Chunqiao, with whom he formed a Red Guards group that wreaked havoc in Shanghai in the first two years of the Cultural Revolution. Regarded as one of Jiang's protégés, he had risen to membership of the Politburo by 1969. By 1973, he seemed to be poised to succeed Zhou Enlai as premier. However, Mao's death left him and the others in the Gang isolated and in the brief power struggle that followed he was arrested, put on trial and later imprisoned.

Yao Wenyuan (1931–2005)

An aggressive ideologue based in Shanghai, Yao came to Mao's attention with his denunciation of Wu Han's play, *The Dismissal of Hai Rai*, in 1965. With Jiang's support, Yao established himself as a leading party propagandist. Working with Zhang Chunqiao, he crushed the 'rightists' in Shanghai before moving to Beijing, where he continued his destructive campaign against radicals who were not radical enough. Elevated to the Politburo, he intensified his criticism of Zhou Enlai and Deng Xiaoping. His charge was that in pursuing a moderate political line and seeking economic reform they were ignoring the necessity of 'continuous revolution', and 'class war against the bourgeoisie'. As with the other three members of the Gang of Four, Yao's influence crumbled when Mao's death showed how little support they could command. Overthrown and arrested, Yao remained mute at his later trial, before being imprisoned.

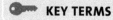 **KEY TERMS**

Packing Controlling the membership of committees in such a way that they always contained a majority of Maoists.

Central Cultural Revolution Group (CCRG) A subcommittee of the Politburo, established in May 1965; its seventeen members included the Gang of Four.

The forum's answer was for the PLA, 'the mainstay and hope of the Chinese people', to lead China in rooting out 'anti-socialist weeds' and eradicating all traces of artistic corruption that delayed the achievement of a truly proletarian culture. Lin Biao spoke of an 'imminent and inevitable' struggle against class enemies. Lin's statement proved to be the beginning of a purge of the party. In April 1966, Peng Zhen and the leading members of the Group of Five were denounced for 'taking the capitalist road'.

The Central Cultural Revolution Group

The ground for this attack had been prepared during the preceding twelve months by Maoists **packing** the key party committees. A striking example of this Maoist control had been the setting up in May 1965 of the **Central Cultural Revolution Group (CCRG)**. This body, which was dominated by the Gang of Four, was the instrument through which Mao would run the Cultural Revolution (see page 129). Such was the influence of the CCRG that by the early summer of

1966, Liu Shaoqi and Deng Xiaoping found themselves being outmanoeuvred and undermined. Acting on information the CCRG had given him, Mao himself in May 1966 issued a 'notification' to the CCP (see Source B) in which he defined the enemy within.

SOURCE B

From Mao's 'Notification', 16 May 1966, quoted in Philip Short, *Mao: A Life*, Hodder & Stoughton, 1999, p. 532.

Some people in authority are taking the capitalist road. These representatives of the bourgeoisie who have sneaked into the party, the government, the army and various spheres of culture are actually a bunch of counter-revolutionary revisionists. Once the conditions are ripe, they will try to seize power, turning the dictatorship of the proletariat into the dictatorship of the capitalist class. Some of the people have already been exposed by us; others have not. Some are still trusted by us, and are being groomed as our successors, people of Khrushchev type who are nestling right beside us. Party cadres at all levels must pay attention to this point.

According to Mao in Source B, what crisis does the CCP face?

Mao's reference to Khrushchev was not a cheap insult. He had convinced himself by early 1966 that Soviet revisionism (see page 91) had infected not merely organisations like SEM but the whole of the party and government, and that the Chinese revolution itself was at risk.

SOURCE C

From a statement of Mao's to the CCP in May 1966, quoted in Roderick Macfarquar and Michael Schoenhals, *Mao's Last Revolution*, Belknap Press, 2006, p. 12. With the Cultural Revolution soon to be launched, Mao is here concerned to impress on party members the necessity of training younger members to follow a true revolutionary path.

The question of training successors for the revolutionary cause of the proletariat is one of whether or not there will be people who can carry on the Marxist–Leninist revolutionary cause started by the older generation of proletarian revolutionaries, whether or not the leadership of our Party and state will remain in the hands of proletarian revolutionaries, whether or not our descendants will continue to march along the correct road or whether or not we can successfully prevent the emergence of revisionism in China. In short it is a matter of life and death for our Party and our country. It is a question of fundamental importance to the proletarian revolutionary cause for a hundred, a thousand, nay ten thousand years.

According to Source C, why is Mao so worried by the development of revisionism in the PRC?

Mao's words were, in effect, an announcement that China had entered the tumultuous period of political and social history known as the Cultural Revolution (see page 128).

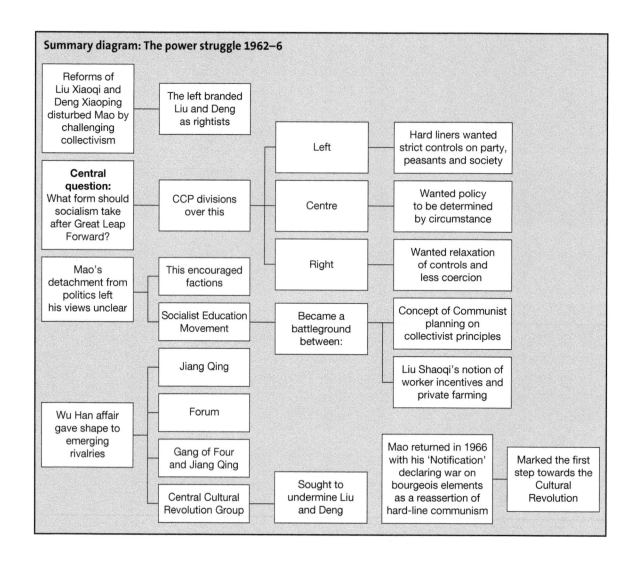

Summary diagram: The power struggle 1962–6

2 The cult of Mao

▶ *What were the principal features of the cult of Mao?*

Mao began to feel that his withdrawing from the political scene had been an error; his absence had enabled factions to develop. It was to regain his dominance that Mao turned to Lin Biao, a dedicated follower. Lin was a field marshal of the PLA and had been defence minister since 1959, when he had replaced Peng Dehuai. His loyalty and leadership of the PLA made him an invaluable ally. He now began to serve his master in a remarkable way.

Lin became, in effect, Mao's propaganda minister. He made it his task to inculcate the notion that Mao Zedong was a unique being whose successful leadership of the Chinese Revolution since the 1920s was proof of his faultless judgement. Mao was projected as the outstanding interpreter of class struggle, the last and the greatest in the line of prophets of revolution that stretched from Marx, by way of Lenin and Stalin, to reach its culmination in him. Lin's aim was to elevate Mao above ordinary politics and put him beyond criticism as the embodiment of wisdom.

The Little Red Book

Lin popularised the concept of Mao as icon in a propaganda campaign that proved brilliantly successful. Early in the 1960s, he collaborated with **Chen Boda** in compiling what became known as the Little Red Book. Formally entitled *Quotations from Chairman Mao Zedong*, the book was a collection of the thoughts and sayings of Mao since the 1920s and was drawn mainly from the volumes of his writings and speeches already published by the CCP. Encased in bold red plastic covers and printed in handy pocket size, its 33 chapters ranged over a wide set of subjects and highlighted such topics as 'The Communist Party', 'Classes and Class Struggle' and 'Culture and Art'. The work was prefaced by Lin's exhortation: 'Study Chairman Mao's writings, follow his teachings and act according to his instructions.'

The Little Red Book, which first appeared in 1964, is best understood as China's **secular bible**, the source of all truth. It was Revelation in plastic covers. Within two years of publication over 740 million copies had been distributed. Under Lin's direction, it became the prescribed source for every subject on the curriculum in the schools and universities. Classes and lectures began and ended with readings from it. It soon became essential for everyone to possess a copy. In factories, the workers were uplifted by continual loudspeaker broadcasts of readings of Mao's words. Specially designed copies were presented as a precious wedding gift to couples, who were urged to read from it before having sex so that the bride might conceive.

The sayings of **Confucius** had once been invoked to settle legal and social disputes. It was now the thoughts of Chairman Mao that were the ultimate reference. Yang Tang, China's table-tennis champion, was asked by foreign journalists what made him such an excellent player. Was it his cunning serve, ferocious backhand or lightning speed? No, he replied, 'it was the progressive thinking of Chairman Mao as expressed in the Little Red Book'.

The PLA

For Mao, the vital feature of all this was the swift adoption of the Little Red Book by the PLA as their inspiration and guide. Lin Biao, as a field marshal of the PLA and head of the armed services, made the book a compulsory and daily part of a soldier's military training. Since the 1920s, Mao had consistently defined the

KEY FIGURES

Chen Boda (1904–89)
A leading Communist intellectual and the editor of the CCP journal, *Red Flag*.

Confucius (BC551–479)
The revered scholar of classical times, whose ideas on how to achieve a fulfilled life had been the main influence on Chinese thought for over 2000 years.

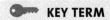

KEY TERM

Secular bible The Little Red Book came to have the same authority in Maoist society as the Bible had in Christian culture or the Qur'an in Islamic.

role of the Red Army, and its successor the PLA, as a political one. 'The Chinese Red Army is an armed force for carrying out the political tasks of the revolution.' Having been the instrument by which the Chinese Communist revolution had been achieved, its historical role was now that of protector of the revolution. 'Without a people's army the people have nothing.' In this way the PLA, the institution with the highest prestige and proudest revolutionary tradition in Communist China, was politicised as a force totally committed to the support of Mao Zedong.

Since 1962, the PLA had attracted many of its new recruits from the SEM, which had been set up to act as a **ginger group** to keep party members focused on revolution (see page 102). Such developments confirmed that, under Lin Biao, the PLA was a force on whose loyalty Chairman Mao Zedong could fully rely. Mao reciprocated by urging the Chinese people to 'learn from the PLA' as the model of revolutionary spirit and integrity. The special relationship between the chairman and the armed services was a major instrument in projecting the cult of Mao and was to prove of vital importance in the development of the Cultural Revolution.

> **🔑 KEY TERM**
>
> **Ginger group** A supportive group whose task was to keep the party committed to true revolution.

> **?** Is there anything about the portrait shown in Source D that explains why it became the iconic depiction of Mao?

SOURCE D

Mao as he appeared on the inside cover of the Little Red Book. This was the most popular image of Mao to appear during his lifetime. The picture was originally painted in 1949, when Mao was 56. It is this picture that still overlooks Tiananmen Square in Beijing. The original, which was priceless in Mao's time, was auctioned in Beijing in 2006 for the equivalent of £90,000.

The Diary of Lei Feng

The Maoist propaganda campaign made further ground with the publication in 1963 of *The Diary of Lei Feng*. It was claimed that this book was the daily journal of a humble PLA lorry driver, whose every thought and action were inspired by his devotion to Mao. The manner in which Lei died, accidentally crushed under the wheels of a truck while faithfully performing his assigned duties, was held up as a symbol of martyrdom for the revolutionary cause. Every Chinese person, no matter how humble or humdrum his role in life, should try to reach Lei's level of dedication. That the story was concocted by the government's propaganda department did not prevent its hero from achieving secular sainthood.

Lei Feng was projected by Maoists as the embodiment of the loyalty of the ordinary Chinese, a loyalty that stood in marked contrast to the time-serving careerism of many of those with soft jobs in the party or government. Lei Feng's diary joined the Little Red Book as an essential text for study in China's schools.

The PRC becomes a superpower

The Chinese were soon given added reason to venerate Chairman Mao. In 1964, the PRC strengthened its claim to equal status with the USSR by exploding its own nuclear bomb; three years later it successfully detonated a hydrogen bomb. China, under Mao, had thus become a superpower. Exulting in having achieved this by their own independent efforts, the Chinese called their nuclear programme 59/6, a pointed allusion to the year and month when Khrushchev had announced that the Soviet Union would no longer provide assistance to the Chinese in developing their nuclear programme (see page 124).

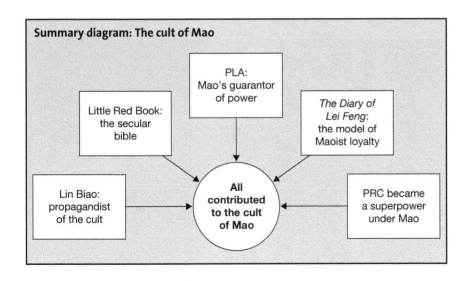

Summary diagram: The cult of Mao

Social change by 1966

▶ *What were the major social changes that occurred under Mao?*

The status of women and the family

Imperial China, the nation in which Mao Zedong grew up, was a patriarchal (male-dominated) system. Confucius had taught that for a society to be harmonious it had to follow the rules of the *san gang* – the three relationships that hold society together:

- loyalty of ministers and officials to the emperor
- respect of children for their parents
- obedience of wives to their husbands.

As a result, it had become traditional for women to be discriminated against in China. There were instances of females playing a leading role in public life – one example was **Cixi** – but she was very much an exception. For the most part women played a subordinate role.

Mao Zedong's own story is illuminating. A striking example of how young women and men were expected to conform to the *san gang* was Mao's betrothal in 1907, when he was barely fourteen, to a woman seven years his senior. Arranged marriages were the practice in rural China. Whether the young couple liked each other or had even met was not a consideration. The arrangement was a financial one between the two families. In the event, Mao, a natural rebel, refused to go through with the betrothal, let alone the marriage, even though the **bride-price** had been paid. Mao's stand over this was later used in CCP propaganda as a stirring example of his fight against a corrupt social system in which women were treated as commodities, not people.

Mao's fight against the practice of forced marriages

It was as a defender of women's rights that Mao had became involved in 1919 in a notorious affair in Changsha, the principal city of his home province of Hunan. A young woman, forced by her family to marry a wealthy man she detested, waited until the wedding morning before cutting her throat and bleeding to death. Mao seized on the incident as evidence of the rottenness of the social system that had driven a young woman to suicide. In a series of articles, he condemned arranged marriages as 'indirect rape'. Women, he said, had been 'relegated to the dark corners of society'. He gave bitter descriptions of how they were exploited by China's marriage customs which turned a wife into the slave of her husband and his family.

Mao's powerful argument suggested that he was a firm believer in women's rights. It was certainly the case that, in the Jiangxi and Yanan soviets in the

KEY FIGURE

Cixi (1835–1908)
The Empress Dowager who in, effect, ruled for most of the final twenty years of the Qing dynasty.

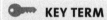

KEY TERM

Bride-price Payment made by the bride's family to the groom's family to seal the marriage contract.

1930s and 1940s, Mao had insisted that women were the equals of men. The party under him formally outlawed the practice of **foot binding**, which had survived in parts of China until the 1940s.

However, in practice Mao and the party often failed to respect the principle of female equality. In his personal life Mao tended either to use women or to patronise them. Having been puritanical as a young man, he became a notorious womaniser in his later years. Whatever their official statements, the Chinese Communists operated what was very much a male-dominated system. Few of the important posts in the party organisation went to women. Foreign visitors to the Communist base at Yanan noted how the domestic chores were invariably carried out by the female comrades. Ding Ling, who had joined the Communists in Yanan, described Mao and the CCP as hypocrites. She asserted that, undermining their claim to be revolutionaries, they lived comfortable lives at Yanan, exploiting the women who worked for them. Although she had been initially supportive of Mao, she came to believe that his brand of socialism did not truly include female emancipation (see page 26).

Marriage reform under Mao in the 1950s

Notwithstanding Ding Ling's accusation, it was to be expected that, in view of his record of supporting female rights, Mao would back measures to help women once he was in power. One of the first acts of the PRC was to introduce a new marriage law in 1950. This laid down that:

- **Concubinage** was abolished.
- Arranged marriages were to be discontinued.
- The paying of bride-price was forbidden.
- Women (and men) who had previously been forced to marry were entitled to divorce their partners.
- All marriages had to be officially recorded and registered.

Many women used their new freedom to divorce and remarry. There were cases of women taking as many as four different husbands in as many years. This threatened to prove so disruptive that a special clause was added to PLA regulations giving the soldiers the legal right to overrule their wives' plea for a divorce.

The impact of collectivisation on women

Further laws were passed in the 1950s giving women the right to own and sell land and property. In the land redistribution which followed the seizure of the properties of the landlords (see page 8), women were actually granted land in their own name. This seemed to be a major advance since it broke the tradition whereby all property dealings had been controlled by the men of the family. However, much of this apparent gain was undermined by Mao's Great

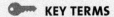

KEY TERMS

Foot binding The tight bandaging of the feet to prevent their growth. This had two purposes: to hobble the women so that they could not get about and to make them more attractive to men, who traditionally regarded small feet as highly erotic.

Concubinage The practice of men keeping women not as wives but as mistresses (concubines).

Leap Forward whose collectivisation programme ended the holding of private property by either men or women and required people to live in communes.

Interestingly, life in the communes did bring women one immediate advantage. The rule now was that everybody should eat in common in mess halls; this meant that women no longer had the daily drudgery of finding food and preparing it for the family. Yet, for every gain that women made, there seemed to be an accompanying disadvantage. Now that they were officially regarded in Mao's China as the equals of men, they could be called on to do the work of men. Between 1949 and 1966, the proportion of women in the workforce rose from 8 to 29 per cent. This might bring women advantages if the work was suitable, but if it was heavy or dangerous physical labour they were worse off than before.

Ingrained prejudice against women

The hard truth was that social values and attitudes could not be easily changed. China was by deep-seated tradition a male-dominated society; no matter how genuine the new Communist regime might be in declaring that the sexes were equal, women were still having to compete with Chinese ingrained notions of their inferiority. This was clearly evident in the common prejudice against female babies. It was the wish of nearly all Chinese couples to have male children. This desire derived from a mixture of pride and economic interest. The birth of a boy was thought to bring honour on the family, and the promise of another source of income; girls were seen as a drain on resources.

Peasants complained that the new marriage laws interfered with the established ways of life. The idea of female subordination was persistent in all China's rural areas but especially so in the western provinces where there was a predominantly Muslim culture. In areas such as Xinjiang, families, in accordance with Muslim teaching, were tightly controlled by the men; female members were subject to the orders of husbands, fathers and brothers, and even brothers-in-law, and were likely to be punished if they disobeyed or showed too much independence of thought.

The representative of the All China Women's Federation described the outlook of Xinjiang's 4 million women as being like a frog in a well: 'All they can see is a tiny bit of sky, so their outlook is very narrow. A woman is treated as a man's possession. It is the duty of a woman to look after him, whether he is working the fields or in the house.'

CCP restrictions on women

There is also the consideration that, as Ding Ling had earlier suggested, the Communist authorities may not have been as committed to gender equality as they claimed. **Soong Qingling**, one of the few women to hold a high position in the PRC government under Mao, later complained that her party colleagues

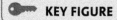
KEY FIGURE

Soong Qingling (1893–1981)

One of a remarkable set of sisters who became prominent in Chinese politics. Qingling had been the wife of the Nationalist leader, Sun Yat-sen, while her sister, Meiling, was married to Mao's great rival, Chiang Kai-shek.

did not really treat her as an equal and did not accept that women comrades could play key roles in government and party. During Mao's time, women made up only 13 per cent of the membership of the Communist Party. The number of women who became members of the National People's Congress did rise during Mao's period of power but never on such a scale as to suggest that the Communist Party had made a priority of promoting females within its ranks.

Women and the family

In addition to women being denied a fuller political role, there was a deeper sense in which Mao's reforms prevented them from making a sustained advance in their status. If anything, the radical and invariably violent character of the reforms increased women's vulnerability. Collectivisation entailed a direct and deliberate assault on the traditional Chinese family. Mao had already prepared the way for this as early as 1944 when he had stated that 'It is necessary to destroy the peasant family; women going to the factories and joining the army are part of the big destruction of the family.' The prohibiting of ancestor worship, which was part of the attack on religion (see page 119), was intended as a blow against the family as a social unit with its historical roots and deep emotional attachments.

No matter how much women wanted emancipation, few of them felt happy that their role as mothers and raisers of families was now to be written off as no longer being necessary. It went against nature. So determined was the Communist Party to undermine the family that in many of the communes men and women had to live in separate quarters and were allowed to meet only for **conjugal visits**. An official party statement of 1958 left no doubts over the purpose of such restrictions: 'It is not the family, but Chairman Mao and the Communist Party, which has given us everything. Personal love is not important.'

While in some respects this might be considered liberating, since women might be freed from restrictive family ties, there was a downside to it. The enforced social change had happened all too suddenly. The Chinese, a profoundly conservative people, became disorientated; women found themselves detached from their traditional moorings. The famine that struck so many parts of China in the wake of the Great Leap Forward deepened this sense of helplessness.

Impact of the famine on women and the family

It was women who suffered most in the famine that devastated China between 1958 and 1962 as they found themselves caught in a tragedy that simply overwhelmed them. Circumstances made it impossible for them to remain the providers for their children. The psychological shock suffered by the mothers caught up in the events is frighteningly described in Source E (page 116), an eyewitness account of the famine in Anhui province.

Table 4.1 Percentage of women deputies in the National People's Congress

1954	14%
1959	14%
1964	17%
1975	23%

KEY TERM

Conjugal visits Time set aside for couples to have sex.

Why, according to Source E, were females considered expendable?

SOURCE E

From an eyewitness account, quoted in Jasper Becker, *Hungry Ghosts*, John Murray, 1996, p. 138.

The worst thing that happened during the famine was this: parents would decide to allow the old and the young to die first. They thought they could not allow their sons to die but a mother would say to a daughter, 'You have to go and see your granny in heaven.' They stopped giving the girl children food. They just gave them water. Then they swapped the body of their daughter with that of a neighbour's. About five to seven women would agree to do this amongst themselves. Then they boiled the corpses into a kind of soup. People had learned to do this during the famine of the 1930s. People accepted this as it was a kind of hunger culture. They said: 'If your stomach is empty, then who can keep face.' One woman was reported and arrested by the Public Security Bureau. No one criticized her when she returned from a labour camp a few years later.

The impossibility of maintaining anything approaching a normal married life in such circumstances was reflected in the divorce figures during the famine period. In Gansu province, for example, the divorce rate rose by 60 per cent. This did not always denote a breakdown of personal relationships, but rather that as the family ran out of food the couple judged it better for the wife to leave and look for a husband elsewhere. Her starving family would at least have the little bit of food that she would have eaten had she stayed. Divorce was an alternative to wife selling, which became common in the famine areas. As one report stated: 'The poorer the region, the more wife selling there was. If the chief family earner died, a teenage daughter might be sold to the highest bidder in a distant place to obtain grain to keep the rest of the household alive.'

The family disruption that buying and selling of wives had often caused became clear after the famine had eased by the middle 1960s. Wives often refused to go back to their original husbands, preferring the new life they had made. In Hebei, Sichuan and Gansu provinces, there was a stream of court cases in which husbands appealed for decisions that would return their former wives to them. In most instances the courts found for the husbands but this was by no means guaranteed. A number of women resisted being forced to return and were supported by the courts.

Consequences for children

One of the most tragic consequences of the wives' leaving home was that the children of the family were left motherless. This often led to their being sold or abandoned. Youngsters who were old enough to be useful were sold as workers, slaves, in effect. But at least such children had a chance of survival. It was the very young who suffered most from being deserted. A nurse in Lanzuo, the main city in Gansu, described how on a hospital stairway she came across a tattered cardboard box; inside this crude manger lay a baby girl. Pinned to the dirty rags in which she was dressed was a roughly pencilled note: 'To kind-hearted people, please look after her. From a mother who regrets her faults.'

At first, it was girl infants who were dumped in hospitals, at railway stations or simply by the roadside, but as the famine grew worse boys, too, were abandoned. Source F is a Gansu villager's description of a heart-rending scene.

SOURCE F

From a report, quoted in Jasper Becker, *Hungry Ghosts*, John Murray, 1996, p. 153. Becker was a Western writer who visited China to make a detailed study of the famine. He interviewed thousands of those who had suffered. Here he quotes a survivor from Anhui province, giving an eyewitness account of the cannibalism that became common practice in some areas during the worst of the famine.

Those who still had the strength left the village begging and many died on the road. The road from the village to the neighbouring province was strewn with bodies, and piercing wails came from holes on either sides of the road. Following the cries, you could see the tops of heads of children who were abandoned in those holes. A lot of mothers thought their children had a better chance of surviving if they were adopted by somebody else. The holes were just deep enough so that the children could not get out but could be seen by passers-by who might adopt them.

What picture of the desperate conditions emerges from the description in Source F?

Abandoned children were obvious targets for exploitation and sexual abuse. One example was a predatory party official in Hefei who bought a young girl from a starving family and proceeded to make her his sexual plaything. His behaviour was too much even for a party that was used to covering up its members' scandals and he was dismissed. The party were also involved in the spread of prostitution, which, like wife selling, became more widespread as the famine bit deeper. In the worst-hit regions women openly offered themselves for sex in return for food. Using the opportunity for exploitation that this provided, CCP workers in Anhui set up a series of brothels reserved for special use by party members.

Birth control

Mao had earlier encouraged the people to have large families, his belief being that industrialisation, based on mass effort, required an ever-growing population. However, the grim experience of the famine suggested that China had too many mouths to feed. In 1963, therefore, the PRC formally introduced a campaign aimed at cutting the birth rate. A Birth Control Bureau was set up to organise this. Teams of medical workers were sent into the countryside to advocate:

- sexual abstinence and late marriage
- couples having no more than two children
- husbands being sterilised after the conception of a second child
- women adopting effective contraceptive methods.

The bureau had only limited success. The idea of family limitation met strong resistance from the peasants, for whom having large numbers of children

Table 4.2 China's population

1953	594,350,000
1964	694,580,000
1976	925,100,000

was traditionally a matter of pride and good fortune. There was also the long-established peasant view that rather than being a drain on resources, children were a source of future family income and a guarantee of care and protection for parents in old age. In the face of this natural conservatism, the health workers were often reluctant or half-hearted in preaching the new ways. It would be some time before the Chinese authorities felt able to go so far as to impose a one-child policy.

Education and young people

Table 4.3 Literacy rates

1949	20%
1960	50%
1964	66%
1976	70%

The education plans of the PRC began with high hopes for raising the educational levels of the Chinese people. In 1949, the majority of the peasants were illiterate or barely literate. They could read a little but write almost nothing. It had been one of Mao's contentions that, under communism, China would see a major spread of education among the people and a sharp decrease in illiteracy. He kept his word. By the middle 1950s a national system of primary education had been set up; its success is evident from the figures in Table 4.3.

Language reform

One fascinating aspect of this was the reform of the Chinese language adopted by the PRC. In 1955, a new form of Mandarin, the language of 80 per cent of the Chinese people, was adopted. Up to that date there had been no standardised form of written Mandarin that everybody could understand. This was because of two factors:

- The pronunciation of Mandarin varied widely from area to area; visitors from one place often could not be understood by speakers in another.
- Mandarin had no alphabet. Whereas all the words in every European language are made up from a basic alphabet (English, for example, has 26 letters), written Mandarin was made up of **ideograms**, not letters. This made writing Mandarin extremely difficult, since all its words had to be learned separately.

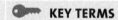

KEY TERMS

Ideograms Pictures. Mandarin symbols had begun as pictures of the ideas they described.

Pinyin A modernised form of Mandarin.

To solve the problem, the PRC decided to introduce a written form of Mandarin that all speakers and writers of it could recognise and use. The result was the adoption of *pinyin*: in this, all the sounds in Mandarin were given a particular symbol. This greatly eased the learning process since all Mandarin speakers could now express the words they said in a standardised, recognisable written form. Here is an example:

- Mandarin Chinese: 三个孩子都上学
- *Pinyin*: sān gè háizi dōu shangxué
- English: All three children go to school.

There was no doubt that through such initiatives Mao's leadership of China saw major advances in education by the mid-1960s. One striking statistic is that in 1949 there were 200 colleges and universities in China; by 1961 that number had grown to 1289. The tragedy was to come after 1966 when the Cultural Revolution practically destroyed education as a public activity (see page 154).

Religion in the PRC

As Marxists, the Chinese Communists considered religious belief and worship to be superstitions that throughout history had been deliberately cultivated by the classes in power to suppress the masses. Religion, with its promise of eternal happiness in the afterlife, was a powerful force persuading the workers to put up with their grim lives without protest; the more they suffered in the here and now the greater would be their reward in heaven. Mao Zedong had declared that religion was poison and had compared the Christian missionaries in China to the Nazis in Europe. Almost immediately after he led his party to power, the attack on religion began. The official rationale was that since the workers were now in power there was no longer any reason for religion to exist; the triumph of the workers had ended the need for such escapism. For religion to continue openly would be an affront to the new Chinese Communist world. Religious worship had now to be replaced by loyalty to the CCP and the state.

Suppression took an organised form:

- Christian churches were forcibly closed.
- Church property was seized or destroyed.
- Clergy were denounced and physically abused.
- Foreign priests and nuns were expelled from China.

SOURCE G

Why should Buddhism have been selected for special attack, as shown in the photo in Source G? **?**

Buddhist monks are paraded to be mocked and humiliated at a temple in Harbin in August 1966. The banners say such things as 'Eradicate the ghosts and demons', 'What are these Buddhist sutras? Just a collection of dog farts'.

Wall posters, the standard way by which Chinese governments spread their propaganda, and loudspeakers at every corner, kept up a running condemnation of religion and those who practised it. Confucianism, **Buddhism** and Christianity were denounced as worthless superstitions that had no place in the new nation. Slogans proclaiming the virtues of the new Maoist China were to be seen everywhere. China, possibly even more than the USSR, became a **slogan-ridden society**. The slogans became more than simply a way of exhorting the comrades to ever greater efforts; they were a means of enforcing solidarity and conformity.

Peasant religion suppressed

The peasants, the largest and most religious segment of China's population, were the first to be targeted. Beginning in 1950, a campaign was launched to eliminate all traces of religion from their lives. The Chinese traditional faiths, Buddhism and Confucianism, were forbidden to be openly practised, as were the major foreign religions, Christianity and Islam. Priests and monks were prohibited from wearing their distinctive dress; any who disobeyed this order were liable to arrest and imprisonment. There were cases of the police encouraging bystanders to strip the clothes off the clergy who dared to walk about in their traditional distinctive dress. Foreign clergy were expelled from China, and temples, churches, shrines and monasteries were closed down or turned into offices and public buildings. **Ancestor worship** was also condemned as a superstition that was no longer acceptable in the new China.

Chinese customs suppressed

It was not merely the formal expressions of belief that were outlawed. The customs and rituals that had helped to shape the life of the peasants were proscribed. These included the songs and dances they had performed at weddings and festivals, the chants that had accompanied their work in the fields, and the sagas and narratives with which wandering poets had entertained whole villages. These traditional ways were replaced with political meetings and discussions organised by the party. The huge social experiment of collectivisation which Mao introduced in 1950s was meant to destroy the time-honoured pattern of rural life.

The peasants were now expected to embrace Maoism as their new faith. Troupes of **agit-prop** performers toured the countryside putting on shows and plays which the villagers were required to attend and sit through. The shows were put on in halls and public spaces. Sometimes the players arrived in brightly painted trucks carrying slogans and images extolling the wonders and benefits of the new Maoist world. The sides of the truck could serve as a screen on which propaganda films were projected after dark or they could be removed to convert the truck into a stage.

The message of the films and the live performances was always the same: the old days of cruel landlords and abused peasant farmers had been replaced with a communal way of life in which the peasants, guided by the wisdom of Mao Zedong and the CCP, had entered an era of happy collective endeavour and achievement. The shows were played at knockabout pantomime level; the baddies were always bad, the goodies were always good. The landlords were obviously the worst of the baddies, but scheming Confucian officials and exploiting priests also appeared to be hissed at and jeered.

The patriotic churches

Mao and the authorities were shrewd enough to realise that there could be advantages for them in permitting some forms of public worship to continue. It would give the appearance of toleration. It was laid down that some churches could remain open provided that they 'did not endanger the security of the state'. What this meant in practice was they became state controlled. Known as the patriotic churches, their clergy had to profess open support for the Communist regime and accept that the authorities had the right to dictate doctrine and appoint clergy.

One consequence of the state sponsoring of the patriotic churches was a sharpening of conflict between the PRC and the **Vatican**. The persecution of the Catholic Church in Mao's China, which involved the seizure and closure of churches and chapels and the imprisonment or expulsion of priests and nuns, was condemned by the **papacy**, which made a particular point of rejecting the notion of the patriotic church as a genuine form of Catholicism. Bishops and priests appointed by the Chinese state would not be recognised by Rome and risked **excommunication**. In 2014, the dispute between Beijing and Rome over this issue had still not been resolved.

Religion and the regional minorities

A basic fear of the PRC government was that religion might encourage the breakaway tendencies in the western provinces. From the beginning of its rule in 1949, Mao's government had confirmed that it would not grant independence to any of the provinces or regions. That is why in 1950 it sent the PLA into Tibet, Xinjiang and Guangzhou to enforce its authority (see page 53). It claimed that the strength, indeed the survival, of the PRC as a nation demanded total unity and obedience to central control.

It was Tibet's Lama faith, a particular form of Buddhism, that inspired Tibetan nationalism in its resistance to Chinese occupation (see page 53). The PRC fretted that religion and nationalism would prove an equally dangerous mix in Tibet's northern neighbour, Xinjiang. Here the majority of the population was made up of the **Uighur, Kazakh, Hui** and **Kirghiz** peoples, who were devotedly Muslim in faith.

KEY TERMS

Vatican The administrative centre of the Catholic Church in Rome, where the Pope has his official residence.

Papacy The Catholic Church's system of government, headed by the Pope.

Excommunication Formal dismissal from the Catholic Church.

Uighur, Kazakh, Hui, Kirghiz Ethnic groups, who, in regard to race, language and religion, were distinct from the Han people who made up over 80 per cent of China's population.

What added to Chinese fears was the strategic position of Xinjiang, on whose western borders lay Pakistan, Turkistan and Kazakhstan, all of them strongly Muslim countries. Beijing's understandable concern was that religious belief would combine with politics to create a dangerous separatist movement in Xinjiang, backed by these border countries. In a major effort to prevent this, the PRC condemned all independence organisations in China's border regions as 'handfuls of national separatists' with 'reactionary feudal ideas', who were in league with 'hostile foreign forces' with the aim of weakening the Chinese nation itself. The government adopted the same policy that it had in Tibet (see page 80); it tried to dilute the Muslim element in the population by settling large numbers of Han Chinese in the region. This proved only partially successful. At the time of Mao's death in 1976, the Muslim proportion still formed a large minority of the Xinjiang population.

Summary diagram: Social change by 1966

The status of women and the family

Mao: an advocate of women's rights	But in practice CCP did not always promote female equality in its own ranks	Marriage reform under Mao in the 1950s	Women's property rights recognised	Concubinage and arranged marriage abolished	Right to divorce and remarriage

Collectivisation brought women

Gains: end of drudgery and more work opportunities	Losses: exposed to unsuitable heavy work	Traditional prejudice against women remained

Great famine

Devastating for women as mothers and providers	Grim consequences for children

PRC

Birth Control Bureau promoted programme to stem population growth

Education and young people

Successful literacy programme	Mandarin language simplified

Religion in the PRC

State attacks on religious worship	Churches and clergy suppressed	Chinese peasant customs ridiculed	PRC's Patriotic Churches led to clash with Vatican	PRC concerned by strength of religion as a destabilising force among regional minorities

4 Sino-Soviet relations: the nuclear issue

▶ *Why were the USSR and China so divided over the question of nuclear weapons?*

The issue of coexistence

The continuing Sino-Soviet dispute over whether coexistence was compatible with true Marxism–Leninism was at its fiercest over the **test ban treaty** of 1963. Mao dismissed the treaty as another betrayal by the USSR of its revolutionary role. Instead of confronting imperialism, it was collaborating with it: 'Soviet revisionists are uniting with the running dogs of capitalism.'

Mao pointed to what he saw as a fundamental flaw in the Soviet pursuit of peace with the West. In a formal statement in 1963, he declared that coexistence could operate only between equal nations, but since, in Marxist logic, all pre-revolutionary states were in subjection to the exploiting capitalist power, true equality did not exist. Therefore, it was impossible 'to practise peaceful coexistence with the imperialists and their lackeys'. It was a betrayal of international socialism to pretend that there could be peaceful relations between 'oppressed and oppressor classes and between oppressed and oppressor nations'.

Khrushchev retorted by accusing the Chinese of irresponsibility; they were being arrogant and dangerous in claiming to speak for the international working class. 'We might ask the Chinese – what right have you to decide for us questions involving our very existence and our class struggle? – We too want socialism, but we want to win it through the class struggle, not by unleashing a world thermo-nuclear war.' Khrushchev's charge was that, rather than seek peace, the Chinese wished to see East and West destroy themselves in nuclear war, leaving China free to dominate what was left of the world. What gave particular irony to Khrushchev's charge was that China was only a year away from exploding its own nuclear bomb.

China's nuclear bomb

Ever since the early 1950s Mao Zedong had been unhappy with the attitude of Stalin and successive Soviet leaders towards the nuclear question. Moscow's position was that if China wanted Soviet assistance in its nuclear programme it must give the USSR a controlling hand in the PRC's defence policy. This was too much for Mao. The Soviet demand redoubled his determination to make China a superpower by achieving nuclear status unaided. In 1959 a particularly low point in Sino-Soviet relations was reached when the USSR decided to withdraw its scientists from the PRC. Nonetheless, China, undeterred, pressed on with

KEY TERM

Test ban treaty Agreement between the USSR and the Western nuclear powers in 1963, in which the parties pledged to end their atmospheric testing of nuclear weapons.

its own research programme. Chinese nuclear physicists painstakingly pieced together the records that the Soviet advisers had shredded before their hurried departure.

Such efforts brought their reward. In 1964, to great rejoicing with massed crowds singing 'The East is Red' in Mao's honour, Communist China detonated its first nuclear device. Three years later it produced its first hydrogen bomb. China's remarkable feat allowed it to mock the USSR's refusal to assist. The first Chinese bomb was codenamed 59/6, a reference to the year and month in which the Soviet technicians had withdrawn from China. Mao recorded gloatingly: 'This is the result of Khrushchev's "help". By withdrawing the experts he forced us to take our own road. We should give him a big medal.'

Mao's attitude to nuclear war

China's emergence as a nuclear power frightened the world. China seemed not to have the same awesome fear of nuclear war that the West and the USSR had. Mao referred to nuclear weapons as 'paper tigers' (see page 97). He told Khrushchev at one of their meetings that despite the awesome destructiveness of these weapons, the PRC was quite willing to contemplate nuclear war with its enemies. To Khrushchev's amazement, Mao casually informed him that China's population was so big that it would soon make up any losses it suffered, no matter how great the disaster.

This was in keeping with an earlier CCP statement which indicated China's belief that it could successfully survive a nuclear war: 'On the debris of a dead imperialism, the victorious Chinese people would create very swiftly a civilisation thousands of times higher than the capitalist system and a truly beautiful future for themselves.' Mao believed that China's emergence as a superpower and its refusal to be frightened of paper tigers had confirmed its position as the true champion of the oppressed peoples of the world.

At the time of his fall from power in the USSR in 1964, Khrushchev was still trying to convince the rest of the Marxist world that the Maoist brand of communism was heretical. His policy of isolating China was continued by the collective leadership that superseded him. In the fierce Sino-Soviet propaganda war each side accused the other of a long list of crimes against communism. The USSR resurrected the spectre of the **'yellow peril'**. The bitter dispute was soon to be further deepened by the onset of China's Cultural Revolution.

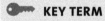 **KEY TERM**

'Yellow peril' A term, with strong racist overtones, first used in the nineteenth century to suggest that China's vast population was preparing to swamp Europe, with Russia as the first victim.

Summary diagram: Sino-Soviet relations: the nuclear issue

Sino-Soviet antipathy over coexistence and test ban treaty 1963

↓

Dismissed by Mao as revisionism and betrayal of the class war

↓

USSR regarded China as wishing to see East and West destroy themselves in nuclear war

↓

China's atom bomb 1964 and hydrogen bomb 1967: achieved without Soviet assistance

↓

PRC claimed its nuclear power status had confirmed its position as champion of all oppressed peoples

↓

Mao prepared to contemplate nuclear war

↓

USSR resurrected the 'yellow peril' fear to suggest that China was preparing to swamp Europe, with Russia as the first victim

---

Chapter summary

In the aftermath of the failure of the Great Leap Forward, the CCP experienced a series of disputes over economic planning. The disagreements were often a cover for political power bids, made possible by Mao's decision to remove himself for a time from the centre of things. Extraordinarily, however, it was during his period of relative detachment that his reputation reached new heights. This was the result of a campaign led by Lin Biao, who skilfully used state propaganda to project the cult of Mao as a unique leader whose peerless judgement rendered all opposition to him both pointless and counter-revolutionary.

By 1966, it was possible to measure the impact Maoism had had on Chinese society since 1949. Women had both gained and lost in status, education had seen significant developments, while religion had been largely suppressed, this last policy leading to resistance from the PRC's ethnic and religious minorities. On the international front, the PRC's successful development of a nuclear bomb by 1964 excited the fears of the USSR and led to renewed hostility between Mao and the Soviet leaders over whether the Soviet policy of coexistence with the West was the true path that international communism should be following.

Refresher questions

Use these questions to remind yourself of the key material covered in this chapter.

1 What explains the intra-party disputes of this period?

2 What motives underlay the creation of the Socialist Education Movement?

3 What methods did Deng Xiaoping and Liu Shaoqi employ to end the famine?

4 Why was the creation of the Central Cultural Revolution Group such a significant political move?

5 How did Lin Biao succeed in turning Mao Zedong into a cult?

6 How committed to female emancipation were Mao and the Communists?

7 Did Chinese women gain or lose in status between 1949 and 1966?

8 Why were women particularly vulnerable during the Great Leap Forward and the famine?

9 How did the Communist authorities tackle the question of basic literacy?

10 Why did the Chinese Communists regard religion as a threat?

11 What measures did the authorities take to suppress religion?

12 How was state propaganda used to undermine traditional ways?

13 What problems did the suppression of religion create between the PRC and its national and ethnic minorities?

14 What influence did the development of China's nuclear weapon have on Mao's attitude to the outside world?

15 What issue was at stake in the Sino-Soviet dispute over coexistence with the West?

 Question practice

ESSAY QUESTIONS

1 How successful were the reform policies of Liu Shaoqi and Deng Xiaoping in the period 1962–6?

2 How significant was the Wu Han affair of 1961–5 in deepening the divide between the left and the right in the Chinese Communist Party?

3 'Under Mao's leadership, the status of women was not elevated but depressed.' Assess the validity of this view.

4 'China's development of an atomic bomb in 1964 fundamentally altered its relations with the Soviet Union.' How far do you agree with this statement?

SOURCE ANALYSIS QUESTIONS

1 With reference to Sources A (**page 105**), B (**page 107**) and C (**page 107**), and your understanding of the historical context, assess the value of these sources to a historian studying the power struggle within the Chinese Communist Party in the period 1961–6.

2 Why is Source C (**page 107**) valuable to the historian studying Mao's revolutionary ideas? Explain your answer using the source, the information given about it and your own knowledge of the historical context.

3 How far could the historian make use of Sources E (**page 116**) and F (**page 117**) together to investigate the particular impact of the famine on China's women? Explain your answer, using the sources, the information given about them and your own knowledge of the historical context.

CHAPTER 5

The Cultural Revolution 1966–76

One of the most remarkable episodes in Chinese history occurred between 1966 and 1976. For a decade, Mao Zedong's Great Proletarian Cultural Revolution convulsed the PRC. Why Mao launched this disruptive movement, who implemented it, why it came to an end and what its effects were are the questions which this chapter covers under the following headings:

★ Origins and aims of the Cultural Revolution

★ The Red Guards

★ The PLA and the winding down of the Cultural Revolution

★ Impact of the Cultural Revolution on Chinese society

★ Impact of the Cultural Revolution on external affairs

The key debate on *page 161* of this chapter asks the question: Was Mao a monster?

Key dates

1966	Mao reappeared in public	1972	Nixon's visit to China
	Liu and Deng dismissed	1973	Liu Shaoqi died in prison
	First Tiananmen Square rally		Deng Xiaoping brought back into government
1966–76	Great Proletarian Cultural Revolution		
1967	Hydrogen bomb exploded by Chinese	1976	Death of Zhou Enlai
1968	'Cleansing the class ranks' campaign		Tiananmen Incident in Beijing
1971	Lin Biao killed in a plane crash		Death of Mao Zedong
1972	Criticise Lin Biao and Confucius campaign began		

1 Origins and aims of the Cultural Revolution

▶ *What were Mao's motives in launching the Cultural Revolution?*

Lin Biao's poster campaign

The official starting date of the 'Cultural Revolution' was May 1966, when Mao announced the beginning of a party purge to be organised by the CCRG (see page 107). However, the event that first brought the Cultural Revolution to the attention of the Chinese people and to the outside world as a great national movement was a mass rally in Tiananmen Square on 18 August. During the intervening months, Lin Biao, acting on Mao's instruction, had organised students and radical teachers in the universities in a wall poster campaign attacking the education system for its divergence from the revolutionary path. The enthusiasm with which the students abandoned their classes and attacked their teachers caused such unrest that Deng Xiaoping and Liu Shaoqi sent special work teams to the campuses in an attempt to contain the trouble.

Zhou Enlai, ever the diplomat, tried to keep the peace between the party factions, between those who wanted to restore order and the Maoist elements who were eager for the disruption to spread. But in an atmosphere of increasing violence even his best efforts were in vain. The work teams were attacked by the students who, in a particularly ominous development, began to take to the streets as **Red Guards** intent on creating a reign of terror.

Mao's return

It was at this critical stage that Mao Zedong made a dramatic public reappearance. In July 1966, in a stage-managed extravaganza, he was seen swimming across the Yangzi River at Wuhan, the scene of the 1911 Revolution against the Qing dynasty (see page 1). Photos of this feat filled the Chinese newspapers, and television and cinema newsreels carried the pictures into every village.

Mao had made a great symbolic gesture that excited the whole of China. The Yangzi had been carefully chosen as the site of his return to public view. In Chinese tradition, the nation's greatest river was regarded as a life force. The 73-year-old chairman had proved that he was very much alive and, therefore, still in control of events. American scholar John King Fairbank has suggested that to understand the impact of the incident on the Chinese imagination one needs to think of the reaction there would be in Britain to 'the news that Queen Elizabeth II had swum the Channel'.

Mao exploited the adulation aroused by his spectacular return to tighten his grip on government and party. In August, he summoned a special meeting of the CCP's Central Committee, at which he condemned the revisionist tendencies

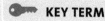

KEY TERM

Red Guards Radical students whose name derived from the red armbands they were given by Lin Biao.

in the party and called on members to rededicate themselves to unwavering class struggle. Mao also announced the downgrading of Liu Shaoqi in the party ranking and the elevation of Lin Biao to second in command. This was, in effect, to nominate Lin as his successor.

The August rally 1966

On 18 August over a million people, the majority of them in their teens or early twenties, packed into Tiananmen Square in Beijing. Waving their Little Red Books, they screamed themselves hoarse in an outpouring of veneration for their idol. They chanted 'Chairman Mao, may you live for a thousand years!' and sang 'Mao Zedong is the red sun rising in the east'.

This massive demonstration, which lasted for a whole day, was evidence of the organising skill of Lin Biao and Chen Boda, who had made the arrangements for filling the square with such huge numbers of Maoist supporters. So effectively had the cult of Mao been developed that Lin and Chen were able to assemble masses of genuinely enthusiastic Maoist demonstrators.

Enlisting the young

It was the ability to manipulate public opinion and behaviour, especially of the young, that allowed Mao to launch the Cultural Revolution, a movement that aimed at nothing less than the creation of a new type of Chinese society. His attempt to do this was to convulse the whole of China for the next decade. Mao had enlisted the youth of China as his instrument for reimposing his will on the nation and reshaping it according to his vision. In August 1966, he presented the students of Qinghai University with a banner inscribed in his own hand, 'Bombard the Headquarters'. It was his way of encouraging China's young people to criticise and attack those ideas and those members in party and government that he wanted to remove.

The decision to exploit the young in this way was no last-minute thought on Mao's part. In discussions he held with Kang Sheng (see page 134) and the Gang of Four late in 1965, he had remarked: 'We have to depend on them, the young, to start a rebellion, a revolution, otherwise we may not be able to overthrow the demons and monsters. We must liberate the little devils. We need more **monkeys to disrupt the palace**.'

The attack on the four olds

The high point of the rally came in a speech given by Lin Biao. In Mao's name, Lin identified 'four olds' as targets for the young to attack:

- old ideas
- old culture
- old customs
- old habits.

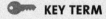 **KEY TERM**

Monkeys to disrupt the palace Mao's imagery is drawn from the practice in the imperial court of having monkeys as pets, whose uncontrolled behaviour could cause mayhem.

SOURCE A

The front page of the *Heilongjiang Daily*, 19 August 1966, reports the news of the great rally held in Beijing the day before. The photos show Mao, Lin Biao and the adoring crowds, and the main headline reads 'Chairman Mao celebrates the Great Cultural Revolution with millions of people'.

There was something bizarre about Mao Zedong, now 73 years old, calling on the young to overthrow the old, but at the time the irony went unnoticed by the youngsters. They rushed to do his bidding with a terrifying intensity and ferocity. It is doubtful whether any other society in peacetime has witnessed organised upheaval on such a scale. China had been told that nothing in its past was worth preserving. Hardly anywhere in China, even the remotest regions, would remain untouched. Nearly every family would be affected by what was to happen. Millions would die; many more millions would have their lives irreparably damaged.

The great rallies 1966

Between August and November 1966, eight mass rallies were held in Tiananmen Square. Mao did not attend all of these; he said he found them exhausting. Nevertheless his was the dominating spirit. Lin Biao, assisted on occasion by Jiang Qing, used the rallies to excite the crowds to ever greater displays of affection and loyalty towards China's leader. Lin appealed to the great throngs to honour Mao Zedong as the outstanding revolutionary genius of the age who was 'remoulding the souls of the people'. It was this very attempt to remould the people of China that was to give the Cultural Revolution its destructive character.

Mao's reasons for launching the Cultural Revolution

So massively disruptive was the Cultural Revolution that it raises an obvious question. Why was Mao Zedong willing to plunge his nation into renewed turmoil when it had only just emerged from decades of foreign occupation, civil war and famine? At its simplest, the answer is that the Cultural Revolution was to be the means by which Mao, conscious at the age of 73 of his mortality, would reassert his authority over China and the CCP. He had a number of interlocking objectives:

- to preserve himself in power for the rest of his life by removing all possible sources of opposition
- to obliterate the damaging record of the failure of the Great Leap Forward
- to ensure that his concept of revolution would continue after his death by remoulding Chinese society and culture in such a way that they could never be changed back
- to prevent China making the same mistakes as the revisionist USSR
- to break the power of the urban bureaucrats and restore the peasant character of China's Communist revolution.

Mao's idea of permanent revolution

Mao believed that the revolution, which he had led to victory in 1949, was being betrayed from within. He was convinced that many in the upper echelons of the CCP were infected by **neo-capitalism** and a desire for personal power that robbed them of their revolutionary purpose. The Great Proletarian Cultural Revolution, to give it its full title, has, therefore, to be seen as an extension of Mao's belief in **permanent revolution**. He believed that if the Chinese revolution stood still it would cease to be a genuine movement, and he feared that after him the CCP would simply become a self-justifying bureaucracy that would destroy all that had been achieved by the PRC since 1949.

To prevent this, Mao planned to circumvent the party bureaucracy and appeal directly to the Chinese people. In a great populist gesture he would enlist them in a campaign to save and consolidate the revolution. Mao used a memorable paradox to describe his policy; he spoke of 'great disorder across the land leading to great order': only by a policy of deliberate disruption could the forces of reaction be exposed and destroyed.

KEY TERMS

Neo-capitalism A return to the corrupt bourgeois system based on greed, individualism and profit-making.

Permanent revolution The notion that revolution is not a single historical event but a developing process.

Mao's reaction to Soviet developments

Mao was also motivated by developments in the USSR, China's great Communist rival. In the late 1950s, he had interpreted the Soviet attack on Stalin's 'cult of personality' as a criticism of his own leadership of China (see page 85). The news in 1964 of the fall from power of the Soviet leader, Nikita Khrushchev, gave Mao further concern. The official reason given by the Soviet authorities for their dismissal of Khrushchev was that he had engaged in **'hare-brained' economic schemes**. Nobody in China had openly dared to use such a term in regard to Mao's policies, but the parallel between the political situations in the USSR and China was too close for comfort.

Mao's anxieties went beyond the purely personal. What he observed in the USSR was a party, originally pure in revolutionary spirit, corrupted by its own exercise of power into a self-satisfied élite. Despite his many personal differences with Stalin, Mao had never been willing to accept the lengths to which de-Stalinisation and liberalising had gone in the USSR. He viewed Khrushchev and his successors as guilty of betraying the revolution by encouraging revisionism and by *détente* with the West. He was determined that such developments would not happen in China after him.

Mao's wish to renew the party's revolutionary spirit

Mao judged that CCP and government officials were already being seduced by the privileges of power. He had convinced himself that the older revolutionaries who had defeated the Nationalists and established the People's Republic had lost their revolutionary fervour. Consequently, the only way to save his revolution was by waging war against the Communist Party hierarchy itself. It was a time for a new generation of party members to replace the old guard.

Testing the younger members of the party

However, Mao also judged that the younger members of the party had yet to be tested. They had not undergone the rigours of the legendary experiences of the CCP: the White Terror, the Long March, the anti-Japanese war and the struggle against the GMD (see pages 2, 23 and 35). They needed hardening in the crucible of revolutionary struggle. Only then would it be certain that they were strong enough to withstand a concerted military attack from the West, an eventuality in which Mao continued to believe throughout the 1960s.

Undermining the bureaucrats and intellectuals

A further aim was Mao's determination to preserve the Chinese Revolution as an essentially peasant movement. It was not that he had a high regard for the peasants as individuals. Indeed, he often expressed contempt for them (see page 75). Nevertheless, he held that as a class the peasants were the main revolutionary force in China. That is why he had built his revolution on them. It was also why he did not want affairs to be run by the bureaucrats and intellectuals in the cities.

KEY TERM

'Hare-brained' economic schemes Khrushchev's unsuccessful attempts to reform Soviet agriculture and industry between 1956 and 1964.

A tension had developed between Mao and the urban intellectuals. It was they who had criticised the Great Leap Forward. Although Mao, judged by his writings and poetry, could be described as an intellectual, he always regarded himself as a man of action. He distrusted the type of political thinker who was more interested in theory than in action. It is possible to interpret his assault on the intellectuals in the Cultural Revolution as an act of revenge on a class which, he felt, had always despised him.

Deng Xiaoping and Liu Shaoqi attacked

At a party Central Committee meeting in August 1966, Deng Xiaoping and Liu Shaoqi were accused of being 'the **spearheads of the erroneous line**'. No immediate action was taken against them since it was reported that Mao had granted them the opportunity 'to correct their mistakes'. However, two months later, following a Red Guard demonstration in Beijing, aimed specifically against them, Deng and Liu were both formally dismissed from their positions in government and party on the grounds that they had adopted 'a bourgeois reactionary line' and had become 'revisionists'. Mao let it be known that he had been offended by the way in which Deng and Liu had previously tried to bypass him.

KEY TERM

Spearheads of the erroneous line Leaders who had tried to persuade the party to follow policies that ran counter to Mao's wishes.

In what ways does the photo in Source B illustrate how the Red Guards behaved in this period? **?**

SOURCE B

Wang Gangmei being manhandled by Red Guards. The garland of ping-pong balls has been put round her neck in mockery of her bourgeois habit of wearing expensive jewellery. Although she had been sentenced to death, Wang was reprieved by the personal intervention of Mao Zedong, who crossed her name off an execution list on which she appeared. It was one of the few occasions when Mao used his personal influence to save a victim of the Cultural Revolution. However, he made no move to save Liu Shaoqi. This may well have been vindictiveness on Mao's part; he was paying Liu back for opposing him earlier.

Wall posters were displayed denouncing both men for their betrayal of Maoist thought. Liu and his wife, Wang Gangmei, were dragged from their government residence and beaten by a jeering mob. Liu was then forced to undergo a series of brutal 'struggle sessions' before being imprisoned in conditions which were deliberately intended to break his health. He suffered from diabetes and eventually died in 1973 in solitary confinement after being refused proper medical treatment for his condition.

Deng Xiaoping's son, Pufang, was thrown from an upstairs window by Red Guards, an act of gratuitous violence that broke his spine and left him permanently paralysed. Deng himself suffered less harshly but he, too, was forced to undergo public humiliation that involved his being ranted at by 3000 Red Guards. He then disappeared into solitary confinement before being sent to perform '**corrective labour**' in Jiangxi province in 1969.

(see page 26)

KEY TERM

Corrective labour In Communist theory, a form of imprisonment that allowed a prisoner to see the error of his ways.

Influence of Lin Biao, Jiang Qing and Kang Sheng

The immediate acceptance by the CCP and the PLA of the dismissal of such prominent figures testified to the power that Lin Biao and Jiang Qing were able to exert in Mao's name. This authority was increased by the appointment of Kang Sheng as head of China's special security forces, the PRC's secret police. Kang, who had a reputation for ruthlessness dating back to the Yanan years (see page 26), was a member of the Shanghai Forum and a devotee of Jiang Qing. Kang became a principal organiser of the purges that continued, at Mao's bidding, to decimate the upper ranks of the CCP throughout 1966 and 1967.

Kang Sheng 1898–1975

Kang was Mao's able but psychotic secret police chief, who took a perverse pleasure in terrifying and persecuting people. A fearsome figure, who dressed permanently in black, rode a black horse and carried a black whip, Kang had a reputation for vicious cruelty that dated back to the Yanan years when, in the early 1940s, he had been the principal organiser of Mao's lethal rectification campaign. A member of the Shanghai Forum and initially a committed follower of Jiang Qing, Kang directed the purges that destroyed the upper ranks of the CCP during the years 1966–8, the deadliest period of the Cultural Revolution. Strongly opposed both to the USSR and to the de-Stalinisation policy, Kang

was a stern critic of the USSR's perceived revisionism and Mao used him as an attack dog in the PRC's ideological disputes with Stalin's successors.

Mao's great trust in his loyalty rendered Kang unassailable in the internal party struggles. A factor that won his master's special favour was his ability to procure a supply of young women for Mao's gratification. In Mao's declining years Kang, himself an ailing man, broke with Jiang Qing and the Gang of Four, but remained as extreme a Maoist as they were. Dying in 1976, the same year as Mao, Kang was posthumously expelled from the CCP as part of a symbolic attempt by the new regime to distance itself from the wilder extremes of Mao's policies.

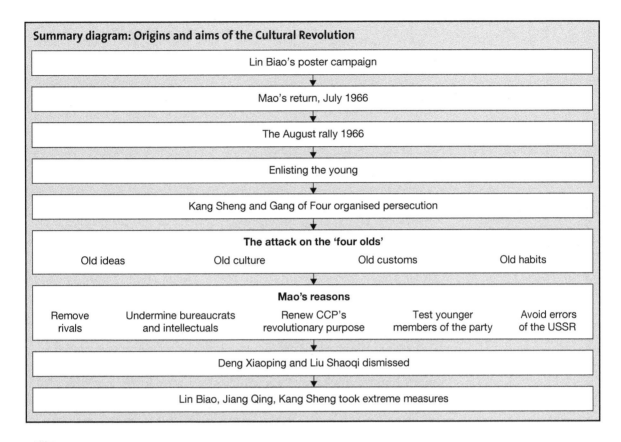

Summary diagram: Origins and aims of the Cultural Revolution

Lin Biao's poster campaign

Mao's return, July 1966

The August rally 1966

Enlisting the young

Kang Sheng and Gang of Four organised persecution

The attack on the 'four olds'

| Old ideas | Old culture | Old customs | Old habits |

Mao's reasons

| Remove rivals | Undermine bureaucrats and intellectuals | Renew CCP's revolutionary purpose | Test younger members of the party | Avoid errors of the USSR |

Deng Xiaoping and Liu Shaoqi dismissed

Lin Biao, Jiang Qing, Kang Sheng took extreme measures

② The Red Guards

▶ *What role did the Red Guards play in the Cultural Revolution?*

The Red Guard movement grew out of prepared soil. Since the Sino-Soviet divide in the 1950s (see page 57), pupils and students had been encouraged to regard themselves as pioneers under Mao Zedong in the advancement of international proletarian revolution. Mass rallies had been used in the Hundred Flowers and anti-rightist campaigns in the 1950s.

Once it was underway, Mao did not take part in the day-to-day direction of the Cultural Revolution. He withdrew from Beijing, leaving the officials at Zhongnanhai to the mercy of the Red Guards. Camped outside in Tiananmen Square for months on end, the guards kept up a constant loudspeaker barrage of insults directed at ministers and officials deemed to be 'rightists'. Anyone trying to break cover and leave the blockaded offices had to run the gauntlet of jeering youngsters, who were eager to turn their insults into blows if given the slightest pretext. Jiang Qing and Lin Biao made sure that the besiegers were kept informed by going down in person to identify the ministers and officials who were to be abused and intimidated.

Why Mao chose the young to lead the revolution

In choosing China's youth to be the instruments of the Cultural Revolution, Mao showed an astute grasp of mass psychology. The young were made to feel that they had a special role to play not only in the regeneration of the nation but also in the creation of a new socialist world order. As one Red Guard later put it: 'We felt that we were defending China's revolution and liberating the world. All the big slogans made a generation of us feel that the Cultural Revolution really was a war, a war to defend Chairman Mao and the new China.'

SOURCE C

> **Why do you think children as young as those shown in Source C became caught up in the revolutionary spirit of the times?**

This 1974 photograph shows young schoolgirls ecstatically portraying their revolutionary fighting spirit by wearing military-style uniform and carrying mock weapons.

Mao's hold over the young

The reminiscences of those who had been Red Guards illustrate the extraordinary hold Mao had over them. The cult of Mao had prepared the way. One young man described how he believed Mao was a god: 'When Chairman Mao waved his hand at Tiananmen, a million Red Guards wept their hearts out as if by some hormonal reaction. He was divine, and the revolutionary tides of the world rose and fell at his command.' Another recalled how willing he had been to give himself totally to Mao: 'I believed in Mao with every cell in my body. You felt you would give Chairman Mao your everything – your body, your mind, your spirit, your soul, your fate.' Another recollected how he had become victim to the power of mass suggestion: 'When you see the red flags and when you see how emotional everybody was you get carried away, you just think

I should be part of that.' One young person offered a new slant on body piercing: 'I cut a small hole in my chest with a penknife and pinned my Mao badge there. That way I thought I would have Chairman Mao engraved on my heart.'

The awe in which Mao was held by the young was extreme but it was not wholly irrational. It was a recognition of what they believed he had achieved for China. The young people who ecstatically chanted Mao's name saw him as the great hero who had freed China from a century of humiliation at the hands of the foreigner. One of the most popular titles given him was 'the red sun rising in the east', an apt metaphor for the man who had made China a great world power, possessing its own nuclear weapon and capable of displacing the Soviet Union as leader of the international socialist movement.

Anthony Grey, a British correspondent for **Reuters** in China, observed that the worship of Mao by the young was not simply a product of official propaganda. There was a sense in which the young felt they had a direct personal relationship with him.

KEY TERM

Reuters An international news agency.

SOURCE D

From Anthony Grey, *Hostage in Peking*, Tagman Press, 2008, p. 56. Grey, a British correspondent, was imprisoned by the Chinese during the Cultural Revolution.

Suddenly he was gone and the still half-hysterical crowd was streaming after the little convoy of jeeps.

Outside the crowd formed up again round the Tien An Men and waited expectantly to see if Mao would make another appearance … but nothing happened. Then a young handsome Chinese of about eighteen who had been standing quietly in front of me turned and said to my great surprise in good English, 'Aren't you English?' … Eventually I said rather inanely, 'Excuse me but what are you waiting here for?' 'To see Chairman Mao of course,' he said and turned back to continue his vigilant watch on the rostrum of the Gate, like the other thousands around us, 'Why?' I persisted. The boy turned and with a polite expression which contained some pity for one who had to ask, he said quietly: 'Because I love Chairman Mao.'

He clearly did. This left a much more vivid impression with me than weeks of official propaganda.

According to Grey in Source D, what impressed him about the way in which the young regarded Mao?

Mao knew that the need to conform to the standards of their peers is very powerful among the young and that this makes them particularly susceptible to suggestion. The more idealistic they are, the more easily led they are. As Grey hinted, when idealism is linked to personal affection it is a powerful force. There are many examples in the West of peer-group pressure creating conformity among the young in such areas as clothing and music. Nor should simple perversity be left out of the account. Marching through the streets chanting slogans is an easier option than working at one's studies. Most students in China were only too willing to believe that by insulting their teachers and burning their textbooks they were in the vanguard of progress.

SOURCE E

What does this photo suggest about the veneration in which Mao was held by the young?

The incident shown in this 1966 photograph, which was one of the high points of the first great rally in Tiananmen Square, was celebrated in the Chinese press as the moment when Mao gave his personal sanction to the Red Guards as the main movement leading the Cultural Revolution. The young girl came on to the balcony and to tumultuous applause fitted a Red Guard armband on Mao. When she told him her name was Song Binbin, which means 'gentle', Mao said it would be better as a Red Guard if her name were 'militant'. This story was often quoted as a sure sign that Mao intended the Cultural Revolution to be an essentially violent movement.

Red Terror

The Red Guards became a terrifying and destructive movement. Mao's policies deliberately brutalised China's idealistic young people. By presenting chaos as more virtuous than order, Mao effectively declared that there was no moral restriction on what could be done in the name of the revolution. Students, trained in the Chinese tradition of obedience to parents and teachers, were suddenly told to insult and abuse them. For children to denounce their elders had enormous significance in a society where respect was ingrained. In a reversal of their traditional deference, they behaved with a particular virulence. They were, of course, still being obedient, but this time to a new master.

Anything that represented the corrupt past was labelled under the blanket term 'Confucius and Co', and was liable to be smashed or torn up. Temples, shrines, works of art and ornamental gardens became obvious targets; many priceless and irreplaceable treasures of Chinese civilisation were destroyed in this wave of organised vandalism. In the words of a Western correspondent: 'Mao told the Red Guards: "To rebel is justified!" They repaid him by crushing almost every semblance of tradition, decency and intellectual endeavour in China.'

Self-criticism and struggle sessions

Given free rein, the Red Guards seized public transport and took over radio and television networks. Anyone showing signs of **decadent tendencies** was likely

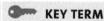 **KEY TERM**

Decadent tendencies
Clinging to bourgeois values, the most obvious examples being the wearing of Western-style clothes, jewellery or make-up.

to be manhandled and publicly humiliated. An especially vulnerable group were the intellectuals, those whose work or privileged way of life was judged to detach them from the people. Schoolteachers, university staff, writers and even doctors were prey to the Red Guard squads, who denounced them as 'bad elements' and made them publicly confess their class crimes. Those regarded as particularly culpable were forced to undergo 'struggle sessions'.

These ordeals, which became a dominant feature of the Cultural Revolution, were in essence an assault on the individual's sense of self and were aimed at provoking and stimulating guilt. **Brainwashing** is an appropriate term to describe the terror tactics. To induce guilt, the victims were made to study Mao's writings followed by periods of intense self-criticism and confession. The first confession was never accepted; the accused had to dig deeper and deeper into their memory to recall all their errors and crimes against the party and the people.

A common practice was for the Red Guards to force the accused to adopt the 'aeroplane' position; with head thrust down, knees bent and arms pulled high behind the back, the unfortunate victims were made to catalogue their past offences against the people. Those who maintained their innocence were systematically punched and kicked. After days of torment and constant denunciation as 'running dogs of imperialism', 'lick-spittle capitalists', 'lackeys of

KEY TERM

Brainwashing Using a combination of physical torture and psychological coercion to disorientate victims so that they become very susceptible to suggestion and direction.

SOURCE F

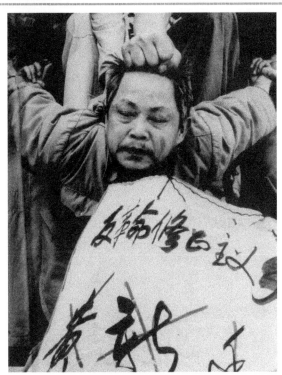

Huang Xinting, the military commander of the Chengdu region, forced by Red Guards into the 'aeroplane' position. The placard around his neck accuses him of being a rightist.

What does the photo in Source F illustrate about the behaviour of the Red Guards?

the USA' and 'betrayers of the people', few had the physical or mental strength to continue resisting.

A victim's past achievements in the revolutionary cause offered no protection. Wang Jinxi had been a hero of the resistance in Gansu province against both the Japanese and the Nationalists, and was also renowned for his prodigious efforts to develop the oil fields of the region. He had been personally honoured by Mao in Beijing and had been visited by Zhou Enlai, Deng Xiaoping and Liu Shaoqi. None of this was sufficient to save him. The Red Guards claimed that since Wang had been working in the oil fields at the time they had been controlled by the GMD this made him a 'traitor-worker'. When he would not confess he was beaten and tortured to death over a three-day period.

Official support for Red Guard terror

Although it often appeared that Red Guard action was spontaneous, it was not only officially sanctioned but also officially directed. Xie Fuzhi, the minister for public security, in addressing the police forces, revealed both why it was that the Red Guards had such a free hand in their terror campaign and how they were able to target their victims so easily.

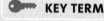

According to Source G, why and how should the police co-operate with the Red Guards?

SOURCE G

From a speech by Xie Fuzhi, September 1966, quoted in Philip Short, *Mao: A Life*, Hodder & Stoughton, 1999, p. 544. Xie Fuzhi, the minister for public security, addresses the police forces:

Should Red Guards who kill people be punished? My view is that if people are killed, they are killed; it's no business of ours. If the masses hate bad people so much we cannot stop them, then let us not insist. The people's police should stand on the side of the Red Guards, liaise with them, sympathise with them and provide them with information especially about the five black categories – the landlords, rich peasants, counter-revolutionaries, bad elements and Rightists.

Victims and victimisers

KEY TERM

Stalinist purges During his leadership of the USSR between 1929 and 1953, Stalin had introduced a series of fierce purges to crush opposition.

The names and whereabouts of all those listed by Xie Fuzhi were passed on to the Red Guard detachments, who then descended on their victims. As had happened during the **Stalinist purges** in the USSR in the 1930s, so, too, in China's Cultural Revolution, the victimisers became in turn the victims. Revolutionaries struggled to prove their proletarian integrity by becoming ever more extreme. Those who faltered or showed signs of being sickened by the horrors were condemned as reactionaries and found themselves subjected to the savagery that they had recently meted out. Genuine idealism was swiftly corrupted into unthinking brutishness. Source I describes a former Red Guard's typical experience.

SOURCE H

From Rae Yang, *Spider Eaters: A Memoir*, University of California Press, 1977, p. 118. Rae Yang was a former Red Guard who recorded a typical experience:

On this day [in 1967] I saw a teacher in the fountain, a middle-aged man. His clothes were muddy. Blood was streaming down his head, as a number of students were throwing bricks at him. He tried to dodge the bricks. While he did so, without noticing it, he crawled in the fountain, round and round, like an animal in the zoo. This teacher survived; another was not so fortunate. Teacher Chen, our art teacher, was said to resemble a spy in the movies. He was a tall, thin man with long hair which was a sign of decadence. Moreover, he seemed gloomy and smoked a lot. In the past he had asked students to draw naked female bodies in front of plaster statues to corrupt them. For these 'crimes' he was beaten to death by a group of senior students.

What does Source H illustrate about the mentality of the Red Guards?

The savagery seemed limitless. In Beijing itself, in addition to the daily scenes of beatings in the street, theatres and sports grounds became the venues of systematic killings of bound victims. During a two-day period in Daxing County, north of Beijing, 300 people were clubbed to death in the public square. In Guangxi province, 67,000 deaths were recorded in the decade after 1966, while in Mongolia, Tibet and Sichuan the figures ran into hundreds of thousands. At the trial of the members of the Gang of Four in 1980 (see page 177), it was charged that the purges they had sanctioned had resulted in the killing of over half a million CCP officials.

SOURCE I

Why did Liu Shaoqi, despite his high position and status, become a victim of Mao's purge (see page 134)?

Protesters publicly demonstrating against Liu Shaoqi at the time of his arrest.

Cultural vandalism

The organised terror created an atmosphere of callousness and brutality. PRC documents record that between 1966 and 1976, in the course of attacking the treasures of China's past, the Red Guards and the other government-sponsored terror squads wrecked, burned or razed 4922 of Beijing's 6843 'places of cultural or historical interest'. The **Forbidden City** only just survived. Forewarned in August 1966 that the Red Guards planned to destroy it, Zhou Enlai moved in a unit of the PLA, which prevented the youngsters running amok.

Arguably the greatest single act of desecration occurred not in Beijing but in Qufu in Shandong province, the home of Confucius. A group of some 200 Beijing University students and teachers went there to join hundreds of local students. Over a four-week period in November 1966, this group committed 6618 organised acts of vandalism. These included:

- the defacing or destruction of 929 paintings
- the tearing up or burning of 2700 books
- the smashing of 1000 statues and monuments
- the desecration of 2000 graves.

After its first two years, 1966–7, the revolution which Mao had unleashed appeared to have got out of hand. The widespread disruption had brought industrial production to a halt and had led to the schools and universities being closed. More immediately disturbing, a series of local civil wars raged in China. The sheer zeal and passion of the Red Guard movement had turned in on itself. Regional groups had begun to clash with one another. Factory workers formed their own units and challenged the claim of the students to be the true leaders of the movement. The various groups began to go to ever-greater lengths to prove the purity of their ideology and the depth of their loyalty to Mao. This convinced the authorities at the top that matters had gone far enough. Orders were given that the work of the Red Guards should be taken over by the PLA.

> **KEY TERM**
>
> **Forbidden City** Beijing's greatest monument, a spacious walled inner city that had been the home and court of the emperors between 1368 and 1911.

Summary diagram: The Red Guards

Why Mao chose the young to lead the revolution
- His grasp of the conformity of the young
- The cult of Mao had prepared the way

Red Guard terror
- enforced self-criticism
- struggle sessions
- mass persecution
- vandalism

Victims
- landlords
- intellectuals
- revisionists
- rich peasants
- reactionaries
- bad elements
- rightists
- decadent tendencies

3 The PLA and the winding down of the Cultural Revolution

▶ *What role did the PLA play in the Cultural Revolution?*

▶ *What was the importance of the fall of Lin Biao in 1971 in the development of the Cultural Revolution?*

Mao and the PLA

Initially, the PLA had tolerated, indeed encouraged, the students and workers in hunting down class enemies but it was unwilling to share its prestige as the creator and defender of China's revolution. The PLA claimed a special relationship with Chairman Mao and with the Chinese people, which entitled it to take over the Cultural Revolution. Army units travelled throughout China in a campaign to impress on the people the totality of the PLA's loyalty to Mao Zedong. They took over from the Red Guards in exposing and terrorising 'counter-revolutionaries'.

There is a strong case for suggesting that the **anarchy** associated with the Red Guards was more apparent than real. They were allowed to run wild only because Mao knew that at any time he could use the PLA to pull them back into line. In all its essentials, the Cultural Revolution was directed from the top by Mao and the CCRG. It may often have had the air of spontaneity, and it is true that once started it seemed to generate a momentum of its own, but there were guiding hands behind the marches and the thuggery. Much of it was orchestrated. The Maoists were prepared to let things run to extremes but always seemed able to call a halt when it suited them. The idealistic youngsters who appeared to lead the Cultural Revolution were pawns in the power struggle in the CCP.

 KEY TERM

Anarchy Often used to describe chaos, but its literal meaning is the absence of government. It was never Mao's intention to allow the situation to get out of hand; his government never lost control.

'Up to the mountains and down to the villages' campaign 1967–72

The ultimate control that the government had through the PLA over China's rebellious youngsters was evident in the ease with which it carried out Mao's decision to redirect the energy and idealism of those who had made up the Red Guard movement. Another great campaign was announced, which called on the youngsters 'to go up to the mountains and down to the villages'. They were urged to go into the countryside and live among the peasants; in this way they would both learn what life was like for 80 per cent of the Chinese people and deepen their understanding of revolution.

However, the real motive behind the slogans was much less idealistic. The government's main aim was to rid the urban areas of the gangs of delinquent youths who had threatened to become uncontrollable in the general turmoil.

The campaign may also be seen as an extension of Mao's policy for making city intellectuals experience the harsh realities of life that were the common lot of the ordinary Chinese. The notion that people of privilege should learn 'the dignity of labour' was one of Mao's constant refrains.

The experience of the young in the countryside

Whatever the ulterior motives underlying the campaign may have been, there was no doubting that it aroused a massive response. Between 1967 and 1972 over 12 million young people moved from the towns into the countryside. Their experience proved to be very different from what they had expected. Most had a very miserable time of it, being wholly unprepared for the primitive conditions they encountered. They had no countryside skills; they did not know how to grow food or rear livestock and the peasants had little food to spare for them.

As to the quality of the contribution the newcomers made to the localities, the peasants were unimpressed. A common complaint among locals was that the students did not really earn their keep and tended to regard themselves as superior beings who were making an act of heroic self-sacrifice in coming to the land. It is true that there were words of praise from some villagers for the efforts of the student visitors to raise literacy standards. However, this was small gain to set beside the hunger and deep homesickness most students felt.

Disillusion among the young

The idealism of those who made up this great experiment rarely survived the misery and appallingly low standards of living that they met; it is doubtful that more than a small minority felt they had gained from the experience. It was this as much as anything that made them doubt what they had never questioned before – the wisdom and good will of Mao Zedong. They began to realise they had been used. As one youngster recalled: 'It was only when I went to the countryside that I suddenly discovered the conflict between language and reality and this gave me a profound distrust of the language of all this state propaganda.'

The PLA's 'cleansing the class ranks' campaign 1968–71

The dispersal of the Red Guards did not mean a weakening of the movement against the anti-Maoists. Indeed, the PLA squads who replaced the Red Guards were if anything even more vicious in their persecution of 'counter-revolutionaries'. The CCRG, with Jiang Qing's Gang of Four playing the most prominent role, developed a new campaign known as **cleansing the class ranks**. Committees were established in all the major regions of China and given the task of 'eradicating once and for all any signs of capitalism'. The result was an orgy of killing and destruction as grim as anything perpetrated by the Red Guards. One official described it as a 'massive **pogrom**, a massive campaign of

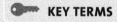 **KEY TERMS**

Cleansing the class ranks A terror campaign to exterminate those whose social background made them real or potential opponents of Maoism.

Pogrom A state-organised persecution of a particular group of people.

torture and murder to uncover wholly imaginary mass conspiracies that could involve tens of thousands'.

The fearful success of the 'cleansing the class ranks' movement as a campaign of terror is evident in the body count:

- In Inner Mongolia 22,900 were killed and 120,000 maimed.
- In Hebei province 84,000 were arrested, 2955 of whom then died after being tortured.
- In Yunnan 15,000 people were 'cleansed'; of these 6979 died from their injuries.
- In Beijing 3731 people were killed; these cases were officially classified as 'suicide'.
- In Zhejiang 100,000 were arrested and 'struggled against'; of these 9198 were 'hounded to death'.
- In Binyang county in Guangxi province 3681 were killed in a mass execution over a ten-day period.

Mao stepped in at this point and claimed that the excesses that were being reported must be checked. He did this for political rather than humanitarian reasons. He wanted his personal rivals and the nation's class enemies removed, but he did not want damage done to his image as China's great benefactor and champion of his people.

Mao's responsibility

It is noteworthy that once Mao had begun the Cultural Revolution, he tended to remain in the background, allowing others to organise it. He spent much of his time away from Beijing. His absence left affairs in the hands of Jiang Qing and her adherents. He said to his doctor: 'Let others stay busy with politics. Let them handle the problem of the movement by themselves.' Mao's absence from the political centre of things meant that while the policies were carried out under his authority, he was rarely involved in the everyday details. The individual acts of brutality were seldom the result of his specific orders. It may even be that, on occasion, the Cultural Revolution was pushed further than Mao had intended. He once said that Jiang Qing and the Gang of Four were more Maoist than he was.

Yet none of this absolves Mao from responsibility for what occurred. Everything was done in his name. He could have called off the terror any time had he so chosen. By leaving Jiang and the extremists in control, he sanctioned what they did to the Chinese people. Mao was the originator of the movement that overtook China. Without him there would have been no Cultural Revolution with all its convulsive consequences.

By the early 1970s, there were signs that many Chinese were becoming disenchanted with the Cultural Revolution. Despite this, there was little open opposition to Mao. Mistakes were blamed on those responsible for implementing his policies, never on Mao himself. The cult of Mao Zedong was by now so well established that, while he lived, there was no realistic chance of undermining his authority. What happened, therefore, was that the power seekers in the CCP declared their wholehearted loyalty to Mao and jockeyed for position and influence while awaiting his death which, judging from the rumours about his declining health, could not be long delayed.

The fall of Lin Biao 1971–2

There was one major exception to the practice of wait and see. In an extraordinary set of events, Lin Biao, the nominated successor to Mao, became a victim of the Cultural Revolution that he had done so much to engineer. As is so often the case with internal Chinese politics, the exact details are difficult to determine. However, what appears to have happened is that by 1971 Mao or those closest to him had become disturbed by the growing influence that Lin Biao and the PLA were acquiring under the Cultural Revolution. The PLA's success in bringing the Red Guards under control had obviously pleased Mao, but it led to increased tension within the party. There was a fear that the PLA, which was now strongly represented on the Politburo, would assert its strength over the politicians. Lin Biao was a key figure in this. Mao remarked with reference to Lin, 'There is somebody who says he wants to support me, elevate me, but what he really has in mind is supporting himself, elevating himself.' As a first step towards removing them, therefore, Lin and other PLA leaders were told that they must submit themselves to self-criticism.

Lin Biao's plot against Mao

Realising that he was a marked man whose time was running out, Lin became a reluctant conspirator in an assassination plot, organised by his son, Lin Liguo, an officer in the Chinese air force. However, when Lin Luguo's sister leaked details of the plan to kill Mao to Zhou Enlai, a full security alert was activated and armed guards hustled Mao away for his own protection. With all chance of the plot's succeeding now gone, Lin Biao made a desperate bid to escape to the USSR. On 13 September 1971, the plane carrying him and his family crashed in Outer Mongolia, killing all on board.

Whether this was an accident or sabotage remains a mystery. Mao insisted that he had not ordered the shooting down of the plane. Indeed, he had expressly rejected Zhou Enlai's suggestion that the aircraft be brought down. 'If we shoot the plane down, how can we explain it to the people of the whole country?' The likeliest explanation is the simplest; the plane, a British-made Trident jet, which had taken off in a great hurry, had simply run out of fuel.

SOURCE J

> What chain of events led to the dramatic death of Lin Biao, as shown in Source J? **?**

The remains of the plane which crashed in Mongolia, killing Lin Biao and his family in 1971.

Mao's reaction to the plot

Whatever the truth relating to the crash, Mao ought to have been happy with the outcome. The man he regarded as his most dangerous rival had been removed. Yet the affair seemed to depress him. He moped and became unwell. His doctor recorded that Mao 'took to his bed and lay there all day, saying and doing little. When he did get up, he seemed to have aged. His shoulders stooped and he walked with a shuffle. He could not sleep.' This may have been because he was a rapidly ageing man, prone to increasing bouts of depression, or it may have been that he truly believed that the thwarted assassination plot was an indication of how widespread the opposition to him in the party had become. It is likely that Mao, after leading his nation for 22 years, was dismayed by the realisation that special security measures were needed to protect him from his people.

The results of Lin Biao's fall

The news of the scandal surrounding Lin's fall was not publicly released until a year later, in 1972. The announcement came in the form of a 'criticise Lin Biao and Confucius' campaign. The name of Lin Biao, 'the great traitor and Soviet spy', was linked with the great reactionary figure of Chinese history. Lin, it was officially declared, had been caught hatching a 'monstrous conspiracy' against Mao and the Chinese people. The memory of his treachery would last 'for ten thousand years'. It was this public denunciation of Lin, a man who only a short while before had been second only to Mao in popular estimation, that led many to question privately whether they could any longer believe the official pronouncements issued by the PRC authorities. Lin Biao, Mao's nominated successor, the compiler of the Little Red Book, the creator and propagator of the cult of Mao, was now to be reviled as a betrayer of his great leader and a traitor to the Cultural Revolution, the very movement that he himself had helped to form. People asked themselves whether this was really credible.

The sudden and baffling changes in the reputation of political leaders created the gravest doubts as to whether any government statement was trustworthy. A party worker later described how she and her husband had reacted: 'Both my husband and I were disillusioned, aware that something was fundamentally wrong with the system in which we had believed so devotedly. I guessed that we were not the only ones whose faith in the party wavered, but no one could communicate his misgivings.' A Chen villager later admitted: 'the Lin Biao affair provided us with a major lesson; we came to see that the leaders up there could say today that something is round, tomorrow, that it's flat. We lost faith in the system.'

At the time it took a very brave or very foolhardy person to say openly what many CCP members and ordinary Chinese were thinking. One who did speak out was Tu Deyong, a CCP member from Chengdu. Early in 1973, he published 'Ten Indictments against the Great Cultural Revolution', the first three of which are shown in Source K.

What, according to Source K, have been the harmful effects of the Cultural Revolution?

SOURCE K

From Tu Deyong's 'Ten Indictments against the Great Cultural Revolution' of 1973, quoted in Roderick Macfarquar and Michael Schoenhals, *Mao's Last Revolution*, Belknap Press, 2006, p. 351. Tu Deyong was a CCP member from Chengdu.

The Great Cultural Revolution has subjected more than 90 percent of cadres and more than 60 percent of the masses to mindless attacks of every possible kind, political persecution, sometimes even physical ruin. It has seriously affected the eagerness with which cadres and the masses build socialism as well as the loyalty they feel towards the party.

The Great Cultural Revolution has had an extremely destructive impact on industrial production, with production stagnating, financial resources drying up, the state treasury being emptied, and people's standard of living declining.

The Great Cultural Revolution has led to an unprecedented degeneration in social morals and has guided young people onto a road of criminality.

The inevitable happened. Tu was arrested and sentenced to life imprisonment. At his trial he said tellingly 'if someone like me, who has really deep feelings for the party and Chairman Mao is now having thoughts like these, one can easily imagine how other people look upon the Great Cultural Revolution'.

The final phase of the Cultural Revolution

The charges made by those such as Tu Deyong against the PRC's government were powerful but they could not be admitted by the authorities. Nevertheless, from 1972 to Mao's death in 1976 there was a noticeable lessening of the extremism with which the pogroms and persecutions were conducted. There are a number of explanations for this:

- There was a general uncertainty in the party about the ailing Mao's true intentions.
- The effect of the Lin Biao affair led to a rethink in the CCP about how severe its policies should be. Initially it had seemed that Lin shared the same extreme ideas that the Gang of Four had, but once Lin came under Mao's suspicion, the Gang members were swift to disassociate themselves from him.
- There was an unacknowledged recognition by the party that the points made by critics such as Tu Deyong were an accurate description of the harmful effects of the Cultural Revolution.
- The party wished to impress the USA, whose President, Richard Nixon, made an official visit to the PRC in 1972 (see page 167).

The return of Zhou Enlai and Deng Xiaoping

Much to the irritation of the Gang of Four, an important effect of Lin Biao's dramatic end was the enhancement of Zhou Enlai's position in the government and party. Zhou, who had played a key part in uncovering the plot against Mao, was one of the great survivors of Chinese politics. His shrewd sense of political judgement and genuine popularity enabled him to evade the attempts made to bring him down during the Cultural Revolution. It was Zhou who had worked to prevent the fracturing of the party during the power struggles of the 1960s and it was he who became recognised as an outstanding international statesman in the 1970s (see page 175).

Lin's fall also benefited Deng Xiaoping, another great survivor in the cut-throat world of PRC politics. His earlier dismissal for having been a **capitalist roader** now worked to his advantage. In 1973, Zhou Enlai, who had great respect for Deng's detailed knowledge of the workings of the CCP, invited him to re-enter the government. By 1975 Deng had regained his place as party secretary. But his rehabilitation did not go unchallenged. Jiang Qing and the CCRG, disturbed by the grip that the moderates appeared to be regaining and aware that their previous association with Lin might damage their position, intensified the 'criticise Lin Biao and Confucius' campaign by turning it into an attack on 'the pragmatist clique', a reference to Zhou and Deng.

The return of Zhou and Deng meant that the Cultural Revolution was less savagely enforced after 1973. But it was far from being abandoned. Arrests of suspected persons continued and the prison camps went on expanding. The truth was that as long as the CCRG, dominated by Jiang Qing's hard-line Gang of Four, had Mao's support the Cultural Revolution would continue.

Tiananmen Incident

The influence that Jiang and the CCRG still exercised during the final phase of the Cultural Revolution was evident in the crisis that followed the death of Zhou

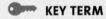

KEY TERM

Capitalist roader
A reference to Deng's wish to see the economy modernised on neo-capitalist lines.

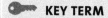
KEY TERM

Heroes' Monument
A large shrine, commemorating the great deeds of China's revolutionary past, at the southern end of Tiananmen Square.

Enlai from lung cancer in January 1976. With his moderating influence now removed, the power struggle took another turn. In April, the memorial service for Zhou, held in the Great Hall of the People facing Tiananmen Square, became the occasion for a large-scale demonstration in favour of the policies that Zhou had advocated. Tens of thousands flocked into the square to lay wreaths and pictures of Zhou around the **Heroes' Monument**. This spontaneous gathering of people was in defiance of the official order that there should be no public displays of mourning. Speeches were made at the monument; these became increasingly bolder in tone, graduating from praise of Zhou Enlai for his wise statesmanship to attacks on the government for its corruption. Fearing that the demonstration might get out of hand, the Mayor of Beijing ordered riot police to remove the flowers and tributes and disperse the crowds. When some of the demonstrators resisted the police used force. Scattered but violent and bloody confrontations took place before the police managed to clear the square.

The Politburo condemned this 'Tiananmen Incident' as the work of rightist agitators and laid a large part of the blame on Deng Xiaoping, whom they dismissed from his position as party secretary. Although he had not been present at the demonstration, Deng chose not to risk defending himself; instead he removed himself from the political scene by hastily leaving Beijing for Guangdong province, from where he would wait on events.

No clear lead came from Mao Zedong on how to handle the Tiananmen Incident for the simple reason that during the final year of his life he was rarely capable of giving one. His doctor, Li Zhisui, subsequently revealed that, during the last three years of his life, Mao was sustained only by massive injections of drugs which left him comatose for much of the time. The term 'helmsman' has a particular irony, for Mao was quite unable to govern. It was this situation that gave influence to his close attendants. They became the interpreters of his barely coherent statements.

Yet, even though Mao was incapacitated, his power remained. In an odd way it was actually increased. Since he was so often enfeebled, it became increasingly difficult to know exactly what his ideas and instructions actually were. This had two conflicting consequences:

- It paralysed the fearful into inaction since they were frightened of taking steps that Mao might later condemn in one of his rational moments.
- It encouraged those who believed that Mao would never recover to try to manoeuvre themselves into a position from which they could subsequently seize power.

Effect of Mao's death

The uncertain situation appeared to leave Jiang Qing and the Gang of Four in effective control. However, their authority depended wholly on their closeness to Mao. Once he had died everything was at hazard and there was no certainty what would happen. Given Mao's god-like status, it was somehow fitting that his death in September 1976 should have been preceded six weeks earlier by what many saw as an omen – a massive earthquake in **Tangshan** which caused the death of a quarter of a million of the city's inhabitants. People recalled that in Chinese lore earthquakes, 'the speaking of the dragon', denoted the advent of great changes in the state. Mao had been deified in his own lifetime and, when gods die, the succession – as events were to show – becomes a troubled affair.

Weakness of the Gang of Four

The hope of the members of the Gang of Four had been that the deaths of both Mao and Zhou would clear the path for them to full power. But they had miscalculated. They did not recognise the irony that, for all their ferocity and ruthlessness in the Cultural Revolution, they had no authority of their own except that bestowed on them by Mao Zedong. He may frequently have drifted into the background and left things to them, yet the reality was that without his support they were defenceless and prey to those they had previously persecuted. This became apparent after Zhou's death and even more so after Mao's. They had hoped the passing of the two party giants would be the prelude to their taking full command. In the event, it exposed how limited was the support they had in the party and in government. They had no constituency and no loyalty on which they could call.

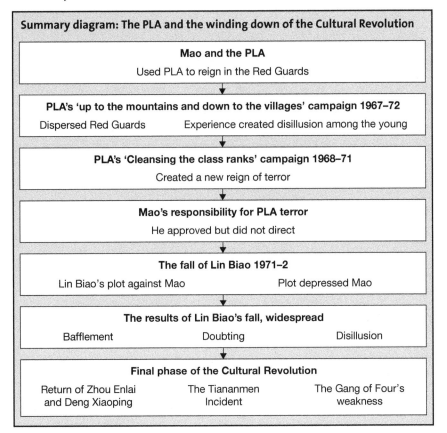

Summary diagram: The PLA and the winding down of the Cultural Revolution

Mao and the PLA
Used PLA to reign in the Red Guards

↓

PLA's 'up to the mountains and down to the villages' campaign 1967–72
Dispersed Red Guards   Experience created disillusion among the young

↓

PLA's 'Cleansing the class ranks' campaign 1968–71
Created a new reign of terror

↓

Mao's responsibility for PLA terror
He approved but did not direct

↓

The fall of Lin Biao 1971–2
Lin Biao's plot against Mao   Plot depressed Mao

↓

The results of Lin Biao's fall, widespread
Bafflement   Doubting   Disillusion

↓

Final phase of the Cultural Revolution
Return of Zhou Enlai and Deng Xiaoping   The Tiananmen Incident   The Gang of Four's weakness

KEY TERM

Tangshan An industrial city, 150 km (90 miles) south of Beijing.

Impact of the Cultural Revolution on Chinese society

▶ *In what ways did the Cultural Revolution affect Chinese society?*

Culture

It is important to understand how Mao interpreted culture. For him, it was never a separate, detached aspect of society. From the 1930s onwards he had taught that:

- Culture was central not peripheral. It was a nation's culture that defined its character.
- Throughout history, the culture of every society was the direct product of the values laid down by the ruling class. It was the means by which rulers imposed their control over the people.
- Now that China was a proletarian society, the culture had to be proletarian. All traces of the previous bourgeois culture had to be eradicated.
- Eradication of bourgeois culture could not be done gently or by persuasion. No ruling class ever gives up its power willingly; it has to be swept aside by force.

On the principle of 'the more brutal, the more revolutionary', Mao demanded that class enemies should be crushed mercilessly. 'A revolution is not a dinner party, or writing an essay, or painting a picture. A revolution is an insurrection, an act of violence by which one class overthrows another.' Culture was not a matter of refined tastes; it was about the life of the people.

Mao's notion of the role of the creative artist

It followed that all creative artists – writers, painters, musicians, film-makers and so on – must accept that their first duty was to serve the people. Their works must further the cause of revolution. Mao had no time for artistic self-expression for its own sake. He asserted that there was 'no such thing as art for art's sake, art that stands above classes, art that is detached from or independent of politics. Proletarian literature and art are part of the whole revolutionary cause.'

The role of Jiang Qing

In a remarkable move, Mao decided that his wife, Jiang Qing, was to be the creator-in-chief of the new Chinese culture he desired. He gave her the responsibility of turning his general denunciation of China's 'four olds' into a definite programme for the suppression of traditional Chinese society. Mao instructed her to become the 'cultural purifier of the nation'.

Believing that her former career as an actress ideally qualified her for such a task, Jiang applied herself to the job with fanatical zeal:

- She imposed a rigid system of censorship which denied a public showing or performance to any work which did not meet her criteria of revolutionary purity.
- Only those writings, art works, broadcast programmes and films which had directly relevant contemporary Chinese themes were permitted.
- Western music, classical and pop, was banned.
- Traditional Chinese opera was ruled out and replaced by a repertoire of specially commissioned contemporary works.

The works which Jiang commissioned were a set of opera-ballets, all concerned in the most naive fashion with the triumph of the proletariat over its class enemies. They were an exact expression of Mao's demand that Chinese culture must be relevant and meaningful to the people by having as its only theme the struggle of the heroic masses. Grindingly tedious though they were, the opera-ballets were loudly applauded by the **privileged audiences** who dared not reveal their true feelings.

Jiang Qing's rejection of all non-proletarian culture was **political correctness** in its most extreme form. This was an intellectually and emotionally destructive process that aimed at the systematic undermining of all sense of tradition. In accordance with Mao's saying 'the more brutal, the more revolutionary', children were urged to knock the heads off flowers in order to show their rejection of bourgeois concepts of beauty. Zhou Guanrun, a professor of music, recalled how Jiang's edicts against bourgeois culture terrorised the staff at the Beijing Conservatoire (a specialist music college) into silence. 'No music sounded any more. The Conservatoire was silent. Everybody was just learning and doing self-criticism or accepting criticism from students.'

 **KEY TERMS**

Privileged audiences
In Mao's time the best seats in the theatres were reserved for party members.

Political correctness
The requirement that people conform to a set of prescribed opinions to show that they have accepted the ideology of the leaders of society.

SOURCE L

Preparing for an open-air performance in Harbin of 'The Red Woman Troop', one of Jiang Qing's specially commissioned opera-ballets, in 1975.

How is the size of the crowd shown in the photo to be accounted for?

The consequences of Jiang's Qing's cultural policies

By the early 1970s Jiang Qing's assault on traditional culture had begun to produce an artistic wasteland. Musicians, painters and writers who showed reluctance to embrace the new rigidities were denounced and sent to 're-educational' labour camps, where they were treated in brutal ways. One example was the denial of tools to the musicians who were sent to work in the fields; pianists and string players were made to scratch at the ground with their hands so that they would lose the vital sensitivity in their fingers and never be able to play well again.

There were rare attempts to question Jiang Qing's suffocating political correctness. On one occasion Deng Xiaoping dared to suggest that culture was about entertainment as well as indoctrination. He remarked caustically, 'After a hard week's work people want to go to the theatre to relax, but they go there and watch Jiang Qing's pieces and find they are on a fucking battle field.'

However, Deng apart, none of the leading politicians was prepared to challenge Jiang's policy of cultural barbarism. They, like the majority of artists, opted publicly to approve her great cultural experiment while privately hoping that her power would be broken once the rapidly ageing Mao had died. One of the most distressing features of Mao's China was the failure of the intellectuals and natural leaders of the community to protest against the crimes of the regime. A mixture of moral cowardice and an understandable fear of what might be done to them and their families led them to accept the unacceptable without complaint.

Jiang's stranglehold on the arts remained for the whole of the decade between 1966 and Mao's death ten years later. By then it was clear that the result of this artistic persecution had been not the creation of a new culture but merely the near destruction of the old one. Writers and artists had been frightened either into inaction or into producing politically correct dross that would not fall foul of the censors.

Describing the profound damage done to China by the artistic destruction, Yan Yen, a poet, commented: 'As a result of the Cultural Revolution you could say the cultural trademark of my generation is that we have no culture.' Twenty years after the events, Deng Xiaoping's son, Pufang, reflected: 'The Cultural Revolution was not just a disaster for the party, for the country, but for the whole people. We were all victims, people of several generations. One hundred million people were its victims'.

The impact of the Cultural Revolution on education

There is a sense in which education in any meaningful form simply stopped for much of the Cultural Revolution. A census compiled in 1982, six years after Mao's death, contained the following revealing figures:

- Less than one per cent of the working population had a university degree.
- Only eleven per cent had received schooling after the age of sixteen.

- Only 26 per cent had received schooling between the ages of twelve and sixteen.
- Only 35 per cent had received schooling up to the age of twelve.

Reasons for lack of educational progress

The principal reason for the sharp decline in qualified youngsters was the disruption caused by the Cultural Revolution. Between 1966 and 1970, 130 million of China's young people simply stopped attending school or university. Nor was it simply a question of numbers. Education itself as an ideal was degraded. The deliberate creation of disorder and the encouragement of pupils and students to ridicule or attack their teachers, tear up the curriculum and reject all forms of traditional learning had the all too obvious consequence of undermining the purpose of education itself.

Everything became politicised. Nothing was regarded as being of intrinsic worth any longer. Learning and study were dismissed as worthless unless they served the revolution. It was more important to train loyal party workers than it was to prepare China's young people to take their place in a modern state. That was why, having used the young as the instrument for waging the Cultural Revolution, Mao then sent 12 million of them not back to school and college but 'up to the mountains and down to the villages' (see page 143).

Table 5.1 Number of universities and colleges operating in China 1959–82. What main trends are indicated in the table? How is the contrast between the figures for 1961 and those from 1965 to 1976 to be explained?

Year	Number
1959	791
1961	1289
1965	434
1970	434
1972	434
1976	434
1982	598

SOURCE M

How is the children's enthusiasm for marching and demonstrating, shown in this photo, to be explained?

Schoolchildren parading in Harbin, Heilongjiang province, 1 October 1966.

Educational standards of CCP members

An embarrassing revelation for the Communist authorities in the late 1970s was that among the officials responsible for running the party and the government only six per cent had been formally educated beyond the age of sixteen. That the PRC under Mao had had such a poorly educated workforce and administration indicated how unrealistic his dreams had been for turning China into a modern state. It is notable that when Deng Xiaoping began to reform China after 1978 one his major priorities was the improvement of education, which had been so neglected under Mao.

7 May cadre schools

Typifying Mao's approach to education was a particular initiative early in the Cultural Revolution. Taking their title from a directive issued by Mao Zedong on 7 May 1966, cadre schools were intended to teach those who attended them 'the dignity of labour' by working on the land to learn how the peasants lived. The schools were essentially primitive farms where soft-living party officials and those suspected of lacking full commitment to the regime's policies were sent. Wang Hongwen, one of the Gang of Four, remarked, 'All the ones who aren't obedient, we send them there.' Organised by Lin Biao, the schools were barely different from labour camps; life was made deliberately hard within them and the average two-year term of 're-education' could be extended if inmates failed to co-operate.

Over 1000 such schools were established across eighteen provinces, holding some 100,000 higher rank cadres. A notable inmate was Deng Xiaoping. Many thousands more schools were set up for lower officials, holding possibly up to a quarter of a million cadres. 'Intellectuals', purged during the Cultural Revolution, were also dumped in these places. Suicide and deaths from malnutrition were not uncommon. With the easing of the severity of the Cultural Revolution following the death of Lin Biao in 1971, the schools began to be closed down. None was in existence at the time of Mao's death in 1976.

Influence of the Cultural Revolution on health provision

Mao and the Communists had begun with high hopes of providing the people with health care. It was the government's policy in the early years of the PRC to train many more doctors and nurses with the specific aim of providing direct medical care in the remoter parts of China. In the 1950s, large numbers of Chinese were treated by a qualified doctor for the first time in their lives. However, the number of qualified doctors never reached the original targets because here, as in so many areas of social life, politics intervened. As with education, so with health, the original good intentions were undermined by the self-inflicted disruption caused by the Great Leap Forward and the Cultural Revolution.

China's doctors attacked

In a repeat of what had happened during the 'anti-campaigns', the Cultural Revolution saw doctors coming under attack as a professional class that lived off the backs of the workers. The accusation was made that, not having learned the 'dignity of labour', they were a privileged élite who used their special skills to make money for an indulgent, bourgeois lifestyle. The consequence was that to survive during the Cultural Revolution, doctors had to subordinate medical considerations to political ones. This produced such absurdities as surgeons cancelling operations in order to show their solidarity with the workers by sweeping floors and cleaning toilets.

Caught up in the politically correct atmosphere, some doctors decided that since showing pain was a bourgeois reaction and that bearing things without flinching was a sign of revolutionary purpose, they would no longer use anaesthetics and **analgesics**. China's maternity wards resounded to the groans of women in labour as, denied any painkillers, they struggled to suppress their agonised cries.

The barefoot doctors

Despite the denigration of the medical profession on political grounds, Mao remained aware of the propaganda value of effective health provision. It was such thinking that lay behind the crash programme for training doctors that was introduced by the late 1960s. In keeping with the notion that it was their long period of academic study that had detached the doctors from the people, the new system was based on short practical courses. Instead of long years of preparation, the trainees would now engage in six-month periods of intensive study with the emphasis wholly on the practical. Once trained in the basics, the new doctors would be sent to work among the peasants. It was very similar to the way in which the ex-Red Guards had been dispersed into the countryside (see page 143).

The scheme had its undoubted successes. By 1973, over a million new doctors had been trained. They contributed greatly to the improvement of the lives of the peasants. Known colloquially as **barefoot doctors**, these idealistic young general practitioners travelled around rural China providing treatment, often free of charge. But impressive though such dedicated doctors were, often performing minor miracles in primitive conditions, they were a stop-gap. They could not provide the full national medical service that a modern state requires.

The impact of the Cultural Revolution on women and the family

Women and society at large had barely had time to recover from the famine (see page 76) when they were plunged into the turmoil of the Cultural Revolution.

KEY TERMS

Analgesics Painkillers.

Barefoot doctors Teams of swiftly trained medics who were sent into the countryside to provide a rudimentary health service.

The rejection of the importance of the individual and the family that came with collectivisation was re-emphasised with particular force during the Cultural Revolution:

- Private property and ownership were now depicted as crimes against Communist society, which was engaged in a great collective effort to build a new world.
- The enforced pooling of resources and effort meant that the economic link that held families together was broken.
- Whereas in traditional China the **extended family**, which might in practice be a whole village, had been the main provider of help in difficult times, in Mao's China that role was taken over by the state.
- The provision of social welfare, such as education and medical care, was now to be organised and delivered by Communist Party officials and appointees.

The bitter irony was that this new state-controlled system collapsed in the face of the great famine that swept through central China after 1958. With the family system of support destroyed and the new state system undeveloped, the starving peasants had nowhere and no one to turn to for relief.

Pressures on the family structure

The excesses of the Cultural Revolution carried to their logical conclusion the process of enforced conformity that had begun with collectivisation and the outlawing of private ownership. The traditional **nuclear family** fell into one of the categories of the 'four olds' that the young were set to destroy. Children were told to look on Mao Zedong and the Communist Party as their true parents and, therefore, deserving of their first loyalty. Normal family affection was replaced by love for Mao. A Beijing student recalled: 'From the first day of my schooling, at seven years old, I learned "I love you Chairman Mao", not "I love you Mamma or Papa". I was brainwashed; the party was purifying us so we would live for Mao's idealism instead of discovering our own humanity.'

The young were urged to inform on those among their relatives who betrayed any sign of clinging, even in the slightest manner, to the decadent values of the past. In such a frenzied atmosphere, it was hard for any semblance of normal family life to survive. The Red Guards who, after terrorising the nation, were dispersed by Mao and sent 'up to the mountains and down to the villages' (see page 143), themselves became bewildered victims. Their bitter experience as they eked out a miserable existence far from home left them disillusioned and resentful. It proved very difficult for them to pick up the pieces and return to anything approaching normal family life. They have been aptly described as China's lost generation.

Religious persecution during the Cultural Revolution

During the Cultural Revolution, religion was denounced as belonging to the 'four olds' and the attacks on it intensified. No public worship or ceremony

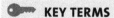

KEY TERMS

Extended family Not just parents and children but all the relatives, including in-laws.

Nuclear family Mother, father and their children, considered as a unit.

Denominations Separate groups within a faith, for example, Catholicism and Protestantism within Christianity.

was allowed and any clergy who had survived the earlier persecutions were rounded up and imprisoned. So severe was the repression that it provoked an international outcry. Representatives of the world's major faiths, **denominations** and philosophies called on the PRC to call off the persecutions and show humanity.

Campaigns against 'Confucius and Co'

There was little response from Mao's government to the appeals, save to describe them as the product of capitalist distortions and anti-Chinese malice. The suppression of religion continued. Confucianism was denounced as representing all that was worst in China's past. The name of Confucius was linked to any person or movement that the authorities wished to denounce. 'Confucius and Co' became a standard term of abuse directed at any suspect group or organisation. Significantly, when Lin Biao came under fire during the Cultural Revolution, the slogan coined to attack him was 'criticise Lin Biao and Confucius' (see page 147).

Economic effects of the Cultural Revolution

The disruption occasioned by the Cultural Revolution inevitably led to serious economic setbacks. In theory, the PRC ran a third Five-Year Plan from 1966 to 1970, but the social turmoil resulted in its being abandoned, even though this was not officially admitted. The statistics between 1966 and 1976 tell their own story:

- Industrial production fell by 13.8 per cent.
- Steel output fell from 15 million tonnes to 11 million.
- Coal output fell from 260 million tonnes to 206 million.
- Oil production fell from 15 million tonnes to 13.9 tonnes.
- Construction fell by 33 per cent.
- Rail freight declined from 555 million tonnes to 421 million tonnes.
- The PRC deficit increased from 1 billion yuan to 2.25 billion yuan.

Since the worst of the disruption was in the urban areas, agriculture suffered less severely:

- Agricultural production fell by 1.6 per cent.
- Cotton production rose from 2.35 million tonnes to 23.8 million tonnes.
- Grain production declined from 213 million tonnes to 209 million tonnes.

The government's response to the shortages was to resort to austerity. It called on the masses to 'practise frugality while making revolution'. Rationing became the norm:

- The assets of state companies were frozen.
- Borrowing from, and lending by, banks were heavily restricted.
- Travel permits were required for travel from one province to another.
- The purchase of cooking oil and rice was restricted to those with special permits.

In introducing the austerity measures, officials quoted Mao's statement: 'the situation in the Great Proletarian Cultural Revolution nationwide is not merely good, but excellent'. It was a falsehood, but one that was sustained throughout the years of disruption.

Mao's prison camps: the *laogai*

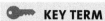
The Cultural Revolution was an intensification of the desire Mao had always had of enforcing conformity and obedience in China. The period witnessed the creation of a vast network of labour camps in which those who opposed him or were suspected of opposing him were imprisoned. As the title *laogai* suggested, the official theory was that the camps were places not of punishment but of re-education. The fiction was maintained that the mass of the people were happy and content in the Communist state created by Mao, and that those who protested against the system were the exceptions who were not so much bad as misguided. It was the state's duty, therefore, to help them towards the truth by putting them in camps where they could be trained into enlightenment.

In reality, the camps became places where the harshest means were used to dehumanise the prisoners, who were forced to do humiliating and backbreaking work while being systematically starved. The camps were set up throughout China, but many of the worst were deliberately built in the most inhospitable parts of the country where the bitter cold of winter or the searing heat of summer made life a torture for the prisoners. To obtain even the bare minimum ration of food, prisoners had to make a full confession of their crimes. Those who persisted in claiming that they were innocent were interrogated, deprived of sleep, held in solitary confinement, beaten and starved until they broke down and conformed.

Very few prisoners had the physical or mental power to resist such treatment for very long, and even those who had exceptional reserves of strength tended to buckle when told that their families would suffer if they did not give in. The desperate state to which the prisoners were brought by their hunger was described by a doctor who visited the camps: 'I noticed a very strange wound at the back of the thigh of many of the dead. First of all I dismissed it as a gunshot wound at close quarters but after seeing a few more I asked a friend and he told me that many of the prisoners were cutting chunks out of the bodies to eat.'

Statistics relating to the camps

- The average number of prisoners held in the camps each year during Mao's time was 10 million.
- Over 25 million prisoners died during that period, the number being composed of those who were officially executed, those who died from hunger and ill treatment and those who killed themselves. Even in death prisoners were treated with contempt. The term used by the prison authorities to describe those who took their own lives was 'alienating themselves from the party and the people'.

The broader purpose of the camps

A factor in the management of the camps was that they were not simply prisons; they were economically important in that they provided a limitless supply of slave labour. The *laogai* also performed a function that went beyond simply the punishment of particular dissidents. The existence of the camps effectively terrified the whole population. Even when prisoners were released after completing their sentence, they remained under constant threat of being rearrested. The feeling prevailed that what had happened to them could happen to anybody. The families of prisoners were also regarded as guilty by association and were shunned by their neighbours.

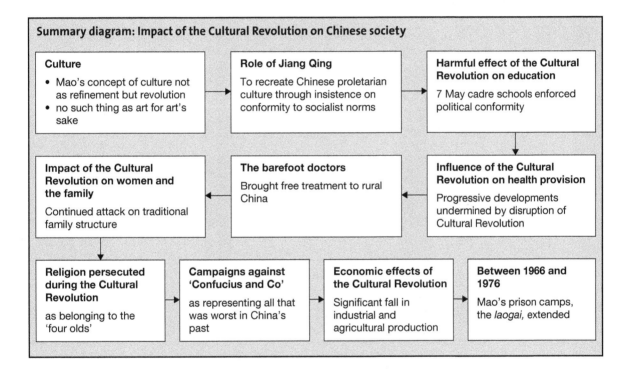

Summary diagram: Impact of the Cultural Revolution on Chinese society

Culture
- Mao's concept of culture not as refinement but revolution
- no such thing as art for art's sake

Role of Jiang Qing
To recreate Chinese proletarian culture through insistence on conformity to socialist norms

Harmful effect of the Cultural Revolution on education
7 May cadre schools enforced political conformity

Impact of the Cultural Revolution on women and the family
Continued attack on traditional family structure

The barefoot doctors
Brought free treatment to rural China

Influence of the Cultural Revolution on health provision
Progressive developments undermined by disruption of Cultural Revolution

Religion persecuted during the Cultural Revolution
as belonging to the 'four olds'

Campaigns against 'Confucius and Co'
as representing all that was worst in China's past

Economic effects of the Cultural Revolution
Significant fall in industrial and agricultural production

Between 1966 and 1976
Mao's prison camps, the *laogai*, extended

5 Key debate

▶ *Was Mao a monster?*

In 2005, a book appeared which claimed to tell the 'unknown story' of Mao. It did not quite do that since many of the 'discoveries' in the book had already been presented in a less dramatic way by scholars in the field, such as Jonathan Spence (*The Search for Modern China*, 1990), Philip Short (*Mao: A Life*, 1999) and Jasper Becker (*Hungry Ghosts: China's Secret Famine*, 1996). Nonetheless, the biography, *Mao: The Unknown Story*, by Jung Chang and Jon Halliday, quickly caught the imagination of students of China in the West, largely because Jung Chang was already a very popular Chinese novelist, whose family had lived and suffered under Mao. Her book's main contention was that Mao was a monstrous, uncaring dictator. A representative passage is given in Extract 1.

EXTRACT I

? What contradictory pictures of Mao emerge from the views of the writers represented in Extracts 1–6?

From Jung Chang and Jon Halliday, *Mao: The Unknown Story*, Jonathan Cape, 2005, p. 509.

What Mao had in mind was a completely arid society, devoid of civilisation, deprived of representation of human feelings, inhabited by a herd with no sensibility, which would automatically obey his orders. He wanted the nation to be brain dead in order to carry out his big purge – and to live in this state permanently. In this he was more extreme than Hitler or Stalin.

Disturbed by the book's lack of balance, a set of experts on China came together in 2010 to produce *Was Mao Really a Monster?*, a collection of essays in which they criticised Jung and Halliday for their unremittingly negative approach. One of the main contributors, the distinguished scholar Jonathan Spence, is quoted in Extract 2.

EXTRACT 2

From Jonathan D. Spence, 'Portrait of a Monster', in Gregor Benton and Lin Chun (eds), *Was Mao Really a Monster?*, Routledge, 2010, p. 39.

By focusing so tightly on Mao's vileness – to the exclusion of other factors – the authors undermine much of the power their story might have had. By seeking to demonstrate that Mao started out as a vile person and stayed vile throughout his life, the authors deny any room for change, whether growth or degeneration, for subtlety or the possibilities of redemption.

Jung Chang's book and the response it aroused drew attention to what biographers had already said about Mao. Lee Feigon, an American analyst, had defended Mao's record.

EXTRACT 3

From Lee Feigon, *Mao: A Reinterpretation*, Ivan R. Dee, 2002, p. 83.

Mao was a great leader who transformed China. In a post-socialist age, Mao still ranks as a socialist hero. In an anti-totalitarian time, Mao can still inspire awe for his struggles against bureaucracy and his efforts to educate and empower the common people.

A celebrated British writer, Delia Davin, while also acknowledging Mao's destructive policies, had pointed to his achievements.

EXTRACT 4

From Delia Davin, *Mao Zedong*, Sutton Publishing, 1997, p. 106.

The revolution that Mao led unified China, began to modernize the economy and made the country a power to reckon with in the world. It also brought enormous improvements to the lives of many, raising life expectancy and standards of living and of health and education. But Mao's utopian dreams, his periodic refusal to engage with reality, also resulted in millions of deaths.

Another British writer had stressed that Mao's failings had to be set against the scale of his ambition.

EXTRACT 5

From Michael Lynch, *Mao*, Routledge, 2004, p. 231.

The vital and ironic point is that Mao's ruthlessness was deployed in pursuit of an inspiring cause – the salvation of China and its people. His outstanding characteristic was his intense nationalism. He wanted the restoration of China's greatness after a century of foreign occupation and internal corruption. Chinese considerations always had primacy.

Philip Short, arguably Mao Zedong's most authoritative biographer, had argued that Mao had to be viewed in a balanced way and suggested that assessment of Mao's true stature was a matter of waiting to see how China developed.

EXTRACT 6

Adapted from Philip Short, *Mao: A Life*, Hodder & Stoughton, 1999, p. 633.

Mao's legacy was to clear the way for less visionary, more practical men to build the shining future that he could never achieve. Mao ruled for twenty-seven years. If the past, as he believed, is indeed a mirror for the present, will the twenty-first century mark the start of a Chinese golden age for which the Maoist dictatorship will have opened the way? Or will he be remembered as a flawed colossus, who brought fundamental change that only a handful of others had managed in all the years of China's history, but then failed to follow through?

6 Impact of the Cultural Revolution on external affairs

▶ *How did the Cultural Revolution affect the PRC's foreign relations?*

Chinese attacks on foreign embassies in China

One of the remarkable aspects of the Cultural Revolution was that its victims were not restricted to the Chinese people. In defiance of all the accepted rules of international diplomacy, eleven **foreign embassies** were attacked and their staff assaulted. With only minimal interference from the police, Red Guards were allowed to besiege foreign embassies and terrorise the people who worked in them. Among the examples were:

- the surrounding of the Soviet embassy by Red Guards, who kept up a 24-hour barrage of insults
- the besieging of the Dutch **chargé d'affaires** and his family in their house for over a month
- the seizure of a French commercial attaché and his wife, who were then screamed at for six hours by Maoists
- two secretaries from the Indian Embassy being grabbed at Beijing airport before they could board their plane and being badly beaten
- the breaking into and burning of the British Embassy in Beijing, accompanied by physical attacks on mission personnel.

Donald Hopson, the head of the British Embassy, sent a vivid dispatch to his government describing what had happened, as shown in Source N.

SOURCE N

From 'The burning of the British office in Peking', a confidential report sent to the Foreign Office, 8 September 1967, quoted in Roderick Macfarquhar and Michael Schoenhals, *Mao's Last Revolution*, Belknap Press, 2006, p. 226.

Outside the crowd broke the glass of the windows, but the bars and plywood shutters held. The mob then started to burn straw at the windows. We threw water through the gaps, but the room began to fill with smoke. We could see the glare of many fires, and it was now clear that the mob would soon be through the wall and there was a danger that we should be burned alive if we stayed. I gave orders for the emergency exit to be opened. We were hauled by our hair, half-strangled with our ties, kicked and beaten on the head with bamboo poles.

*Most of the staff had similar experiences to my own. Some were paraded up and down, forced to their knees and photographed in humiliating positions. All were beaten and kicked, and the girls were not spared lewd attentions from the prying fingers of the mob. So much for the **morals of the Red Guards**. Most of the staff were eventually rescued by the army and plain-clothes police agents.*

❓ What are the likely explanations for the attack on the British Embassy and staff described in Source N?

Chinese attacks abroad

The attacks on foreigners were not confined within China. Disregarding the damage it did to its image abroad, the PRC carried its Cultural Revolution ferociously into other countries. By 1967, Chinese militants had caused violent incidents in over 30 countries around the world. In some of these the local people hit back; in Burma and Indonesia, Chinese expatriates were attacked in retaliation.

It had been a consistent feature of Asian history for large numbers of Chinese to live and work in other Asian countries. This pattern continued after 1949. Rather than integrate into the local culture, the Chinese settlers tended to regard themselves as a discrete group whose first loyalty was to the PRC. This was encouraged by Beijing, which granted its expatriates full Chinese citizenship. The result was particularly evident in Indonesia and Burma. In any dispute that those countries had with the PRC the expatriates took the side of Communist China and became a source of subversion. The resentment aroused abroad by the presence of large numbers of Chinese expatriates in many Asian countries was intensified at the time of the Cultural Revolution, when Maoist fanaticism made the Chinese in the various countries in which they had settled a highly volatile and disruptive element.

Amazing scenes occurred in London in August 1967 when scores of staff members, all shouting Mao's name, came out of the Chinese Embassy in Portland Place armed with sticks and machetes, which they waved threateningly at the police. Safe from arrest because of their diplomatic immunity, they demonstrated loudly and went back into their embassy building only after they had caused major disruption in the area.

Trouble in Hong Kong

Mao used the opportunity provided by the Cultural Revolution to make trouble for Britain over its continuing possession of **Hong Kong**. In May 1967, he tried to turn a workers' strike in the colony into an anti-British demonstration, in the hope that the police would fire on the demonstrators, thus illustrating the evils of British colonialism in China. When the local police declined to act in this way, Mao instructed Zhou Enlai to send Chinese terrorists into the colony to murder policemen and so create the desired retaliation. In an eight-week period the terrorists killed five policemen and exploded over 160 bombs which caused civilian deaths and extensive damage to property. The Hong Kong authorities still did not resort to the extreme measures that Mao had expected. He had wanted a massacre but he did not get one.

The cynical aspect of the whole affair was that although Mao wished to frighten the British into thinking that the PRC was preparing to take Hong Kong by force, he had no intention of going through with such a plan. He wanted to embarrass the British but not to push things to the point where he would have to

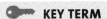 **KEY TERM**

Hong Kong The Chinese city-port that had been a British Crown colony since 1898 and was not scheduled to return to China until 1997.

carry out his bluff. He told Zhou Enlai to stop short of actions that 'might lead to our having to take Hong Kong back ahead of time'.

The Cultural Revolution and the Soviet Union

Sino-Soviet relations, which were already at a low ebb, were made worse by the Cultural Revolution. Moscow condemned the excess and extremism of Mao's programme. Mao resented this as another example of Soviet 'great power chauvinism'. He soon had the chance to turn the tables. In 1968, Leonid Brezhnev, the Soviet hard-line leader, acting in accordance with the pseudonymous **Brezhnev doctrine**, sent Soviet forces into the Czechoslovak capital to suppress the **Prague spring**.

While Mao had no time for counter-revolution in Communist states, he was unwilling to accept the right of the USSR, by his reckoning itself guilty of revisionism, to impose Soviet authority on the members of the Marxist camp. Mao's confidence in speaking out against the Soviet Union had undoubtedly been buoyed by that fact that China was now a superpower. In 1969 Brezhnev called an international Communist conference in Moscow with the aim of outlawing China. However, the Soviet invasion of Czechoslovakia in 1968 had weakened the USSR's moral leadership and the conference was largely a failure from Brezhnev's perspective; he did not get the outright condemnation of China that he had wanted.

The fact was that international communism had seriously fragmented. The low point in the relations of the two Communist superpowers came in 1969. Serious border incidents threatened to escalate into full-scale war. In an extraordinary development, the PRC and the USSR repositioned their nuclear-armed rockets so that they now faced inwards towards each other rather than outwards towards their Western enemies. This may have been bluff and counter-bluff but there was no doubting that Sino-Soviet relations had reached their lowest ebb. This was powerfully expressed by Lin Biao's 1969 denunciation of the Soviet 'revisionists', whom, in a reverse insult, he called **social fascists**. Mao's death in 1976, which was soon followed by the overthrow of the fanatically anti-Soviet Gang of Four, effectively removed the immediate danger of Sino-Soviet nuclear confrontation.

Sino-American relations

In a remarkable development, the deterioration in Sino-Soviet relations coincided with a major improvement in Sino-American relations. Indeed, the developments were more than coincidences, they were connected. A precipitating factor was the USA's reversal of its position on Chinese representation in the UN; in 1971 it formally recognised mainland China's right to replace Taiwan in the UN (see page 54). It has been suggested that this may have been motivated by the USA's reaction, part fear, part admiration, to the PRC's successful development of its own hydrogen bomb in 1967. Better to be on good rather than bad terms with China now that it was a full superpower.

KEY TERMS

Brezhnev doctrine The demand that all international Communists should toe the Soviet line or risk being disciplined by the other Marxist states acting under Soviet leadership.

Prague spring The attempt of the Czech Communist government to liberalise some of its policies and assert its independence of Soviet control.

Social fascism A term first used by Stalin to denote those Communists and socialists who were willing to compromise with their political enemies.

Regardless of what prompted it, the US diplomatic concession over Taiwan certainly encouraged the PRC to soften its approach to the USA. Talks between the two countries began in 1971. The initial diplomacy was conducted by Zhou Enlai and **Henry Kissinger**, whose negotiations prepared the way for the visit of President **Richard Nixon** to Beijing in February 1972.

The parting of the bamboo curtain

That Nixon's visit took place at all made it a momentous event. For the leader of the USA, 'the number one enemy nation', to be invited to China would have been unimaginable only a few years earlier. The ailing Mao, who was suffering from motor neurone disease, was genuinely excited by the thought of meeting the US president, arguably the most powerful man in the world. The two men genuinely took to each other; their talks and those between their officials went very well. Overall, the visit was a major diplomatic success. A joint declaration was issued in which the two nations expressed:

- the hope that there would be continuing Sino-American contacts
- the desirability of commercial, cultural and educational exchanges
- their joint agreement to give further consideration to ways in which the previously intractable Taiwan issue could be resolved.

SOURCE O

Photo showing Mao and Nixon shaking hands in Beijing in 1972.

KEY FIGURES

Henry Kissinger (1923–)

The US president's special adviser on foreign affairs.

Richard Nixon (1913–94)

US president from 1969 to 1974.

Why might this photo be described as iconic?

Nixon's visit was more than merely symbolic. As their communiqué showed, the PRC and the US sides remained guarded in their approach. But the visit had indicated that China, after the upheavals of the Cultural Revolution, was prepared if not to lift the **bamboo curtain**, at least to part it.

> 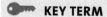 **KEY TERM**
>
> **Bamboo curtain**
> A figurative way of describing China's hostile attitude towards the non-Communist world.

Mao's aim of undermining the USSR

China's willingness to improve its relations with the USA had a deeper purpose than merely a desire to be on better terms with the West. The softening of China's previously hard line was part of its strategy to undermine the USSR. The Chinese resented the Soviet policies of *détente* and coexistence, which they interpreted as a tactic to leave China internationally isolated. The PRC decided to outplay the USSR at its own game by achieving a Sino-American *détente*. The Chinese were undoubtedly assisted in this by the more understanding approach of the Americans and by their mutual readiness to do down the USSR. Relations continued to improve during Mao's remaining years and laid the basis for further diplomatic and commercial contacts.

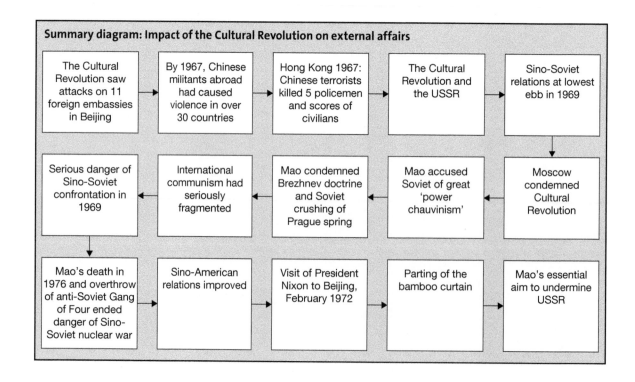

Summary diagram: Impact of the Cultural Revolution on external affairs

Chapter summary

In 1966, Mao, now in his seventies, embarked on an extraordinary programme for leaving his stamp permanently on the PRC. Calling on the young to attack the 'four olds', he aimed to remove all those elements he saw as preventing the fulfilment of the revolution that he had begun in 1949. Using the Red Guards and the PLA as his instruments, he implemented a destructive purge that left no major aspect of Chinese society untouched, the most striking effects being wrought by Mao's wife, Jiang Qing, in the field of culture itself.

Mao put the running of the Cultural Revolution into the hands of the Central Cultural Revolution Group, an offshoot of the Politburo, on which the most radical of the hard liners had a prominent place. The attempt of the ultra-radicals, the Gang of Four, to impose its ideas and policies on the more moderate leaders such as Zhou Enlai and Deng Xiaoping, led to years of infighting. Despite the internal turmoil, the period was of major significance in foreign affairs, as it saw the PRC achieve diplomatic success in improving its relations with the USA, a deliberate move to disadvantage and undermine the PRC's great national and ideological rival, the USSR.

 # Refresher questions

Use these questions to remind yourself of the key material covered in this chapter.

1 What were Mao's motives for subjecting his people to the Cultural Revolution?

2 Why did China's young people prove so willing to follow Mao's lead?

3 Why were Deng and Liu attacked?

4 What methods did the Red Guards use to terrify the population?

5 What role did the PLA play in the Cultural Revolution?

6 In what sense was the Lin Biao affair a turning point in the Cultural Revolution?

7 How did Lin Biao's fall benefit Zhou Enlai and Deng Xiaoping?

8 How did the Gang of Four try to assert its authority during Mao's final days?

9 What did Mao understand by the term 'culture'?

10 What impact did Jiang Qing have on Chinese culture?

11 How socially disruptive was the Cultural Revolution?

12 How did the Cultural Revolution affect the Chinese economy?

13 What in theory was the purpose of the *laogai*?

14 In what sense was the lifting of the bamboo curtain an anti-Soviet move?

15 Why was Nixon's 1972 visit to the PRC such a major event in East–West relations?

Question practice

ESSAY QUESTIONS

1 How successful were the Red Guards in carrying out the mission that Mao Zedong set them between 1966 and 1967?

2 'For all their ability to strike terror into their opponents, the Gang of Four never held real power.' Assess the validity of this view.

3 'Without the PLA there would have been no Cultural Revolution.' How far do you agree with this statement?

4 How far do you agree with the view that Jiang Qing did not reform Chinese culture, she destroyed it?

5 To what extent was the achievement of improved Sino-American relations in 1972 intended by Mao to be a slight to the USSR?

SOURCES

1 Why is Source K (**page 148**) valuable to the historian looking for evidence of opposition to the Cultural Revolution among ordinary Chinese?

2 How far could the historian make use of Sources G (**page 140**) and H (**page 141**) together to investigate the extremes of behaviour that occurred in response to Mao's call for a Cultural Revolution in China? Explain your answer using the sources, the information given about them and your own knowledge of the historical context.

8 With reference to Sources D (**page 137**), G (**page 140**) and H (**page 141**), and your understanding of the historical context, assess the value of these sources to a historian studying the commitment of China's young people to the Cultural Revolution.

CHAPTER 6

The Deng era 1976–97

Deng Xiaoping emerged from the power struggle after Mao's death as the paramount figure in Chinese politics. Deng set about reforming the economy through four modernisations. However, he made no political concessions. A democracy movement formed, which climaxed with the occupation of Tiananmen Square, a protest that was violently crushed by Deng. Undeterred by the protest, Deng continued his reform programme. By the time of his death, he had made China an economic giant. These themes are covered under four headings:

★ The power struggle after Mao's death

★ Economic reform: the Four Modernisations

★ Political stagnation and the pro-democracy movement 1979–89

★ China as a global power

Key dates

1976	Gang of Four arrested	1989	Death of Hu Yaobang
1977–8	Deng returned to prominence		Mikhail Gorbachev visited China
1978	Third Plenum convened		Tiananmen Square pro-democracy demonstration crushed
	Sino-Japanese peace and friendship treaty	1993	Tibetan rising
1979	Pro-democracy movement began	1994	PRC granted 'Most Favored Nation' status
	Wei Jingsheng imprisoned		
1981	Sentencing of the Gang of Four	1997	Death of Deng Xiaoping
1986	Protests in China's leading universities		

The power struggle after Mao's death

▶ *Who were the main contenders for power in party and government after Mao's death?*

The rivals

With the death of Mao Zedong in September 1976, the power struggle within the party that had gone on behind the scenes became an open conflict. There were three principal contestants:

- the moderate **Hua Guofeng**, whom Mao had nominated as his successor
- the Gang of Four, a small group of hard liners led by Mao's widow, Jiang Qing
- the pragmatist Deng Xiaoping, who had survived being purged and demoted during the Cultural Revolution.

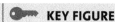

KEY FIGURE

Hua Guofeng (1921–2008)

A diligent but unspectacular CCP member from Mao's home province of Hunan.

At Mao's funeral, which was accompanied by displays of mass lamentation, there were indications that the jockeying for position among the party leaders had already begun. Appearances matter greatly in Chinese politics. How prominent a role individuals played in the funeral ceremonies was a good indication of their place in the party hierarchy. That Hua Guofeng delivered the main funeral eulogy was a clear sign that he had taken precedence over Jiang Qing, whose unseemly behaviour at the lying in state, when she had fought with one of her cousins over the right to lay a wreath, had led the organisers of the ceremony to entrust her with only a minor role in the proceedings.

Hua Guofeng

'With you in charge, my heart is at ease': these were the last intelligible words that Mao Zedong was reported to have uttered before he fell into a final coma. They were addressed to Hua Guofeng, whom Mao, in the month before his death, had nominated as his successor as party chairman. Before then, Hua had been a little-known official with no substantial following in the party. In so far as Mao was capable of rational judgement in the final months of his life, his thinking appears to have been that with Zhou Enlai now dead, and Deng Xiaoping again demoted, there was no longer an obvious heir to the leadership of China. It was far better therefore to give authority to someone whose record, while undistinguished, had been one of unswerving Maoist loyalties.

The Gang of Four

It is noteworthy that Mao Zedong had not considered entrusting power to the Gang of Four. This suggests that despite the ferocity with which Jiang Qing and her followers had tried to enforce their concept of Maoist orthodoxy on

China, Mao himself had always been suspicious of their motives. His personal estrangement from Jiang – they lived apart for at least the last ten years of Mao's life – may well have been caused in part by their political differences.

Immediately following Mao's death, the sixteen-member Politburo split into two identifiable groups: the Gang of Four and the supporters of Hua Guofeng. Since the Gang was in a minority, it was bound to lose in any straight vote. But while the Politburo was undoubtedly the dominant body politically, there was always the possibility that its power could be neutralised by a direct resort to military force. This was where Hua Guofeng's previous dealings with the army stood him in good stead. He was able to outflank the Gang of Four. His work as co-ordinator of the relief effort that had followed the Tangshan earthquake in 1976 (see page 151) had consolidated his close relationship with a number of generals. In particular, he had gained the support of **Wang Dongxing** and Marshall **Ye Jianying**.

Military opposition to the Gang of Four

Wang had earlier been an associate of the Gang of Four but had never fully committed himself to its side. This was largely because he found Jiang Qing's hectoring style deeply distasteful. A similar personal dislike of Jiang had also helped to push Marshall Ye into direct opposition to the Gang of Four. It was also significant that Mao, during his final year, had made Ye a close confidant, warning him of Jiang's overweening ambitions. At Mao's death, therefore, both Wang Dongxing and Marshall Ye were prepared to prevent the Gang of Four from seizing power.

As had invariably been the case in China in a disputed succession, it was the military who held the key. Had the Gang of Four been able to command enough army support it might well have been able to assert political control. Realising this, the Gang tried to exploit its provincial connections. The Gang hoped to be able to use its influence in Shanghai, where it had its strongest following, to raise an army from the city's militia. The Gang members had some success but the troops available to them were never sufficient to match their political ambitions. The reality was that the Gang's provincial base was too detached from the real source of power in Communist China: Beijing.

How little influence the Gang had in the capital was shown when Jiang Qing's main military supporter, **Mao Yuanxin**, a nephew of Mao Zedong, was dismissed from his Beijing post by Marshall Ye. Mao Yuanxin had been given responsibility for collecting his late uncle's papers; Jiang had tried to bribe him into either finding evidence among these that Mao Zedong had entrusted his revolution to the Gang of Four or providing reliable forgeries to the same effect. (This was to be one of the allegations against Jiang at her later trial.) But with Mao Yuanxin's removal this particular ruse was blocked.

 KEY FIGURES

Wang Dongxing (1916–)
Head of China's special security forces and Mao Zedong's chief bodyguard during the Cultural Revolution.

Ye Jianying (1897–1986)
Chief of Beijing's armed forces.

Mao Yuanxin (1941–)
Acted as Mao Zedong's liaison officer before his death.

Gang of Four outmanoeuvred

Jiang Qing's other main hope had been that Wang Hongwen, from his government post in Beijing, would be able to organise support for the Gang of Four in other parts of China. It was the fear that Wang's efforts might begin to succeed that precipitated the next move by its opponents. Fearing an attempted coup by the Gang, Marshall Ye and Wang Dongxing joined Hua Guofeng in a pre-emptive strike. Ye and Wang deployed selected units of the armed forces in Beijing and other key areas to forestall possible 'counter-revolution'.

Hua then invited the Gang of Four to a rearranged Politburo meeting on 6 October. Each of the four was given a different time for the start of the meeting. When the three male members of the Gang arrived at their separate times, they were immediately arrested. Before she had time to leave for the meeting, Jiang Qing was seized in her own home and bundled off to prison, shouting obscenities at her captors. For a brief period it seemed that the Gang's supporters in Shanghai might actively challenge the turn of events in Beijing, but by the time the news of the Gang's fall was officially announced nationwide on 15 October all signs of resistance had disappeared.

Re-emergence of Deng Xiaoping

The ousting of the Gang of Four seemed to indicate that Hua Guofeng had inherited Mao Zedong's authority. But appearances proved deceptive. The real beneficiary of the events proved to be someone who had played no direct part in them: Deng Xiaoping. Despite his withdrawal to Guangzhou following his earlier demotion, Deng retained the highest reputation and the largest following in the party and in the PLA. This allowed him to play a waiting game during the power struggle. He did not need to challenge Hua Guofeng openly; he felt he could rely on Hua's lack of a committed following in the party to deny him full power. It proved a shrewd calculation. Hua found his newly acquired authority within the party hard to sustain. There was a broad feeling among members that his position as chairman was not permanent; he was merely a caretaker.

In contrast, Deng's strength lay in his reputation and his range of personal contacts with leading figures in the party and the PLA. Although he had been demoted during the Cultural Revolution, Deng had never lost his party membership. Now that Mao had gone and the Gang of Four had been removed, there was no one who could match Deng Xiaoping's personal standing.

Deng's military backing

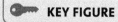 **KEY FIGURE**

Xu Shiyou (1905–85)
PLA general and the military governor of Guangzhou.

Deng was a natural survivor; he had an instinctive feel for politics, an ability to read situations and befriend the right people. One such was General **Xu Shiyou**. Following his strategic withdrawal from Beijing, Deng had put himself under the protection of Xu, a determined opponent of the Gang of Four and no supporter of Hua Guofeng. Xu's influence was strong throughout the southern and eastern provinces, which were the most prosperous and economically advanced areas of China. He used his contacts with the leading CCP officials in these regions to press for Deng's reinstatement in the Politburo. Since Deng's earlier dismissal could be blamed on the intrigues of the now disgraced Gang of Four, this proved relatively easy to achieve.

The most significant figure at this juncture was Marshall Ye Jianying. His support for Hua Guofeng had been provisional. He had backed him in order to overthrow the Gang of Four; this accomplished, his allegiance passed from Hua to Deng Xiaoping. In the Politburo, Ye became the chief spokesman for all those regional party leaders who demanded that Deng's value to the party and the nation should be recognised by his readmittance. Deng bided his time, not returning to Beijing until he was convinced that the Politburo's invitation to him to rejoin provided a genuine opportunity for him to regain power at the centre of things.

Hua's isolation

Hua Guofeng tried to retain the initiative but he was becoming increasingly isolated. Deng's supporters were growing in number throughout the party. By March 1977, the Politburo had been persuaded to make two critical decisions which effectively saw Deng Xiaoping return to centre stage. In January, in a tense atmosphere, heightened by a pro-Deng wall-poster campaign, the Politburo agreed to drop the criticism that had led to Deng's earlier expulsion; namely, that he had been guilty of **antagonistic contradiction**. With this achieved, Deng's supporters pressed for a special meeting of the Politburo to be convened in order to determine his position in the party hierarchy. In March, after weeks of lobbying, it was formally decided that Deng should be restored to his place on the Politburo and to his position as vice-chairman of the state council. Deng returned to Beijing in April 1977. By July he had resumed his role as CCP general secretary.

Deng's leadership qualities

For the next two years, Deng's influence in the party continued to grow at the expense of Hua's. Hua did not step down immediately. He retained his position as premier until 1978, but his political strength was leaking away. The majority of new members elected to provincial and national party committees were Deng's supporters. Hua attempted a rear-guard action by appealing for support to the PLA, but Deng's popularity with the army was too strong to be seriously undermined. What added to Deng's strength was his record as an economic planner, having worked with Liu Shaoqi to end the Great Famine (see page 101) and with Zhou Enlai in the early 1970s on a major programme for industrial growth. Deng's record in foreign affairs was also a great asset. Having served as assistant to China's great statesman, Zhou Enlai, the PRC's chief spokesman and negotiator from 1949 to 1976, Deng had gained an experience and reputation in foreign policy that far outstripped Hua Guofeng's.

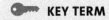 **KEY TERM**

Antagonistic contradiction Aggressive opposition to party policy.

So it was that when Deng returned to the political fore he had attributes and successes to his name that no party rival could match in his bid for leadership:

- long experience at the heart of Chinese politics
- exceptional political skills
- genuine popularity within the CCP
- support among leading party officials at the centre and in the provinces
- close relations with key military leaders
- success in ending the famine in the 1960s
- high standing as a representative of the PRC in international affairs.

Within two years of Mao Zedong's death in 1976, Deng Xiaoping, having survived denunciation and exile during the Cultural Revolution, had returned to become the dominant force in China. By the time of his death in 1997, Deng would prove to have been as remarkable a leader as Mao. Believing that Mao's economic policies had been fundamentally mistaken, Deng restructured Chinese agriculture and industry in such a way that he laid the basis for China's development as a modern nation, capable of competing commercially with the advanced nations of the world. The process began with his victory at the Third **Plenum** in 1978.

The Third Plenum 1978

The first major meeting of the CCP to gather after Mao's death became known as the Third Plenum of the Central Committee of the Chinese Communist Party. Convened in December 1978, it proved to be a landmark in China's post-Mao reformation. The decisions reached at the plenum meant a new departure for the PRC:

- The resolution 'to restore party democracy' began the process of rehabilitating those who had been wrongly condemned during the Maoist purges of the 1960s and 1970s.
- The plenum confirmed Deng's leadership of China by appointing him chairman of the People's Political Consultative Conference (PPCC), an organisation that was given the principal responsibility for economic reform in China.
- The plenum accepted Deng's Four Modernisations (see page 179), plans for the reform of agriculture, industry, defence and education, as the basis for China's development.

These resolutions of the Third Plenum clearly meant that the Cultural Revolution had been abandoned. Deng Xiaoping's personal success at the plenum, in obtaining the full support of the CCP for his proposals, also showed that he was now the outstanding figure in Chinese politics. This was soon recognised by the CCP by its conferring on him the honorary title of **paramount leader**. He feigned humility by declining to accept formal positions while knowing that he had the influence and connections to remain in control of developments. He was now in a position to begin what was to become known as the Deng revolution.

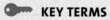

KEY TERMS

Plenum A full, authoritative gathering of the CCP.

Paramount leader The title conferred no specific powers on Deng, which made it all the more valuable to him since it placed no restrictions on him.

Undoing Mao's legacy

Since the early 1960s, when he had tackled the famine in China (see page 101), Deng had regarded the policies of the Great Leap Forward as basically wrong; he believed they had produced not growth but stagnation. Now that he was in power he was resolved to remove the remnants of Maoism that barred the path of China's economic progress. However, Deng was very conscious that Mao's impact had been so powerful that, if it were to be suddenly denounced, it would cause disruption in China. Deng judged that the Chinese people would not be able to understand an attack on Mao, the leader who had come to be regarded as a god. In the USSR, Stalin's record and reputation had become reviled within three years of his death in 1953. But there was to be no equivalent to de-Stalinisation in China. Any criticisms of Mao would have to be muted and subtle.

The Central Committee resolution 1981

Deng was also well aware that any attack on Mao would by implication be an attack on those who had served him. This would include all the current leaders of the government and the party. Far safer, therefore, to subject Mao's reputation to the **drip effect**. A CCP Central Committee resolution of 1981, drafted by Deng Xiaoping himself, revealed the compromise the party was obliged to seek. It observed that Mao Zedong had indeed been a great leader, but one who had made errors which China was now entitled to correct: 'It is true that he made gross mistakes during the Cultural Revolution, but, if we judge his activities as a whole, his contribution to the Chinese Revolution far outweighs his mistakes.' The party then declared that Mao in his policies had been 70 per cent right and 30 per cent wrong. This subtle formula left Deng and the government free to abandon Mao's policies while still appearing to be loyal to his memory.

KEY TERM

Drip effect Letting Mao's reputation gradually erode rather than formally attacking it.

The trial of the Gang of Four 1980–1

The Central Committee resolution came after another event which provided Deng and the reformers with a convenient opportunity to condemn the old Maoist ways while still appearing to honour Mao himself. In November 1980, over four years after their arrest, the members of the Gang of Four were at last put on trial. The aim was to use them as scapegoats to explain why China had gone wrong. The general accusation was that they had betrayed Mao and the Chinese Revolution. Among the specific charges against them were that during the course of the Cultural Revolution they had been individually and collectively responsible for the deaths of 35,000 people and that they had 'framed and persecuted' a further three-quarters of a million.

Jiang Qing, the principal defendant, remained totally defiant, refusing to accept the charges against her and shouting abuse at her accusers. She asserted repeatedly that she had Mao Zedong's support in everything she had done and that the Cultural Revolution had been carried out in accordance with his wishes.

SOURCE A

Caricatures of the Gang of Four hang from a Shanghai building after their failed attempt to overthrow Hua Guofeng in October 1976. The top banner reads: 'Strongly demand the reform of Shanghai Revolutionary Committee'.

? What impact would the posters shown in Source A have had on the Chinese people?

At one point she cried out: 'I was Mao's dog. Whoever he told me to bite, I bit.' Jiang's spirited resistance throughout her three-month trial embarrassed the court but it did not save her. The trials ended in January 1981 with guilty verdicts on all those charged. Jiang was sentenced to death. Subsequently, the sentence was reduced to life imprisonment in order to give her 'time to repent'. But Jiang Qing was not the repenting kind; at the time of her death ten years later in 1991 she was still angrily proclaiming her innocence.

Whatever their weakness as a public relations exercise, the trials marked a fitting final closure of the Great Proletarian Cultural Revolution. The sentencing of the Gang of Four was the new regime's way of admitting that Mao's extraordinary political and social experiment had been a lethal failure.

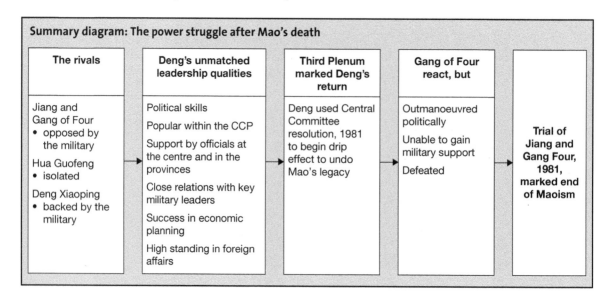

Summary diagram: The power struggle after Mao's death

The rivals	Deng's unmatched leadership qualities	Third Plenum marked Deng's return	Gang of Four react, but	
Jiang and Gang of Four • opposed by the military Hua Guofeng • isolated Deng Xiaoping • backed by the military	Political skills Popular within the CCP Support by officials at the centre and in the provinces Close relations with key military leaders Success in economic planning High standing in foreign affairs	Deng used Central Committee resolution, 1981 to begin drip effect to undo Mao's legacy	Outmanoeuvred politically Unable to gain military support Defeated	Trial of Jiang and Gang Four, 1981, marked end of Maoism

Economic reform: the Four Modernisations

▶ *What was Deng's basic approach in economic matters?*

Deng's economic aims

Throughout the 1970s, Deng had urged that realism, not theory, ought to prevail in the planning of China's economy. If a plan worked, keep it; if it did not, scrap it. If the **market** produced better results than rigid adherence to **socialist concepts**, then let the market operate freely. If contact with the capitalist West increased China's trade and commerce, then encourage such contact. This essentially practical approach was summed up in Deng's favourite saying: 'It does not matter whether a cat is black or white, so long as it catches mice.'

During Mao's time, such apparent disregard for strict socialist planning was thought too extreme and was one of the reasons why Deng had become politically suspect. But with Mao gone and the Gang of Four, fierce opponents of the liberalising of the economy, removed, the time to apply Deng's ideas had come. In 1982 he defined China's economic aims as:

- invigorating China's domestic economy
- opening Chinese trade to the outside world
- allowing the development of individual enterprises
- encouraging joint ventures with both Chinese and foreign investment.

Deng's 'hands-off' policy

It was to be an essentially 'hands-off' policy. The state would not entirely detach itself from economic planning. The state-owned enterprises (SOEs) that had been set up in Mao's time (see page 71) would remain, but much greater freedom and initiative would be granted to managers and experts on the spot. **Dogma** would give way to practicality. Purely administrative concerns would not be allowed to overrule economic considerations. Bureaucracy would be the servant, not the master of the Chinese economy. In explaining his reforms to the party, Deng stressed that the various adjustments he was pressing for all rested on two essential changes:

- the restoration of the market as the chief mechanism by which the Chinese economy operated
- the opening of China to foreign trade.

Deng intended that the methods he was adopting would be directed towards Four Modernisations within the Chinese economy. The designated areas for reform were:

- agriculture
- industry

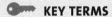

KEY TERMS

Market The operation of supply and demand without interference by the state.

Socialist concepts The structuring of the economy by the government with the aim of spreading equality.

Dogma Rigid belief in a particular approach.

- education
- defence.

The reforms can be divided into two key sections and periods. Between 1978 and 1984, the main emphasis was on the improvement of agriculture and the rural economy. After 1984, attention shifted to the development of industry and commerce.

Modernisation of agriculture

In the countryside, the commune was abandoned and replaced by the *xiang*. The *xiang* would still be required to meet food production output quotas, but, instead of these being achieved by collective work units, individual peasants and their families would contribute their due share under a new 'household responsibility system'. Provided the peasants paid their taxes and contributed to the local quotas, they were left free to sell any surplus produce for private profit. As the figures in Table 6.1 show, this policy of privatisation had notable success in the early 1980s.

Table 6.1 China's agricultural record 1978–89

Year	Grain production (million tonnes)	Meat production (million tonnes)	Index of gross output compared to base of 100 in 1952
1978	304.8	8.6	229.6
1979	332.1	10.6	249.4
1980	320.6	12.1	259.1
1981	325.0	12.6	276.2
1982	354.5	13.5	306.8
1983	387.3	14.0	330.7
1984	407.3	15.4	373.1
1985	379.1	17.6	385.7
1986	391.5	19.2	398.9
1987	404.7	19.9	422.0
1988	394.1	21.9	438.5
1989	407.8	23.3	452.0

Problems created by land reform

The undoubted benefits that the ending of collectivisation brought the peasants were offset by the continuing uncertainty about their property rights. The great majority of farmers in China held their farms on a fifteen-year lease. In most cases, privatisation did not grant permanent ownership. The legal position was that after fifteen years the land would revert back to the state. It is true that the government promised to consider extending the leases, but the bitter experiences of the Chinese peasants in the twentieth century had taught them to distrust government promises.

Doubts about the security of their land holding deterred the peasants from improving their farms or investing for long-term growth. Hence, the traditional but inefficient methods continued to prevail at the very time when the government believed its land reforms would lead farmers to embrace modernisation and expansion.

Industry and education

The relative success that had been achieved in agriculture by the mid-1980s enabled Deng and the government to turn their attention to industry. Here, he combined two of the modernisations. With the aim of promoting industrial growth and scientific education, the universities were greatly expanded in size and number. The plan was to train a million technical students to become the managers and administrators of the new economy. The same objective underlay the schemes for sending thousands of Chinese students to study abroad; this was the means by which China would gain direct knowledge of Western technology and industrial expertise.

The intention was that the students would then return to China to apply their training and experience to the development of the **Special Economic Zones (SEZs)**. The first four SEZs were Shantou and Xiamen in the north, and Shenzen and Zhuhai in the south. The SEZs became China's chief commercial outlets, modelled, although this was not officially acknowledged, on the Hong Kong pattern (see page 195). They were given regional autonomy and granted special tax concessions and financial freedoms to enable them to fulfil Deng's plea that the nation open up its commerce to the world. The SEZs proved to be one of modern China's success stories. Between 1978 and 1989 China's international trade flourished; exports grew by over 500 per cent and foreign investment in China quadrupled (see Table 6.2).

Deng's **pragmatism** in economic matters was evident in all this. He had observed that where the younger and more progressive party officials had been allowed to put their ideas into practice the results had been strikingly successful. Two particular provinces, Sichuan and Guandong, had witnessed major increases in output. Deng was impressed by the way the young managers in these regions had achieved greater output and improved quality of product by introducing wage incentives to encourage the workers to attain higher skill levels.

Problems

It was in regard to incentives that a major problem arose for Deng's reformers. Although the methods followed in Mao's SOEs had not encouraged genuine growth, they had provided the workers with an iron rice bowl (see page 71). Deng's changes, however, meant that workers and companies no longer enjoyed guaranteed incomes. Freedom from state control also meant the end of **state subsidies**. The SOEs were now expected to become efficient and competitive. Cost-saving schemes were to be introduced as means of achieving higher and cheaper output. New short-term contracts aimed at improving productivity meant that employees would now be paid according to performance and would

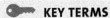

KEY TERMS

Special Economic Zones (SEZs) Areas, containing China's main export industries and companies, which were earmarked for immediate and concentrated development.

Pragmatism A way of tackling problems based on the actual situation rather than on abstract theory.

State subsidies A scheme of payments, introduced in Mao's time, to supplement the income of workers and companies.

Table 6.2 China's imports and exports balance 1978–89 (in billions of US$)

Year	Imports	Exports
1978	10.9	9.8
1979	15.7	13.7
1980	20.0	18.1
1981	22.0	22.0
1982	19.3	22.3
1983	21.4	22.2
1984	27.4	26.1
1985	42.3	27.4
1986	42.9	30.9
1987	43.2	39.4
1988	55.3	47.5
1989	59.1	52.5

retain their jobs only if they contributed genuinely to the enterprise. There were no guaranteed jobs any more.

Not surprisingly, the modernisation schemes met strong resistance from the SOEs. No matter how much the reformers emphasised the virtues of the new proposals, the workers were unwilling to lose their iron rice bowl and were slow to co-operate. This reluctance meant that the intended reforms took far longer to implement than had been planned. It took until 1986 to get a modified **labour-contract scheme** operating and then it applied only to new employees, not to established workers. The government offered further concessions in the form of unemployment insurance, but six years later the scheme covered barely one-fifth of the 80 million employees in the SOEs.

Such resistance to new ideas did not prevent progress towards industrial modernisation but it did slow it down. This indicated that in a country the size of China, with its conservative attitude among the workers and its regional variations, centralised economic planning would always be difficult to achieve. The actual success that was made is evident in Table 6.3.

Table 6.3 China's industrial performance 1979–89

Year	GDP (yuan, millions)	Yearly GDP growth rate (%)	Yearly inflation rate (%)	Yearly manufacturing output growth rate (%)
1979	732.6	7.6	6.1	8.6
1980	790.5	7.9	−1.5	11.9
1981	826.1	4.5	7.0	1.6
1982	896.3	8.5	11.5	5.5
1983	987.7	10.2	8.3	9.2
1984	1130.9	14.5	12.9	14.5
1985	1276.8	12.9	1.8	18.1
1986	1385.4	8.5	3.3	8.3
1987	1539.1	11.1	4.7	12.7
1988	1713.1	11.3	2.5	15.8
1989	1786.7	4.3	3.1	4.9

National defence

The Four Modernisations were treated by Deng not as discrete items but as parts of an interlocking programme. Defence, like education, was integrated into his overall economic strategy. A number of considerations shaped his approach towards the issue.

One consideration was that compliant and co-operative armed services were essential politically. Deng was well aware that the PLA had held the key both to the Cultural Revolution and to his successful leadership bid after Mao's death. His defeat of the Gang of Four and his ousting of Hua Guofeng could not have been accomplished without the backing of the military.

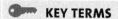

KEY TERMS

Labour-contract scheme An agreement between employers and workers, offering higher wages for increased productivity.

GDP Gross domestic product. The total value of the goods produced in a country in a year.

A second was that Deng also regarded a modernised army with up-to-date weaponry as an essential requirement for China. It was not a matter of choice. If China was to achieve growth and parity with the other world powers it had to be militarily strong. Having developed a hydrogen bomb by 1967, the PRC had become a superpower.

However, a third consideration entered the equation. In terms of funding, defence was the last of the Four Modernisations. Deng judged that, to invigorate the economy in the way he intended, priority expenditure had to go on industry and infrastructure; the PRC could not afford heavy military spending.

Deng's solution to the problem of allocating resources was to cut the military budget. He stressed that this would not weaken the military since the cut would be accompanied by a streamlining of the armed services to make them more efficient. In pursuit of this objective, troop numbers were cut in stages so that by 1990 the PLA had been reduced by a million to a national force of 3.5 million. The reduction was made less painful by absorbing the laid-off soldiers into an expanded **People's Armed Police**. Deng coined the slogan 'People's defence in modern conditions', his way of suggesting that, despite financial constraints, China's defence forces would be equipped with the sophisticated weaponry necessary in modern warfare.

Deng's argument about the need for reform of the services was given weight when the PLA performed poorly after invading Vietnam in 1979 in support of Pol Pot's Cambodia in its war with Vietnam (see page 195).

Overall economic impact of Deng's economic policies

An idea of the impact of Deng's reforms on China's economy can be gained from the following figures. The PRC was undergoing a construction boom. A foreign visitor in 1995 remarked that urban China was a vast building site.

- Between 1981 and 2000, China's economic growth averaged nine per cent every year.
- By 2000 China had become a net creditor of the USA.
- In 2000, fourteen per cent of the USA's imports were from China.

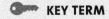

KEY TERM

People's Armed Police
Technically a civilian police force, but essentially a wing of the PLA.

Table 6.4 Production of major resources in the PRC: 1969 and 1986

	1969	1986
Coal (tonnes)	61,875,000	870,000,000
Steel (tonnes)	923,000	52,050,000
Electricity (kW-hours)	5,955,000	445,500,000
Oil (tonnes)	0	131,000,000
Sulphuric acid (tonnes)	227,000	7,700,000
Cereals (tonnes)	138,700,000	391,000,000

What growth trends during Deng's period of leadership can be identified in these figures?

By 1997 China was consuming:

- 28 per cent of the world's steel
- 35 per cent of the world's rice
- 53 per cent of the world's cement.

Between 1995 and 2010 China's:

- exports grew in value from $572 billion to $768 billion
- imports dropped from $770 billion to $650 billion
- total trade rose from $1065 billion to $1480 billion
- trade surplus tripled from $33 billion to $107 billion.

Summary diagram: Economic reform: the Four Modernisations

Deng's basic aims	Means	Methods	Reforms
To stimulate China's domestic economy To open Chinese trade to the outside world	The Four Modernisations: • agriculture • industry • defence • education	Allowing market forces to operate Subordinating theory to practical considerations Allowing the development of individual enterprises Encouraging joint ventures with both Chinese and foreign investment	**Land** End of commune, return of the *xiang* **Industry** Training of students Creation of SEZs End of the 'iron rice bowl' Export drive Drive for efficiency and productivity

---

 3 # Political stagnation and the pro-democracy movement 1979–89

▶ *Why was Deng so determined to resist political reform in China?*

Deng Xiaoping's opposition to political reform

An important point to stress is that Deng's programme for regenerating China was as much concerned with political conservatism as it was with economic progress. He had emphasised this strongly when introducing his reforms. Deng balanced the Four Modernisations with the 'Four Cardinal Principles', which he defined as:

- keeping to the socialist road
- upholding the people's democratic dictatorship
- upholding leadership by the Communist Party
- upholding Marxism–Leninism and Mao Zedong thought.

What is noticeable about these principles is that, unlike the Four Modernisations, they were a formula not for change but for the maintenance of the existing political structure. They were essentially a restating of the concept of democratic centralism, the idea that the CCP as the voice of Marxist correctness was entitled to the absolute obedience of the people (see page 45). 'We are striving for socialist modernization, rather than other modernizations. We should take a clear-cut stand to uphold the Four Cardinal Principles and carry out a protracted struggle against bourgeois liberalization.'

As Deng saw it, China's first need was for internal stability; without this the nation could not modernise and take its proper place in the world. He said that China, having just gone through the bitter experience of the Cultural Revolution, needed a rest from politics. He meant by this that China should move away from debate and discussion and devote itself to the task of making itself a powerful economic nation. 'Our task is to build up the country, and less important things should be subordinated to it.'

It was Deng's thinking that inspired a 1980 resolution of the National People's Congress which condemned the liberal view that the people 'have the right to speak out freely, air their views fully, and hold great debates'. China could not afford to indulge in popular democracy along Western lines. It would merely cause distraction and disruption.

Deng's basic political attitude

Deng Xiaoping was a committed reformer but only in the economic sphere. In politics, he was a Communist hard liner. His aim was to restore the morale and standing of the CCP after the disruptive decades of the Great Leap Forward and the Cultural Revolution. He wanted to show that the Communist Party was still capable of governing China and had the right to the loyalty of the people. Like Mao, he was part product, part creator, of the turbulent history of China through which he had lived since the 1920s. His belief in the authority of the CCP as the only party with the right to hold power was unshakeable. It was this conviction that made a major showdown between the old-guard CCP and the supporters of democracy increasingly likely.

The 'democracy wall'

In the Avenue of Eternal Peace, near Tiananmen Square, there stretched a 200-metre brick wall. In the late 1970s, the avenue became a common gathering place for students, who established the practice of affixing to the wall a mass of literature from small personal letters to large posters. The writings covered every conceivable subject and gave an obvious opportunity for the public expression of anti-government and anti-party feelings. Periodically, the government forbade the 'democracy wall' to be used in this way; it ordered the posters to be torn down and had the more outspoken of the critics arrested.

One such occasion occurred early in 1979 when **Wei Jingsheng**, a former Red Guard, used the wall as part of his personal campaign to call the government to account for its failure to introduce real democratic freedoms into China. He was particularly critical of the PRC's recent foreign policy blunders. When Wei sought to reveal details of China's disastrous showing in Vietnam (see page 195), he was arrested and sentenced to fifteen years in prison.

The democracy movement

Wei may be regarded as the first martyr in what became known as the democracy movement. This was never an organised party and its numbers and strength fluctuated, but it broadly represented those intellectuals who saw in Deng's reforms the opportunity not only to modernise the economy but also to liberalise the political system. The movement did not initially challenge the authority of the CCP, but it urged that Deng and the government should honour the Communist principles that they supposedly espoused. In particular, it asked that the party's commitment to the rule of the people should not merely be a slogan but should be genuinely upheld by extending Deng Xiaoping's 'Four Fundamentals' to include a fifth: the adoption of democracy. Wei Jingsheng had been the first to ask on a wall poster why there was no fifth modernisation (see Source B).

According to Source B, what are the characteristics of the 'fifth modernisation'?

SOURCE B

From the 'Fifth Modernization' essay posted on the democracy wall in 1978, quoted in Wei Jingsheng, *The Courage to Stand Alone: Letters from Prison*, Penguin, 1997, p. 208.

Of course, internal problems cannot be solved overnight but must be constantly addressed as part of a long-term process. Mistakes and shortcomings will be inevitable, but these are for us to worry about. This is infinitely better than facing abusive overlords against whom there is no redress. Those who worry that democracy will lead to anarchy and chaos are just like those who, following the overthrow of the Qing dynasty, worried that without an emperor the country would fall into chaos. Their decision was to patiently suffer oppression because they feared that without the weight of oppression, their spines might completely collapse! To such people, I would like to say, with all due respect: We want to be the masters of our own destiny. We need no gods or emperors and we don't believe in saviors of any kind. We do not want to serve as mere tools of dictators with personal ambitions for carrying out modernization. We want to modernize the lives of the people. Democracy, freedom, and happiness for all are our sole objectives.

For long periods, the democrats were broadly tolerated but they were always likely to be turned against whenever the government felt objections had gone too far. This explains the severity of Wei Jingsheng's punishment. It was intended as a warning to those intellectuals and journalists who mistakenly believed that it had become permissible in post-Mao China to criticise the party and government.

Charges of corruption against the government

The charge which most disturbed the authorities was that government in China had become corrupt. In the late 1970s a notorious case of racketeering came to light in Heilongjiang province when it was revealed that the managers of a state-owned fuel and power company had been diverting large sums of public money into their own pockets. The chief embezzlers were put on public trial and executed.

The government expected to gain credit from this widely publicised example of its resolute response. Yet the fact was that the scandal had come to light only through the tenacity of an investigative journalist whose exposé forced the authorities to take action. Furthermore, the chief culprits in the Heilongjiang case were all leading members of the provincial CCP. Critics began to ask just how widespread was corruption within the party.

Demonstrations spread

The belief that there was something implicitly corrupt about the CCP's management of China underlay the series of student demonstrations that occurred sporadically throughout the 1980s. The common demand of these protests was for greater political democracy and economic opportunity. Major disturbances occurred in 1986 in universities in Hefei, Wuhan and Shanghai. Thousands of students followed Fang Lizhi (who was both a professor at Hefei and a CCP member) in calling for the open government and democracy that the authorities continually talked of but never delivered.

The government quelled the disturbances by sacking Fang, arresting the ringleaders and dismissing the troubles as the work of an anti-social minority. But how deeply the government had been shaken was evident in its removal of **Hu Yaobang**, the CCP general secretary. The party blamed Hu for having encouraged the student troubles by criticising the slow pace of political change.

Deng's rejection of democracy

After the crushing of the 1986 protests, Deng thought it appropriate at this point to restate his rejection of 'bourgeois liberalisation'. He defined this as the mistaken notion which had developed among some party members since the defeat of the Gang of Four that modernisation involved moving towards Western-style democracy. Deng spelled out why genuine democracy was not an option for the Chinese. It was essentially a matter of practicalities, as described in Source C.

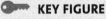

KEY FIGURE

Hu Yaobang (1915–89)

A protégé of Deng Xiaoping, he had been a prominent figure in the party until his dismissal for being too sympathetic to the dissident students.

On what grounds does Deng Xiaoping argue that China must not 'liberalize', as described in Source C?

SOURCE C

From Deng's speech in 1986, quoted in Deng Xiaoping, *Fundamental Issues in Present-Day China*, Foreign Languages Press, 1987, p. 43.

Since the defeat of the Gang of Four an ideological trend has appeared which we call bourgeois liberalization. It exponents worship the 'democracy' and 'freedom' of Western capitalist countries and reject socialism. This cannot be allowed. China must modernise, but it must absolutely not liberalize or take the capitalist road.

China is such a huge country, with such an enormous population, so many nationalities and such varied conditions that it is not yet possible to hold direct elections at higher levels. Furthermore, the people's educational level is too low. So we have to stick to the system of people's congresses, in which democratic centralism is applied. Without the leadership of the Communist Party, there can be no building of socialism.

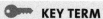

KEY TERM

Progressive thinkers
Those with a forward-looking attitude, who were beginning to demand that power and privilege in China should not be the monopoly of the leaders of the CCP.

Deng's statement captured the fundamental difference of outlook between the CCP hard liners and the **progressive thinkers** who made up the pro-democracy movement. What Deng was declaring was that there was no need for greater participation by the people in Chinese politics; the uninformed people should be content to let their enlightened government lead them. However, for Chinese progressives this was no longer an acceptable attitude; as they saw it, developments in China had shown that left to itself the government was incapable of providing those advances that they had come to expect and to which they believed they were entitled.

Mounting frustration

For many Chinese, the reforms introduced by Deng in the period 1979–89 proved deeply disappointing. This was the result of a number of factors:

- After the initial economic spurt of the early 1980s, there had been a serious downturn in agricultural and industrial production.
- The ending of the subsidy system had created uncertainty and anxiety among the workers and had removed the shield which had protected the urban dwellers from high prices.
- Inflation had reduced the workers' real wages.
- The growing population and the continuing movement of people from the countryside into the urban areas had led to severe overcrowding in the major cities.

These developments had undermined the improved standards of living that had been experienced in the early years of Deng's reforms. It seemed that aspirations had been raised only to be dashed. Students and intellectuals felt that, despite the promise of progress and reform held out by the modernisation programme, the Communist Party under Deng Xiaoping had failed to deliver.

Poor job prospects were a particular anxiety among the students. In the late 1970s, in accordance with the Four Modernisations programme, there had been an explosion in the numbers entering higher education. But a decade later it was evident that employment opportunities had failed to keep pace with the rising number of graduates. There was resentment that such jobs as were available were reserved for party members and their children. It was this grievance that fuelled the anger over government corruption.

The Tiananmen Square Massacre, June 1989

In Beijing, in the summer of 1989, an event took place that shocked the world: the shooting on government orders of thousands of unarmed demonstrators in Tiananmen Square. The massacre was a violent climax to the tensions that had been building up since Mao's death. It was a product of basic problems in China that Deng's reforms, far from solving, had intensified.

The path to the massacre

On 15 April 1989, the death of Hu Yaobang focused the minds of all those who were unhappy with the economic and political system under Deng Xiaoping. Hu had not always been sympathetic to the demands for greater democracy, but all that was forgotten at his passing. What was remembered was his removal from government in 1987 for daring to support the student protests. He had been forced to undergo self-criticism and had received such harsh treatment that his health had broken. Posthumously he was elevated by the students into a symbol of resistance whose death from a heart attack was blamed on the harassment he had suffered for having upheld democratic values.

By the time of Hu's memorial service, a week after his death, large crowds had gathered in Tiananmen Square. They demonstrated noisily as three kneeling students tried to press a petition into the hands of Premier **Li Peng** and other government officials making their way into the **Great Hall of the People** to attend the service. The refusal of Li and his colleagues to accept the petition was taken as a sign of how far the government had become detached from the people. A series of sit-ins and boycotts of university classes quickly followed.

Demonstrators occupy Tiananmen Square

The number of protesters rose as students from over 40 universities in China then came to join their fellows in Tiananmen Square. A worrying sign for the government was the solidarity the transport workers showed with the students by allowing them to travel to Beijing without charge. The *People's Daily*, the official CCP newspaper and the government's mouthpiece, raised the temperature by denouncing all this as the work of 'a small handful of plotters' who must be crushed immediately (see Source D).

SOURCE D

An extract adapted from an editorial, 'It is Necessary to Take a Clear-cut Stand Against Disturbances', in the *People's Daily* editorial, 26 April 1989, retrieved from the Foreign Broadcast Information Service, 25 April 1989, p. 23.

If we are tolerant of this disturbance and let it go unchecked, a seriously chaotic state will appear. Then, the reform and opening up; the improvement of the economic environment and the rectification of the economic order, construction,

KEY FIGURE

Li Peng (1928–)
A Soviet-trained, hard-line Communist, totally opposed to any concessions to the democracy movement.

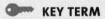

KEY TERM

Great Hall of the People
A large parliament building overlooking Tiananmen Square.

According to the *People's Daily* in Source D, what threat to the PRC do the Tiananmen Square protesters represent?

and development; the control over prices; the improvement of our living standards; the drive to oppose corruption; and the development of democracy and the legal system expected by the people throughout the country, including the young students, will all become empty hopes. Even the tremendous achievements scored in the reform during the past decade may be completely lost, and the great aspiration of the revitalization of China cherished by the whole nation will be hard to realize. A China with very good prospects and a very bright future will become a chaotic and unstable China without any future. … Bans should be placed on unlawful parades and demonstrations.

All comrades in the party and the people throughout the country must soberly recognize the fact that our country will have no peaceful days if this disturbance is not checked resolutely. This struggle concerns the success or failure of the program of the four modernizations, and the future of our state and nation.

🔑 KEY FIGURES

Zhao Ziyang (1919–2005)

CCP general secretary (1986–9), he became distrusted by government colleagues because of his sympathy towards the protesters.

Mikhail Gorbachev (1931–)

The reforming leader of the Soviet Union between 1985 and 1991.

A prominent government figure, **Zhao Ziyang**, tried to appease the protesters by making a public statement in which he suggested that the *People's Daily* had gone too far. But the demonstration in Tiananmen Square had begun to develop a momentum. By the second week of May a group of 300 students had gone on hunger strike. For the first time, the government made direct contact with student representatives, urging them to call off the strike. A number of China's leading writers added their voice to this appeal but at the same time pleaded with the government to recognise the protest as a genuinely patriotic movement.

The demonstrators declined to abandon their protest because they believed that events had given them two advantages that they could exploit:

- The wide international media coverage that they were receiving, with many foreign camera crews and journalists having taken up residence in the square, would restrict the Chinese government's freedom of action.
- The government's hands would also be tied by the imminent arrival in Beijing of **Mikhail Gorbachev**, the Soviet leader, on an official visit. The students revered Gorbachev as the progressive socialist leader who was introducing into his country the very reforms that they were demanding for China. They believed that while he was present in China the government would not dare to crush their demonstration.

Government attitudes harden

The protesters had overestimated the strength of their position. The visit of Gorbachev may have indeed delayed the authorities taking firm action but their anger at having to change his schedule made the hard liners still more resolute against the protesters. With Tiananmen Square now occupied by rebellious students, the plan to impress Gorbachev with the type of organised mass rally which the PRC customarily put on for important foreign visitors had to be curtailed. The talks between the Soviet and Chinese leaders did go ahead but in a strangely unreal atmosphere.

On 19 May, the sixth day of the hunger strike and the day that Gorbachev left China, Zhao Ziyang again went down to the Square to address the students. He tearfully promised them that the issues over which they were protesting would eventually be resolved. Li Peng also spoke briefly to the students, but his was a perfunctory visit; it seems that he and Deng Xiaoping had already decided that the demonstrations were to be ended by force. It was this that gave particular poignancy to Zhao's parting words to the students, 'I came too late, too late. We are too old to see the day when China is strong. But you are young. You should stay alive.'

Martial law imposed and the reaction of Beijing residents

That same evening Zhao was dismissed from his post, and Li Peng, in a broadcast speech in which he condemned the students as 'rioters', formally declared the imposition of martial law. The news of the government's intention to apply 'firm and resolute measures to end the turmoil' rallied the students who had begun to waver. They voted to continue their occupation of the square. It is arguable that this is what the hard liners in the government had wanted. Were the demonstrators to have peacefully dispersed at this point it would have deprived the authorities of the chance to make an example of them.

However, things did not go entirely the government's way. When news of the demonstrators' determination to stay in the square became known thousands who had earlier given up now returned, their numbers swelled by the ordinary people of Beijing. It was these Beijing residents who blocked the roads and avenues leading to Tiananmen Square and prevented the first wave of troops, sent to impose martial law, from reaching the square. The troops were bewildered by this show of popular resistance. After discussions with the leaders of the demonstration their commanders ordered their men to withdraw to the outskirts of Beijing.

The PLA moves in

These events proved to be merely the lull before the storm. With Zhao removed and Li Peng and Deng now prepared to exercise full authority, the plans for ending the protest were activated. Crack troops led by commanders specially appointed by President **Yang Shangkun** and Deng Xiaoping advanced on Beijing. By 2 June, 350,000 PLA soldiers had surrounded Tiananmen Square and had secured the routes leading to it. This time the troops were not to be deterred by the pleas of the local people.

The PLA commanders described the action as a 'full military campaign' to overcome the determined resistance of the 'rebels' occupying Tiananmen Square. The troops were instructed to reclaim the square 'at all costs'. Tanks and armoured personnel carriers rumbled into position. At 10.00p.m. on the night of 3 June the first shots were fired into the demonstrators. Shooting continued

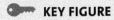

KEY FIGURE

Yang Shangkun (1907–98)
President of the PRC and a leading figure in the PLA; he gave Deng his strong-arm support in crushing the student protest.

intermittently through the hours of darkness and into the morning. By mid-day on 4 June the occupation was over.

The scene was one of carnage. Twisted barricades crushed by the PLA tanks lay strewn around, mixed with the accumulated garbage of the six-week occupation. At regular intervals, lines of exhausted, injured and broken-spirited students were marched away for interrogation and imprisonment.

The number of dead and injured will probably never be precisely known but calculations suggest that the figure ran into thousands. Included in the figures are the people killed in the surrounding streets and the PLA soldiers beaten to death by outraged crowds. Despite the news blackout that the government immediately imposed, the information that leaked out regarding the number of victims treated in Beijing's hospitals confirmed that a massacre had occurred.

In the following weeks, demonstrators who had escaped from Tiananmen Square but had not been able to flee the country were rounded up. Reprisals followed. Those identified as ringleaders were given stiff prison sentences. CCP officials who had shown sympathy for the protesters were dismissed for their wrong-headedness, while those who had resisted the demonstrators were promoted for their loyalty to the party.

The significance of the massacre

The strong likelihood is that Deng and the Chinese leaders wanted a violent end to the affair. The protesters were to be made to atone in blood for their two months' defiance of the government. The resort to tanks and bullets was intended to impress on the Chinese both the seriousness of the challenge of

> The photo in Source E has become one of the most immediately recognisable images relating to the Tiananmen Square massacre. Why is this?

SOURCE E

A lone man halts a line of tanks in Beijing on 5 June 1989. Details of who he was and his subsequent fate are still obscure, but it is thought that having been pulled away and smuggled back into the crowd he was later arrested by the authorities and imprisoned for a lengthy period. It is known that a number of the demonstrators rounded up after the massacre were still being held in prison as late as 2014.

the 'plotters' to civil order and the determination of the government not to tolerate such rebellion. The massacre in Tiananmen Square was very much in the Chinese tradition of crushing opposition by the severest means in order to emphasise the illegitimacy of opposition itself. It was the surest confirmation that Deng Xiaoping's reforms did not include an extension of political freedoms. The CCP was willing to consider sweeping economic change in China. What it would not contemplate was giving up its authority over the Chinese people.

Deng's attitude after Tiananmen Square

The massacre confirmed that under Deng the PRC remained an authoritarian Communist regime. Yet there were strains within the government and party. Deng was aware that what he called a left and a right had developed within the CCP. By the left, he meant those members who were unhappy about the pace at which China was embracing economic liberalism and did not want reform to undermine the PRC's Communist character. By the right, he meant those in the party keen to move even faster towards economic growth, towards 'total Westernization'. Deng saw it as his task to hold a balance between these two, for if either influence became too strong it could destroy what had been achieved by his reforms. In a sense, Deng had defined the basic problem that had confronted the PRC since its foundation in 1949: how to modernise the nation and at the same time be true to the principles of Chinese communism.

By the early 1990s this had become an even more difficult problem. The **velvet revolutions** in Europe suggested that communism was a spent political force. But where did that leave Communist China? Should it cling to the belief that it was a leader of international revolution or should it return to China's traditional view of itself as a unique culture separate from all others? Of one thing Deng was sure: China could not detach itself from the world economically. Its survival as a nation depended on its capacity to produce and to trade.

Deng Xiaoping was a realist and a pragmatist. His own bitter experiences during the Chinese civil war, the Great Leap Forward, the Cultural Revolution, and now Tiananmen Square, had convinced him that China's greatest need was stability. He further believed that the only way to preserve this was by retaining the Communist system in China. Communism, for Deng, mattered less as a revolutionary ideology than as a practical system for preserving China from internal chaos. Communism was the new Confucianism; it was a set of common values that enabled China to function as a harmonious society. It followed, as it had in Confucian times, that those who disrupted that harmony were deserving of the severest punishment by the state.

Continuing repression under Deng

One of Deng's observations after Tiananmen Square was that China suffered from 'too much politics'. His meaning was that the PRC, having gone through the troubles of its first four decades of existence, now had an established socialist

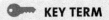
KEY TERM

Velvet revolutions
The non-violent popular movements in the Soviet-controlled Eastern bloc countries in the late 1980s, which brought down the Communist governments and led to the collapse of the USSR itself in 1991.

governmental system. It was time, therefore, for the people to abandon thoughts of political conflict. The politics had been settled; the CCP would guide the people, whose task now was to build China into a great economic power. What outsiders might call political stagnation, Deng saw as the natural political conservatism which maintained the revolution. If that sounded paradoxical, it was the type of paradox that was basic to Marxism.

It was because he was, in Chinese terms, a political conservative that Deng Xiaoping presided over an increasingly repressive regime. A notable victim was Wei Jingsheng, who in 1979 had been the first martyr in the government's crackdown on the protests that began at the democracy wall in Beijing. Wei's original sentence of eighteen years was increased by another fourteen years in 1993 for 'subversion'. His crime this time was that in June 1989, while in prison, he had condemned the government for its massacre of the demonstrators in Tiananmen Square.

At the time of his second sentence in 1993, *The Observer's* Hong Kong correspondent wrote: 'Wei is the nightmare scenario made flesh, the man who more than anyone else proves Beijing to be incapable of tolerating dissenting views, even if they are peacefully expressed.' Wei was eventually released in 1997. This was not an act of remission, but simply that the Chinese authorities did not want the embarrassment of Wei, who appeared to be seriously ill, dying in prison. The political rigidity of Deng's outlook was further illustrated by the statistic that at his death in 1997, there were more political prisoners held in China than there had been in 1976 at the time of Mao's passing.

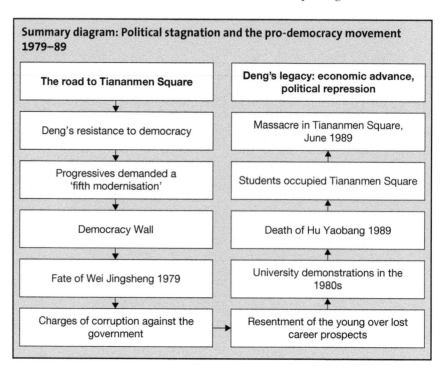

Summary diagram: Political stagnation and the pro-democracy movement 1979–89

The road to Tiananmen Square	Deng's legacy: economic advance, political repression
Deng's resistance to democracy	Massacre in Tiananmen Square, June 1989
Progressives demanded a 'fifth modernisation'	Students occupied Tiananmen Square
Democracy Wall	Death of Hu Yaobang 1989
Fate of Wei Jingsheng 1979	University demonstrations in the 1980s
Charges of corruption against the government	Resentment of the young over lost career prospects

China as a global power

▶ *How did the PRC's international standing and status change under Deng Xiaoping after 1978?*

Deng Xiaoping's greatest success as leader was undoubtedly the transformation of the PRC into a world economic and commercial power. But before that status could be achieved, he felt it necessary to seek to resolve a number of issues, which he had inherited. He regarded them as regional or border problems but they overlapped at many points with foreign policy.

Deng and Vietnam

In 1975, a Marxist revolution had also taken place in Cambodia. **Pol Pot** had seized power after a successful guerrilla war modelled on Maoist strategy. The regime Pol Pot led was a savage one, but his Maoist credentials made him a hero to the Chinese. When the Soviet-backed Vietnamese launched a major offensive into Cambodia in 1979 to overthrow Pol Pot, Deng's China came to his aid by invading Vietnam, with the principal aim of preventing the Soviet Union from establishing its authority there.

The official PRC version of what followed led the Chinese people to believe that the PLA had gained a resounding military success, thereby illustrating the success of Deng's fourth modernisation: China's military reorganisation. This was the opposite of the truth. The PLA suffered heavy casualties and was forced to withdraw from Vietnam, having failed to prevent Pol Pot's defeat by the Vietnamese. Although it was withheld from public knowledge in China, the PRC had undergone a serious reverse. Nevertheless, it was a clear sign of the PRC's determination to establish its influence over its southern neighbours in Asia. The problem of Soviet influence resolved itself a decade later when the USSR collapsed.

The PRC and Hong Kong

More obvious diplomatic and strategic success came to Deng in his recovery of **Hong Kong**. In 1842, China had granted Britain the island of Hong Kong on a permanent basis. In 1860 Britain formally added Kowloon, the harbour directly facing Hong Kong island, to its permanent possessions. The third piece of territory, Kowloon peninsula, on which the harbour stood, was gained by Britain in 1898. This last piece, known as the New Territories, was not granted to Britain permanently but only on a 99-year lease.

The British colony of Hong Kong so formed in 1898 was to develop over the following century into a highly prosperous city. After the Communist takeover of mainland China in 1949 it became a haven for those fleeing from the PRC. Thousands of businessmen and bankers, who brought their wealth with them, settled in Hong Kong and quickly turned it into a world commercial

 KEY FIGURE

Pol Pot (1925–98)
Notorious for the brutality of his dictatorial rule in Cambodia (1975–9), which killed a quarter of the 8 million population.

Hong Kong.

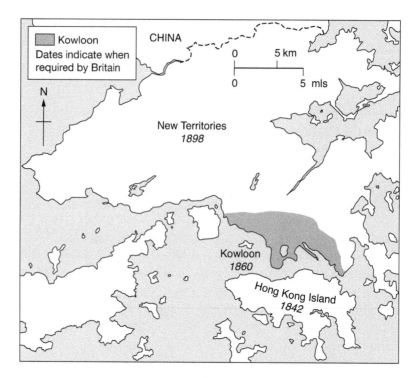

CHINA

Kowloon
Dates indicate when
required by Britain

N

New Territories
1898

0   5 km

0   5 mls

Kowloon
1860

Hong Kong Island
1842

and financial centre. This produced a mixture of resentment and admiration in China's Communist rulers. Nowhere in the PRC was there anything to match Hong Kong's capitalist economic miracle. Yet, the PRC could take deep satisfaction from the thought that under the terms of the 1898 agreement, Hong Kong, 'the pearl of the orient', would return to China in 1997. Deng Xiaoping anticipated that it would add a huge asset to his modernisation plans for China.

There was a problem, however. Opinion polls showed that 95 per cent of the Hong Kong people wanted to remain British. Would Britain use this as a justification for resisting China's claim? In strictly legal terms, Britain had a case for doing so. According to the earlier treaties, Kowloon and the island of Hong Kong were permanent British possessions. It was only the New Territories that were leased. The PRC expected to meet difficulties and prepared for a long diplomatic battle. PRC–UK talks began in 1979. British Prime Minister **Margaret Thatcher** was personally involved in the negotiations from 1982 onwards. Deng Xiaoping took a hard line. He told Mrs Thatcher that the PRC regarded Hong Kong as a part of sovereign Chinese territory and there was no question of Britain's lease being extended. 'I would rather see Hong Kong torched than leave Britain to rule it after 1997', he told her.

Deng knew that he also held the moral high ground. His argument was that, whatever the legal niceties involved, Britain's claim to Hong Kong was founded on dated imperialist concepts. The British had originally acquired the colony through superior military strength, forcing China to sign away Hong Kong against its will. It was, said Deng, an example of colonialism at its most

KEY FIGURE

**Margaret Thatcher
(1925–2013)**

British prime minister between 1979 and 1990, the first British premier to go to China while in office.

exploitative. The *People's Daily* commented bitterly: '150 years ago, to maintain its drug trafficking in China, Britain launched the aggressive **Opium War** against China, during which it carried out burning, killing, rape, and plunder on Chinese soil.'

The Joint Declaration of 1984

Aware of its weak bargaining position, all Britain could work for was a compromise that would give Hong Kong some protection after it returned to China. This came in the form of the Sino-British Joint Declaration, signed in December 1984:

- Britain agreed that on the expiry of the lease on the New Territories in 1997 all the areas that made up Hong Kong would return to the PRC.
- In return, the Chinese Communists declared that Hong Kong after 1997 would be treated as a Special Administrative Region (SAR) until 2047. This would leave its capitalist economic structure unaltered.

Whatever the British concerns over the future of Hong Kong may have been, it was clear that its concessions to the PRC had given Deng all that he had wanted. He had asserted his country's sovereignty and regained what was now Asia's most prosperous city. Deng Xiaoping described the planned 50-year coexistence of the Communist mainland with the SAR as 'one country, two systems'.

Deng and Tibet

The PRC's relations with Tibet, which it regarded not as a separate nation but as one of its outlying provinces, had been strained since the PLA had first imposed itself on the region in 1950 (see pages 47 and 53). Under Deng Xiaoping there was an apparent easing; his government tried to emphasise to the Tibetans the great advantages of co-operation with Beijing. The benefits that 'reunification' could bring were dangled before them: education, health care, modern transport, and an end to Tibet's backward and inefficient ways.

The majority of the Tibetan people remained unimpressed. They knew that beneath the allure of such things was the same Chinese determination to intensify the occupation and destroy Tibet's separate identity. In 1985 the Tibetans' refusal to celebrate the twentieth anniversary of the **TAR** became the prelude to further open resistance that went on into the late 1980s. There were violent clashes when China sent in further detachments of the PLA to crush what threatened to become a Tibetan national revolt. From exile, the Dalai Lama denounced China's actions in Tibet as 'cultural genocide'. To the anger of Beijing, his passionate defence of his country led to his being awarded the Nobel Peace Prize in 1989. This was more than a personal tribute; it was an implicit international recognition of the justice of Tibet's cause. It was also a rebuff to Deng Xiaoping's hopes of gaining international acceptance of the PRC's Tibetan policies by persuading the Dalai Lama to end his self-imposed exile and return to his homeland.

 **KEY TERMS**

Opium War In the nineteenth century, Britain had sent warships to force China to buy large quantities of the opium produced in British Burma, a humiliation which remained a basic historical reference point for many Chinese in their distrust of the West.

TAR Tibetan Autonomous Region, dating from 1965 when Mao's government tried to give a semblance of legality to its control of Tibet by declaring it to be a self-governing region.

The Lhasa rising 1993

That the PRC's methods had not totally crushed Tibetan resistance became evident in 1993 when the largest protest in China since the 1989 Tiananmen Square demonstration occurred in Lhasa, Tibet's capital. The same predictable Chinese response followed; the PLA were sent in and thousands of arrests were made. Those imprisoned were treated brutally. The **Panchen Lama** was seized by the Chinese and taken into 'protective custody'; a euphemism for house arrest. Through its contacts in Tibet, **Asia Watch** was able to give the Western media detailed accounts of the lethal actions of the Chinese in Lhasa.

Tibetan refugees visited the UN headquarters in New York to present the horror story. Great concern was shown by the international community about China's affront to human rights but no concerted action was taken. From 1950, when it was first invaded, it had been clear Tibet lacked the strategic and economic importance to make it an area for intervention by the great powers. Deng could be confident that the Tibetan issue would not seriously compromise China's international standing.

Xinjiang

In Deng's time, Xinjiang continued to be a concern as the predominantly Muslim Uighur people grew increasingly restless with control from Beijing (see page 121). Incidents of protest multiplied and both sides accused the other of using excessive force. The severity of Chinese suppression of Uighur demonstrations was one of the violations that international bodies such as Human Rights Watch condemned.

The Taiwan issue

When Deng Xiaoping began addressing the Taiwan question, he was encouraged by a particular development that had occurred: increasing economic contact between the island and mainland China. Although this was unofficial, it was of major importance since it suggested that China and Taiwan were not irretrievably separated. Deng appeared willing to reverse the idea that the PRC would never tolerate the existence of two Chinas. In 1984, he declared: 'The main system in China must be socialism. The one billion people on the mainland will continue to live under the socialist system, but a capitalist system will be allowed to exist in certain areas, such as Hong Kong and Taiwan.'

Sovereignty

The tone of Deng's remarks was very much in accord with the 'nine principles' presented by the PRC in 1981 which set out a programme for 'the return of Taiwan to the motherland for the peaceful reunification of China'. A key principle had read: 'After the country is unified, Taiwan can enjoy a high degree of autonomy as a special administrative region.' At first sight this clause seemed to suggest that the PRC was willing to recognise Taiwan's independence. But this was a misreading. Communist China may have softened its tone but on one essential it had not changed. Behind the more accommodating words there was the same resolution not to budge on the matter of the PRC's absolute right to govern the whole of China. Deng had made this clear in 1983 when he insisted in a formal statement that it was 'the People's Republic of China that alone represents China'.

Thus, despite the better relations that had emerged between Taiwan and the mainland in the 1980s, the basic position remained unchanged; neither side was prepared to concede any substantial ground on the issue of sovereignty. In the 1990s the PRC and Taiwan, each in its separate way, remained wholly committed to the notion that it was the legitimate China. They both wanted reunification but they had totally contrary understandings of what that meant. The PRC had recovered Hong Kong in 1997. That success inspired the Chinese Communists to believe that the return of Taiwan was also possible. That was why Deng's government resolutely resisted Taiwan's appeals in the 1990s for diplomatic recognition and re-entry into the UN. It was an unresolved issue that would long outlive Deng Xiaoping.

The PRC in Africa

Hong Kong, Tibet and Taiwan could be regarded as falling within the PRC's regional concerns. But under Deng, the PRC began to extend its influence into the wider world. It began to make inroads into Africa in a policy that Deng's successors were to expand greatly. Confident that there was unlikely to be any major resistance from the Western powers, which were inhibited by their **post-imperial guilt**, China made a series of commercial and financial deals with the leaders of a large number of African states. Disregarding the legitimacy or human rights record of the regimes they dealt with, the PRC was concerned only with establishing an economic hold. As a Ugandan academic put it: 'Wherever there are resources the Chinese are going to go there. They see no evil. They hear no evil.'

By the time of Deng's death in 1997, the PRC was in the early stage of what would become a huge expansion into Africa. An area of central Africa stretching from Sudan to Namibia had been targeted. China's chief economic aim was to obtain cheap raw materials: Chinese companies negotiated lucrative contracts allowing them to extract oil, metal ores, diamonds and timber. China also provided aid and cheap loans as a way of establishing a strong commercial foothold. One of China's advantages in seeking influence in Africa is that it presented itself as having a special historical link with Africa, claiming that from Mao onwards, revolutionary China has been a beacon for the emergent nations struggling to throw off their colonial masters. It is certainly the case that the PRC had sent economic and military assistance to a number of African countries. Deng's China now began to reap the benefits of this policy.

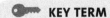 **KEY TERM**

Post-imperial guilt The notion that the exploitative record of the ex-colonial powers denied them the moral right to interfere in the regions they had once held.

China's international standing

Deng Xiaoping's impact on China's standing as an international power was as significant as his impact on its domestic situation. In the post-Mao years, under his modernisation programme, China chose not merely to look out on the world but, in Deng's words, 'to open itself to it'. He was not being high-minded and internationalist. He truly believed that China's future as a nation depended on expanding its commercial contacts throughout the world. The gains to China's reputation which this brought appeared to have been blighted, if not undone, in 1989, when the Tiananmen Square massacre reminded the West that China, for all its economic advances, was still run by a hard-line Communist regime.

Yet, surprisingly, in view of the international condemnation of the Chinese government for its brutality, the event did not cause long-term damage to the PRC's expanding commercial contacts with the USA. The truth is that the USA and the West generally were willing to swallow their misgivings about China's internal politics and to continue trading. The US State Department summed up the approach as 'engagement without endorsement'; it enabled the West to keep its commercial links with China while remaining critical of the violation of human rights by the Chinese government.

China and the USA

In advancing his programme for China's opening itself to the world, Deng Xiaoping was undoubtedly assisted by the more pliant attitude of the USA. Sino-American rapprochement, which had begun with the PRC's switching its recognition from GMD's Taiwan to the PRC (see page 167), and continued through the 1970s, reaching its highest point so far in 1979 with the establishment of full diplomatic relations between the two countries. In that year, Deng Xiaoping accepted a presidential invitation to visit the USA, where he made a favourable impression on the politicians and enthusiastic crowds who greeted him. Such events did not immediately wipe out the mutual suspicion created by years of East–West hostility, but the machinery for diplomatic contact and trade was now in place. A key result was the granting of **Most Favored Nation** status to the PRC in 1994 (see Source F).

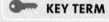 **KEY TERM**

Most Favored Nation An arrangement in which the USA offers a selected country privileged commercial and financial terms.

In Source F, how does President Clinton acknowledge China's position as a global power?

SOURCE F

Adapted from 'Remarks by President Clinton during the Announcement of the Renewal of MFN [most-favoured nation] Status for China', 26 May 1994, quoted in Pei-kai Cheng and Michael Lestz, editors, *The Search for Modern China: A Documentary Collection*, W.W. Norton, 1999, pp. 514–15.

Our relationship with China is important to all Americans. We have significant interests in what happens there and what happens between us. China has an atomic arsenal and a vote and a veto in the UN Security Council. It is a major factor in Asian and global security. We share important interests, such as in a nuclear-free Korean peninsula and in sustaining the global environment. China is also the world's fastest growing economy. Over $8 billion of United States exports to China last year supported 150,000 American jobs.

I have decided that the United States should renew Most Favored Nation trading status toward China. The decision, I believe, offers us the best opportunity to lay the basis for long-term sustainable progress in human rights, and for the advancement of our other interests with China. I am moving, therefore, to delink human rights from the annual extension of Most Favored Nation status for China. That linkage has been constructive during the past years, but I believe we have reached the end of the usefulness of that policy.

What Clinton was, in effect, saying was that in a tough competitive global market, human rights considerations, while important, could not be allowed to interfere with trade. It became the standard approach adopted by all the Western nations in their dealings with China; commercial necessities came first. This might be described as a two-way shift. Both China and the West were prepared in practical terms to move away from their rigid ideological positions. China under Deng had been willing to adopt neo-capitalism at home and eagerly engage in trade with the world's capitalist nations. The West for its part was prepared to ignore the illiberalism of China's Communist regime and enter fully into trading relations with it. Both West and East adapted to the world as it was, rather than as they might have liked it to be.

China's response to the collapse of the USSR

By a remarkable twist in international history, which occurred in Deng's time and few had foreseen, China was left as the world's only major Communist power after the disintegration of the USSR in 1991. The end of the Soviet Union meant that China was the sole leader of the Marxist world. The question everyone now asked was whether the PRC would pursue international revolution, which according to its Marxist principles it was pledged to do. But Deng Xiaoping was a pragmatist and a realist. He looked at the failure of the 75-year-old Soviet experiment and noted why it had collapsed. He judged that the Soviet system had:

- been unable to develop a consumer economy that could reward its people for their efforts
- been incapable of reforming its agriculture sufficiently to feed its population
- pursued an arms race with the USA that it could not afford
- lost belief in itself.

Deng was resolved not to make the same errors. He approached foreign questions primarily as a defender of his country's interests, not as an international revolutionary. His chief aim was to ensure the CCP's political survival by consolidating China's position as a major nation that had embraced modernity. That is what determined his attitude towards foreign affairs.

China and the Pacific Rim

It so happened that China made a number of vital strategic gains under Deng that neither he nor the PRC had initiated. The Russian Federation that replaced

Pacific Rim The lands around the Pacific Ocean.

Spratly Islands Islands in the South China Sea that were believed to have large oil deposits; the islands had also been claimed variously by Indonesia, Malaysia, the Philippines and Vietnam.

Yasukini Shrine A traditional site in Tokyo dedicated to the remembrance of Japanese war dead.

the USSR in 1991 decided that it would have to cut back on many of the former Soviet commitments. One area it withdrew from was the **Pacific Rim**; it gave up its naval base at Vladivostok. By chance, this coincided with the decision by the USA not to retain its naval base in the Philippines. Since Japan's fleet was negligible by international standards, this by default left China dominant over a large area of the western Pacific Ocean.

Freed by all this from any likely international intervention, the PRC chose to take possession of the **Spratly Islands**. Ignoring all counter-claims, China took the islands by force, sinking two Vietnamese vessels and frightening the other claimants off by sending nuclear-armed submarines to the area. Victory over the Vietnamese was particularly satisfying for China since it was the settling of an old score.

India

Beginning in Deng's final years, the PRC sought to settle its border disputes with India. Not all the issues were resolved, but the negotiations between the two countries did ease Sino-Indian tensions.

Japan

The PRC's greater commercial openness helped to prepare the way for better relations with its traditional enemy, Japan. Despite the record of the savage Japanese occupation of China in the 1930s and 1940s, which was locked into China's collective memory (see page 21), national interests required that this should not stand in the way of lucrative Sino-Japanese commercial contracts being agreed. Deng had himself visited Japan in 1978 and top-level ministerial visits and diplomatic exchanges followed. The outcome was a Sino-Japanese peace and friendship treaty signed in 1978, an agreement that laid the basis for the growing trade contacts that followed throughout Deng's period of leadership. Significantly, the treaty contained a clause in which the two countries agreed to oppose 'hegemonism', their codeword for Soviet expansionism. The disintegration of the Soviet Union in 1991 meant that that aspect of the agreement became a dead letter, but it had indicated a mutual awareness of each other's strategic concerns.

Notwithstanding the improved formal relations, there were frequent occasions when the bitterness of Sino-Japanese history reasserted itself. There was still a residual fear among the Chinese of a resurgence of Japanese militarism. A particular issue was the reluctance of Japan to acknowledge its war crimes against China. The Chinese were angered by Japan's practice of omitting any reference in its history books to its brutal behaviour during the 1931–45 occupation. An episode that proved especially contentious was the decision of Japan's prime minster Nakasone to visit the **Yasukini Shrine** in 1985. Since the shrine contained the names of a number of Japan's wartime leaders who had committed war crimes, the visit was resented by the Chinese as being, at best, tasteless, at worst deeply insulting. Such incidents meant that Sino-Japanese relations often became strained, but this did not seriously interfere with their increasing trade contacts. The PRC's readiness not to allow moral outrage to get in the way of commercial growth was a reflection of Deng's determination to approach the economic question from a purely pragmatic standpoint.

China and international organisations

Deng was aware that some of his colleagues were highly doubtful of the benefits of the PRC's belonging to international bodies, since they were Western dominated. He shared some of the doubts but his conviction was that membership of the UN and of the UN Security Council, which had passed to the PRC in the early 1970s, when the USA had dropped its allegiance to Taiwan (see page 166), gave mainland China a prestige and status that far outweighed any dangers of its being subjected to Western whims. In any case, that risk became increasingly remote the stronger financially and economically the PRC became.

By 1997 the PRC had become a member of the **International Monetary Fund** (IMF) and **World Bank**, had accumulated over $130 billion in foreign currency reserves and was the largest recipient of World Bank loans. Nevertheless, Deng had to face resistance within the CCP over this since some of the more hard-line Communists regarded these moves as subordinating China to the USA's global economic policies. Deng managed to stifle the criticism but it was still being voiced around the time of his death. One Beijing academic wrote in 1998, 'Globalization is really Americanization. The IMF, World Bank, and the UN are controlled by the US government.' Despite such criticisms Deng's posthumous will prevailed and the PRC pressed its claim for membership of the **World Trade Organization** (WTO). The stumbling block was the USA, which took a strangely ambiguous approach towards the PRC. For some fifteen years after 1985, the USA vetoed the PRC's application to join GATT (the original title of WTO), but, eventually, in line with its earlier granting of Most Favored Nation status, it withdrew its opposition and China duly became a WTO member in 2001. Although this happened four years after Deng's death, it may be regarded as essentially his achievement since it was the outcome of his determination to make the PRC a modern commercial power.

China's suspicion of Western values

While China under Deng was eager to play its role as a world power, it declined to see things other than on its own terms. China's particular understanding of its past explains its unwillingness to go with the tide on international issues. Having, as it saw it, thrown off 150 years of subjection to the West, it was not going to compromise its independence by falling in with Western notions. A short time before his death, Deng and China were criticised for their reluctance to commit themselves to international schemes such as the promotion of human rights and the prevention of environmental damage.

KEY TERMS

International Monetary Fund Created in 1947 with the main intention of preventing countries from going bankrupt; member states make deposits into a central fund from which they are entitled to draw in times of difficulty.

World Bank A UN financial body, similar in operation to the IMF, that provides loans to developing countries to enable them to embark on growth programmes requiring large amounts of capital.

World Trade Organization Originally formed in 1948 as GATT (the General Agreement on Tariffs and Trade), a body to oversee and regulate international trade agreements, it became the WTO in 1995, its 160 member states representing over 96 per cent of global trade.

The PRC's rejoinder was to point out that when the Western imperialist powers were expanding uninvited into foreign countries, including China, they had paid scant attention to human rights. The Chinese view of the West's lectures to them about respecting political freedoms and behaving responsibly towards the environment was that it was hypocrisy. Deng stressed that the Western powers had been quite prepared in their heyday to pollute the world and enslave its peoples. Having made themselves rich by doing so, they then developed a conscience and wished to prevent anyone else from growing rich in a similar way. This attitude, drawn from its deep sense of historical grievance, means that Deng's China viewed issues in a fundamentally different way from its international critics.

Deng Xiaoping's final years

Deng died in 1997 at the age of 92. Frailty meant that in his last five years, although he remained the paramount authority, he played little direct part in government. His last major contribution was the 'southern journey', a 1992 campaign in which he travelled through a number of southern states urging the local leaders not to misinterpret the Tiananmen Square massacre as a sign of the failure of the Four Modernisations programme, but to see it as a warning of what could happen again if they did not implement them. He declined to accept stories that under the cover of the modernisation programme, corruption had become endemic in China as individuals and companies did shady deals with government officials and administrators.

On Deng Xiaoping's death, the Western press referred to the passing away of the last emperor of China, one who had succeeded the penultimate emperor, Mao Zedong. But Deng's influence survived in ways that Mao's had not. Deng, through his reforms, had laid the basis for the PRC's astonishing economic growth in the twenty-first century. Because of Deng Xiaoping, China accepted that its future was not as an inward-looking Asian nation but as an expansive global power. The paradox was that this would be achieved without the extension of political freedom to the Chinese people. None of the leaders who have followed him has diverged from the twin policies he bequeathed to China: modernisation of the economy accompanied by an implacable refusal to relax the authority over the nation of the Chinese Communist Party.

Deng's legacy may be summarised as follows:

- rejection of Mao Zedong's collectivist principles at home and isolationism abroad
- economic growth based on neo-capitalist methods of incentives and profit making
- CCP's insistence on its sole right to govern China
- endemic corruption
- rejection of Western-style democracy for China
- political suppression in China
- opening up of China to the world as a global commercial power

- the PRC a full member of World Bank, the IMF and poised to joined the WTO
- China's acknowledged international standing as a superpower
- workable relationships with China's previous enemies, India, Japan and the USA
- PRC dominance over the Pacific Rim.

Summary diagram: China as a global power

Deng's approach	**Deng's legacy in foreign affairs**
Defend his country's interests and not pursue international revolution	Opening up of China to the world as a global commercial power PRC internationally acknowledged as a superpower

Regional and border policies

Vietnam
- PRC support of Pol Pot failed
- Forced to withdraw in 1979
- A serious reverse

Hong Kong
- Joint Agreement 1984 on Hong Kong's return to China in 1997
- Great success for Deng

Tibet
- 1993 Lhasa rising
- Crushed by PLA
- Deng uncompromising

Taiwan
- PRC–GMD relations eased
- But PRC sovereignty reasserted
- Deng 'only the PRC represents China'

Wider world

Africa
- PRC's move into Africa under Deng
- The first early stage of massive expansion into the continent

USA
PRC gained 'Most Favored Nation' trading status with USA 1994

Soviet Union
- Collapse of USSR 1991
- Confirmed Deng's resolve that PRC must not go down same path

Pacific Rim
PRC under Deng dominated large area of western Pacific

Deng's abiding suspicion of Western values
Declined to commit PRC to international schemes, e.g. promotion of human rights and environmentalism

---

Chapter summary

Using the highly valuable political and military contacts that he had made, Deng first physically removed the Gang of Four and then outmanoeuvred the only other contender, Hua Guofeng. Acknowledged as paramount leader by the party, Deng began to undermine Mao's policies, not by an open attack on his reputation but by the drip effect. At the Third Plenum in 1978, Deng persuaded the party to accept the Four Modernisations, his strategy for economic reform. His plan was to follow an essentially capitalist line offering incentives and allowing profits to peasants and workers. His ending of the iron rice bowl aroused resentment but the overall effect of his reforms was spectacular. Under pressure to grant a fifth modernisation – democracy – Deng forcibly scattered the pro-democracy protesters in Tiananmen Square in 1989.

Despite these domestic problems, Deng led China into becoming a major world commercial and industrial force, and was accorded international recognition and respect. He also had considerable success in tackling the PRC's regional and border problems and in gaining membership of international economic organisations. At his death in 1997, Deng left China poised to become the twenty-first century's dominant economic power.

Refresher questions

Use these questions to remind yourself of the key material covered in this chapter.

1 How had Deng established himself as Mao's successor by 1978?

2 In what ways was the Third Plenum a turning point in post-Maoist China?

3 How did Deng plan to undermine Mao's policies and reputation?

4 What part did the trial of the Gang of Four play in undermining Maoism?

5 In what sense was Deng's industrial policy a 'hands-off' approach?

6 What economic aims underlay the Four Modernisations programme?

7 Why did so many Chinese people feel let down by Deng's economic reforms?

8 What were the aims of the democracy movement?

9 How significant an event for China was the Tiananmen Square massacre?

10 What steps did Deng take to resolve the issues of (a) Hong Kong and (b) Taiwan?

11 Why was Tibet an intractable problem for the PRC?

12 Why was Deng's China regarded as a 'Most Favored Nation' by the USA?

13 How did the PRC adapt to the collapse of the Soviet Union in 1991?

14 How did Sino-Japanese relations develop under Deng?

15 How did the PRC's membership of international organisations contribute to its status as a global power?

16 What were the main features of Deng Xiaoping's legacy?

 Question practice

ESSAY QUESTIONS

1 To what extent was the Third Plenum of the CCP in 1978 a turning point in post-Maoist China?

2 'Of Deng's Four Modernisations, the one that mattered above all the others was industrial reform.' Assess the validity of this view.

3 How successful was Deng Xiaoping in dealing with the regional and international questions that faced the PRC during his period as paramount leader?

SOURCE ANALYSIS QUESTION

1 With reference to Sources B (**page 186**), C (**page 187**) and D (**page 189**), and your understanding of the historical context, assess the value of these sources to a historian studying the democracy movement in the PRC between 1978 and 1989.

Edexcel A level History

Essay guidance

Edexcel's Paper 2, Unit 2E.1: Mao's China, 1949–76 is assessed by an exam comprising two sections:

- Section A tests the depth of your historical knowledge through source analysis (see page 213 for guidance on this).
- Section B requires you to write one essay from a choice of two from your own knowledge.

The following advice relates to Paper 2, Section B. It is relevant to A level and AS level questions. Generally, the AS exam is similar to the A level exam. Both examine the same content and require similar skills; nonetheless, there are differences, which are discussed below.

Essay skills

In order to get a high grade in Section B of Paper 2 your essay must contain four essential qualities:

- focused analysis
- relevant detail
- supported judgement
- organisation, coherence and clarity.

This section focuses on the following aspects of exam technique:

- understanding the nature of the question
- planning an answer to the question set
- writing a focused introduction
- deploying relevant detail
- writing analytically
- reaching a supported judgement.

The nature of the question

Section B questions are designed to test the depth of your historical knowledge. Therefore, they can focus on relatively short periods, or single events, or indeed on the whole period from 1949 to 1976. Moreover, they can focus on different historical processes or 'concepts'. These include:

- cause
- consequence
- change/continuity
- similarity/difference
- significance.

These different question focuses require slightly different approaches:

Cause	1 How far was Mao's ideology the main reason for the introduction of the Great Leap Forward in 1958?
Consequence	2 To what extent did the First Five-Year Plan of 1952–6 lead to the modernisation of the Chinese economy?
Continuity and change	3 'The position of women in China improved radically in the years 1950–76.' How far do you agree with this statement?
Similarities and differences	4 'The Great Leap Forward reflected radically different economic priorities from the First Five-Year Plan.' How far do you agree with this statement?
Significance	5 'The Hundred Flowers campaign 1957 was the most significant of Mao's campaigns against his political opponents in the years 1949 to 1962.' How far do you agree with this statement?

Some questions include a 'stated factor'. The most common type of stated factor question would ask how far one factor caused something. For example, for the first question in the table:

How far was Mao's ideology the main reason for the introduction of the Great Leap Forward in 1958?

In this type of question you would be expected to evaluate the importance of 'Mao's ideology' – the 'stated factor' – compared to other factors.

AS and A level questions

AS level questions are generally similar to A level questions. However, the wording of AS questions will be slightly less complex than the wording of A level questions.

A level question	AS level question	
To what extent did the first Five-Year Plan of 1952–6 lead to the modernisation of the Chinese economy?	To what extent did the first Five-Year Plan of 1952–6 improve the Chinese economy?	The A level question focuses on the complex notion of 'modernisation' whereas the AS question focuses on the relatively simple issue of 'change'.
'The Great Leap Forward reflected radically different economic priorities from the First Five-Year Plan.' How far do you agree with this statement?	How far did Mao's economic priorities change from the launch of the first Five-Year Plan to the launch of the Great Leap Forward?	The AS question asks how far Mao's economic priorities changed. The A level question asks you to make the more complex judgement: how far were his priorities 'radically different'?

To achieve the highest level at A level, you will have to deal with the full complexity of the question. For example, if you were dealing with question 4, about Mao's changing economic policy, you would have to deal with the question of how far his policies were 'radically different', not merely how far they changed.

Planning your answer

It is crucial that you understand the focus of the question. Therefore read the question carefully before you start planning. Check:

- The chronological focus: which years should your essay deal with?
- The topic focus: what aspect of your course does the question deal with?

- The conceptual focus: is this a causes, consequences, change/continuity, similarity/difference or significance question?

For example, for question 3 you could point these out as follows:

'The position of women in China[1] improved radically[2] in the years 1950–76[3].' How far do you agree with this statement?

1 Topic focus: the position of women.
2 Conceptual focus: continuity/change.
3 Chronological focus: 1950–76.

Your plan should reflect the task that you have been set. Section B asks you to write an analytical, coherent and well-structured essay from your own knowledge, which reaches a supported conclusion in around 40 minutes.

- To ensure that your essay is coherent and well structured, your essay should comprise a series of paragraphs, each focusing on a different point.
- Your paragraphs come in a logical order. For example, you could write your paragraphs in order of importance, so you begin with the most important issues and end with the least important.
- In essays where there is a 'stated factor' it is a good idea to start with the stated factor before moving on to the other points.
- To make sure you keep to time, you should aim to write three or four paragraphs plus an introduction and a conclusion.

The opening paragraph

The opening paragraph should do four main things:

- answer the question directly
- set out your essential argument
- outline the factors or issues that you will discuss
- define key terms used in the question – where necessary.

Different questions require you to define different terms, for example:

A level question	Key terms
To what extent did the first Five-Year Plan of 1952–6 lead to the modernisation of the Chinese economy?	Here it is worth defining 'modernisation'
'The Great Leap Forward reflected radically different economic priorities from the first Five-Year Plan.' How far do you agree with this statement?	In this example, it is worth defining 'radically different'

Here's an example introduction in answer to question 2 in the table on page 207: 'To what extent did the first Five-Year Plan of 1952–6 lead to the modernisation of the Chinese economy?'

The first Five-Year Plan led to partial economic modernisation between 1952 and 1956[1]. Mao believed that modernisation meant industrialisation, urbanisation, greater economic efficiency and the production of high-tech goods[2]. Clearly, the first Five-Year Plan led to some aspects of modernisation, notably industrialisation, more than others such as efficiency and the production of high-tech goods[3].

1 The essay starts with a clear answer to the question.
2 This sentence simultaneously defines modernisation and sets out the four key areas the essay will consider.
3 Finally, the essential argument is stated.

The opening paragraph: advice

- Don't write more than a couple of sentences on general background knowledge. This is unlikely to focus explicitly on the question.
- After defining key terms, refer back to these definitions when justifying your conclusion.
- The introduction should reflect the rest of the essay. Don't make one argument in your introduction, then make a different argument in the essay.

Deploying relevant detail

Paper 2 tests the depth of your historical knowledge. Therefore, you will need to deploy historical detail. In the main body of your essay your paragraphs should begin with a clear point, be full of relevant detail and end with an explanation or evaluation. A detailed answer might include statistics, proper names, dates and technical terms. For example, if you are writing a paragraph about the modernisation of the Chinese economy during the first Five-Year Plan, you might include statistics dealing with industrialisation, such as how much coal, iron and oil were produced.

Writing analytically

The quality of your analysis is one of the key factors that determines the mark you achieve. Writing analytically means clearly showing the relationships between the ideas in your essay. Analysis includes two key skills: explanation and evaluation.

Explanation

Explanation means giving reasons. An explanatory sentence has three parts:

- a claim: a statement that something is true or false
- a reason: a statement that justifies the claim
- a relationship: a word or phrase that shows the relationship between the claim and the reason.

Imagine you are answering question 1 in the table on page 207: 'How far was Mao's ideology the main reason for the introduction of the Great Leap Forward in 1958?' Your paragraph on Mao's ideology should start with a clear point, supported by a series of examples. Finally, you would round off the paragraph with some explanation:

Therefore, Mao's ideology was one reason for the introduction of the Great Leap Forward[1] because[2] it led him to reject the Soviet model of industrialisation and adopt a more radical alternative[3].

1 Claim.
2 Relationship.
3 Reason.

Make sure of the following:

- the reason you give genuinely justifies the claim you have made
- your explanation is focused on the question.

Reaching a supported judgement

Finally, your essay should reach a supported judgement. The obvious place to do this is in the conclusion of your essay. Even so, the judgement should reflect the findings of your essay. The conclusion should present the following:

- a clear judgement that answers the question
- an evaluation of the evidence that supports the judgement
- finally, the evaluation should reflect valid criteria.

Evaluation and criteria

Evaluation means weighing up to reach a judgement. Therefore, evaluation requires you to:

- summarise both sides of the issue
- reach a conclusion that reflects the proper weight of both sides.

So for question 2 in the table on page 207: 'To what extent did the first Five-Year Plan of 1952–6 lead to the modernisation of the Chinese economy?', the conclusion might look like this:

In conclusion, the first Five-Year Plan of 1952–6 led to partial economic modernisation[1].

Clearly, the Chinese economy was significantly modernised as industrialisation grew. The industrial economy grew by at least sixteen per cent, and industrial output doubled during the plan. Similarly, the plan increased urbanisation by 30 per cent[2]. However, in terms of efficiency the plan was much less successful. The plan led to centralisation and growing bureaucracy which made the economy less efficient[3]. Therefore, the first Five-Year Plan led to the partial modernisation of the Chinese economy because although the economy became more modern in the sense that it was more industrial and more urban, it was also less efficient because of the growing bureaucracy of Mao's government planners[4].

1. The conclusion starts with a clear judgement that answers the question.
2. This sentence considers the ways in which modernisation was achieved, presenting a summary of the evidence.
3. The conclusion also considers evidence of the limits of modernisation.
4. The essay ends with a final judgement that is supported by the evidence of the essay.

The judgement is supported in part by evaluating the evidence, and in part by linking it to valid criteria. In this case, the criterion is the definition of modernisation set out in the introduction. Significantly, this criterion is specific to this essay, and different essays will require you to think of different criteria to help you make your judgement.

Sources guidance

Edexcel's Paper 2, Unit 2E.1: Mao's China, 1949–76 is assessed by an exam comprising two sections:

- Section A tests the depth of your historical knowledge through source analysis.
- Section B requires you to write one essay from a choice of two from your own knowledge (see page 207 for guidance on this).

The following advice relates to Paper 2, Section A. It is relevant to A level and AS level questions. Generally, the AS exam is similar to the A level exam. Both examine the same content and require similar skills; nonetheless, there are differences, which are discussed below.

The questions in Paper 2, Section A, are structured differently in the A level and AS exams.

AS exam	Full A level exam
Section A: contains one compulsory question divided into two parts.	Section A: contains a single compulsory question worth 20 marks. The question asks you to evaluate the usefulness of two sources for a specific historical enquiry.
Part a) is worth 8 marks. It focuses on the value of a single source for a specific enquiry.	
Part b) is worth 12 marks. It asks you to weigh the value of a single source for a specific enquiry.	Together the two sources will comprise about 400 words.
Together the two sources will comprise about 350 words.	
Questions will start with the following stems:	Questions will start with the following stem:
a) Why is Source 1 valuable to the historian for an enquiry about …	How far could the historian make use of Sources 1 and 2 together to investigate …
b) How much weight do you give the evidence of Source 2 for an enquiry into …	

Edexcel style questions

AS style question

a) Study Sources 1 and 2 before you answer this question.

Why is Source 1 valuable to the historian for an enquiry about the causes of the Cultural Revolution?

Explain your answer using the source, the information given about it and your own knowledge of the historical context.

b) How much weight do you give the evidence of Source 2 for an enquiry into popular attitudes to the Cultural Revolution in 1966?

Explain your answer using the source, the information given about it and your own knowledge of the historical context.

A level style question

Study Sources 1 and 2 before you answer this question.

How far could the historian make use of Sources 1 and 2 together to investigate the causes of the Cultural Revolution?

Explain your answer, using both sources, the information given about them and your own knowledge of the historical context.

Sources 1 and 2

SOURCE I

From the 'Ninth Anti-Soviet Polemic', a document written in 1963 by the Anti-Revisionist Writers Group (ARWG). The ARWG was assembled by Mao in the late 1950s to develop an ideological criticism of the USSR under Khrushchev. It continued to work up to the outbreak of the Cultural Revolution. The ARWG included Mao's wife, Jiang Qing, and Chen Boda, chair of the Cultural Revolution Group. The ARWG worked under Mao's supervision.

In the final analysis, the question of training successors for the revolutionary cause of the proletariat is one of whether or not there will be people who can carry on the Marxist–Leninist revolutionary cause started by the older generation of proletarian revolutionaries, whether or not the leadership of our Party and state will remain in the hands of proletarian revolutionaries, whether or not our descendants will continue to march along the correct road laid down by Marxism–Leninism, or, in other words, whether or not we can successfully prevent the emergence of Khrushchev's revisionism in China. In short, it is an extremely important question, a matter of life or death for our Party and our country. It is a question of fundamental importance to the proletarian revolutionary cause for a hundred, a thousand, nay ten thousand years.

SOURCE 2

From Gao Yuan's autobiography *Born Red: A Chronicle of the Cultural Revolution*, Stanford University Press, 1987. Gao was a 14-year-old student when the Cultural Revolution began. He attended a school in Yizheng, in east China. Gao joined the Red Guard early in the Cultural Revolution. This extract is his account of the early stages of the revolution in the spring of 1966.

Students began to scrutinize textbooks, teaching methods, and even teachers themselves. One poster criticized a literature textbook for spreading decadent bourgeois ideas because it included a poem about young people's minds turning to love in the spring. Many students tried to imitate the prose style of the Shanghai essayist Yao Wenyuan, who had written the first critique of the play Hai Rui Dismissed from Office. *Posters went up questioning various teachers' backgrounds. What were the circumstances surrounding Teacher Li's defection from the Kuomintang to the Communists?*

The movement had acquired a name: the Great Socialist Cultural Revolution. The newspapers and radio brought us news from the centre of the movement, Beijing. One day, the central radio station attacked the top authorities of the school and called on all revolutionary intellectuals to plunge into the Cultural Revolution. Posters said that 'monsters' and 'demons' and Khrushchev-like counterrevolutionary revisionists were undermining socialism. There were rumours of an important Central Committee document that said that representatives of the bourgeoisie had infiltrated the Party, the government, and the army, as well as the cultural arena.

The next news from the capital was even more exciting: the entire Beijing Party Committee and the two top leaders of [Beijing University] had been dismissed. The reconstituted Party Committee had sent a work team to [the university] to make sure students could carry on the movement unimpeded. The People's Daily *celebrated these events with editorials headlined 'Sweep Away All Monsters and Demons!' and 'We Are Critics of the Old World!'*

Understanding the questions

- To answer the question successfully you must understand how the question works.
- The question is written precisely in order to make sure that you understand the task. Each part of the question has a specific meaning.
- You must use the source, the information given about the source, and your own knowledge of historical context when answering the question.

Understanding the AS question

  a) Why is Source 1 valuable to the historian for an enquiry[1] about Mao's reasons for launching the Cultural Revolution[2]?

1 You must focus on the reasons why the source could be helpful to a historian. Indeed, you can get maximum marks without considering the source's limitations.
2 The final part of the question focuses on a specific topic that a historian might investigate. In this case: 'Mao's reasons for launching the Cultural Revolution'.

  b) How much weight do you give the evidence of Source 2[1] for an enquiry[2] into popular attitudes to the Cultural Revolution in 1966[3]?

1 This question focuses on evaluating the extent to which the source contains evidence. Therefore, you must consider the ways in which the source is valuable and the limitations of the source.
2 This is the essence of the task: you must focus on what a historian could legitimately conclude from studying this source.
3 This is the specific topic that you are considering the source for: 'popular attitudes to the Cultural Revolution in 1966'.

Understanding the A level question

How far[1] could the historian make use of Sources 1 and 2[2] together[3] to investigate the causes of the Cultural Revolution[4]?

Explain your answer, using both sources, the information given about them and your own knowledge of the historical context[5].

1 You must evaluate the extent of something, rather than giving a simple 'yes' or 'no' answer.
2 This is the essence of the task: you must focus on what a historian could legitimately conclude from studying these sources.

3 You must examine the sources as a pair and make a judgement about both sources, rather than simply making separate judgements about each source.
4 The final part of the question focuses on a specific topic that a historian might investigate. In this case: 'the causes of the Cultural Revolution'.
5 This instruction lists the resources you should use: the sources, the information given about the sources and your own knowledge of the historical context that you have learnt during the course.

Source skills

Generally, Section A of Paper 2 tests your ability to evaluate source material. More specifically, the sources presented in Section A will be taken from the period that you have studied, 1949–76, or be written by people who witnessed these events. Your job is to analyse the sources by reading them in the context of the values and assumptions of the society and the period that produced them.

Examiners will mark your work by focusing on the extent to which you are able to:

- Interpret and analyse source material:
  - At a basic level, this means you can understand the sources and select, copy, paraphrase and summarise the source or sources to help answer the question.
  - At a higher level, your interpretation of the sources includes the ability to explain, analyse and make inferences based on the sources.
  - At the highest levels, you will be expected to analyse the source in a sophisticated way. This includes the ability to distinguish between information, opinions and arguments contained in the sources.
- Deploy knowledge of the historical context in relation to the sources:
  - At a basic level, this means the ability to link the sources to your knowledge of the context in which the source was written, using this knowledge to expand or support the information contained in the sources.
  - At a higher level, you will be able to use your contextual knowledge to make inferences, and

to expand, support or challenge the details mentioned in the sources.

- At the highest levels, you will be able to examine the value and limits of the material contained in the sources by interpreting the sources in the context of the values and assumptions of the society that produced them.
- Evaluate the usefulness and weight of the source material:
  - At a basic level, evaluation of the source will be based on simple criteria about reliability and bias.
  - At a higher level, evaluation of the source will be based on the nature and purpose of the source.
  - At the highest levels, evaluation of the source will be based on a valid criterion that is justified in the course of the essay. You will also be able to distinguish between the values of different aspects of the sources.

Make sure your source evaluation is sophisticated. Avoid crude statements about bias, and avoid simple assumptions such as that a source written immediately after an event is reliable, whereas a source written years later is unreliable.

Try to see things through the eyes of the writer:

- How does the writer understand the world?
- What assumptions does the writer have?
- Who is the writer trying to influence?
- What views is the writer trying to challenge?

Basic skill: comprehension

The most basic source skill is comprehension: understanding what the sources mean. There are a variety of techniques that you can use to aid comprehension. For example, you could read the sources included in this book and in past papers:

- read the sources out loud
- look up any words that you don't understand and make a glossary
- make flash cards containing brief biographies of the writers of the sources.

You can demonstrate comprehension by copying, paraphrasing and summarising the sources. However, keep this to the minimum as comprehension is a low-level skill and you need to leave room for higher-level skills.

Advanced skill: contextualising the sources

First, to analyse the sources correctly you need to understand them in the context in which they were written. People in China in the 1960s saw the world differently to people in early twenty-first-century Britain. The sources reflect this. Your job is to understand the values and assumptions behind the source:

- One way of contextualising the sources is to consider the nature, origins and purpose of the sources.
- An alternative is to consider two levels of context. First, you should establish the general context. In this case, Sources 1 and 2 refer to a period in which Mao was trying to regain control of China by attacking his rivals.

Second, you can look for specific references to contemporary events or debates in the sources. For example:

Sources 1 and 2 both refer to Khrushchev. This reflects criticisms of Khrushchev's Russia, which emerged in the mid-1950s and became increasingly important in the 1960s during the Sino-Soviet split. Moreover, the reference to Khrushchev may be a disguised reference to Liu Shaoqi, Mao's main rival in government in 1966, who was nicknamed 'the Chinese Khrushchev' by his enemies. Another important contextual reference in Source 2 is 'Hai Rui Dismissed from Office', a play performed in 1962 which implicitly criticised Mao. Indeed, Jiang Qing's criticisms of the play were an important part of the origins of the Cultural Revolution. Notably, Jiang Qing was one of the people involved in writing Source 1.

Use context to make judgements

- Start by establishing the general context of the source:
  - Ask yourself, what was going on at the time the source was written, or the time of the events described in the source?
  - What are the key debates that the source might be contributing to?
- Next, look for key words and phrases that establish the specific context. Does the source refer to specific people, events or books that might be important?
- Make sure your contextualisation focuses on the question.
- Use the context when evaluating the usefulness and limitations of the source.

For example:

Source 1 is valuable to a historian investigating the origins of the Cultural Revolution because it shows how concerned Mao was about the future of socialism in China and his desire to stop China from following the path of Khrushchev's Russia. Moreover, Source 2 is valuable because it shows the extent to which young people of school age were aware of debates over the future of China. According to Source 2, 14 year olds wanted to write like one of Mao's defenders. This indicates that they sided with radicals like Jiang Qing rather than moderates like Liu Shaoqi. From this we can infer that debates about the future of the revolution were widespread, as they influenced children in schools.

AQA A level History

Essay guidance

At both AS and A level for AQA Component 2: Depth Study: The Transformation of China 1936–97 you will need to answer an essay question in the exam. Each essay question is marked out of 25.

- for the AS exam, Section B: answer **one** essay (from a choice of two)
- for the A level examination, Section B: answer **two** essays from a choice of three.

There are several question stems which all have the same basic requirement: to analyse and reach a conclusion, based on the evidence you provide.

The AS questions often give a quotation and then ask whether you agree or disagree with this view. Almost inevitably, your answer will be a mixture of both. It is the same task as for A level – just phrased differently in the question. Detailed essays are more likely to do well than vague or generalised essays, especially in the Depth Studies of Paper 2.

The AQA mark scheme is essentially the same for AS and the full A level (see the AQA website, www.aqa.org.uk). Both emphasise the need to analyse and evaluate the key features related to the periods studied. The key feature of the highest level is sustained analysis: analysis that unites the whole of the essay.

Writing an essay: general skills

- *Focus and structure.* Be sure what the question is asking and plan what the paragraphs should be about.
- *Focused introduction to the essay.* Be sure that the introductory sentence relates directly to the focus of the question and that each paragraph highlights the structure of the answer.
- *Use detail.* Make sure that you show detailed knowledge, but only as part of an explanation being made in relation to the question. No

knowledge should be standalone; it should be used in context.
- *Explanatory analysis and evaluation.* Consider what words and phrases to use in an answer to strengthen the explanation.
- *Argument and counter-argument.* Think of how arguments can be balanced so as to give contrasting views.
- *Resolution.* Think how best to 'resolve' contradictory arguments.
- *Relative significance and evaluation.* Think how best to reach a judgement when trying to assess the relative importance of various factors, and their possible interrelationship.

Planning an essay

Practice question 1

To what extent was the Third Plenum of the Chinese Communist Party in 1978 a turning point in post-Maoist China?

This question requires you to analyse the extent of changes made by the Third Plenum. You must discuss the following:

- The character of the new policies introduced at the Third Plenum (your primary focus).
- How the policies differed from the ones they replaced (your secondary focus).

A clear structure makes for a much more effective essay and is crucial for achieving the highest marks. You need three or four paragraphs to structure this question effectively. In each paragraph you will deal with one factor. One of these *must* be the factor in the question.

A very basic plan for this question might look like this:

- Paragraph 1: a description of the main policies introduced.
- Paragraph 2: the aims behind the policies and how far they differed from preceding policies.

- Paragraph 3: the extent to which the new policies marked a turning point in post-Maoist China, and any policies that continued.

It is a good idea to cover the factor named in the question first, so that you don't run out of time and forget to do it. Then cover the others in what you think is their order of importance, or in the order that appears logical in terms of the sequence of paragraphs.

The introduction

Maintaining focus is vital. One way to do this from the beginning of your essay is to use the words in the question to help write your argument. The first sentence of question 1, for example, could look like this:

The Third Plenum of the Chinese Communist Party met in order to prepare the way for the modernisation of China by modifying the policies that Mao had followed.

This opening sentence provides a clear focus on the demands of the question.

Focus throughout the essay

Structuring your essay well will help with keeping the focus of your essay on the question. To maintain a focus on the wording in question 1, you could begin your first main paragraph with 'turning point'.

The party members gathered at the Third Plenum with the intention of turning away from Mao's policies. It was this that marked the Third Plenum as a 'turning point'.

- This sentence begins with a clear point that refers to the primary focus of the question (the abandonment of Mao's policies) while linking it to a factor (the modernisation of China).
- You could then have a paragraph for each of your other factors.
- It will be important to make sure that each paragraph focuses on analysis and includes relevant details that are used as part of the argument.

- You may wish to number your factors. This helps to make your structure clear and helps you to maintain focus.

Deploying detail

As well as focus and structure, your essay will be judged on the extent to which it includes accurate detail. There are several different kinds of evidence you could use that might be described as detailed. These include correct dates, names of relevant people, statistics and events. For example, for question 1 you could use terms such as Cultural Revolution and the Four Modernisations. You can also make your essays more detailed by using the correct technical vocabulary.

Analysis and explanation

'Analysis' covers a variety of high-level skills including explanation and evaluation; in essence, it means breaking down something complex into smaller parts. A clear structure which breaks down a complex question into a series of paragraphs is the first step towards writing an analytical essay.

The purpose of explanation is to provide evidence for why something happened, or why something is true or false. An explanatory statement requires two parts: a *claim* and a *justification*.

In question 1, for example, you might want to argue that one important reason was the need to move away from Mao's restrictive policies. Once you have made your point, and supported it with relevant detail, you can then explain how this answers the question. You could conclude your paragraph like this:

So the resolution to restore party democracy was vitally important[1] since[2] it allowed rehabilitation of Deng Xiaoping, whose political and economic ideas would provide the basis for modernisation[3].

1 The first part of this sentence is the claim and the second part justifies the claim.
2 'Since' is a key word to use when writing an explanation, as it shows the relationship between the claim and the justification.
3 The justification.

Evaluation

Evaluation means considering the importance of two or more different factors, weighing them against each other, and reaching a judgement. This is a good skill to use at the end of an essay because the conclusion should reach a judgement which answers the question. Your conclusion to question 1 might read as follows:

Clearly, the Third Plenum's rehabilitation of Deng and the acceptance of his Four Modernisations was a final rejection of the Mao's Cultural Revolution. It was a move away from centralised control and the 'iron rice bowl', towards an open economy that promoted local decision-making, incentives and individual initiative. However, Deng was anxious not to make the rejection too obvious since, given the reverence in which Mao had been held, this would create political difficulties. Therefore, the result was that the political and economic changes were achieved without unnecessary disruption, truly a political and economic turning point in post-Maoist China.

Words like 'however' and 'therefore' are helpful to contrast the importance of the different factors.

Complex essay writing: argument and counterargument

Essays that develop a good argument are more likely to reach the highest levels. This is because argumentative essays are much more likely to develop sustained analysis. As you know, your essays are judged on the extent to which they analyse.

After setting up an argument in your introduction, you should develop it throughout the essay. One way of doing this is to adopt an argument–counterargument structure. A counterargument is one that disagrees with the main argument of the essay. This is a good way of evaluating the importance of the different factors that you discuss. Essays of this type will develop an argument in one paragraph and then set out an opposing argument in another paragraph. Sometimes this will include juxtaposing the differing views of historians on a topic.

Good essays will analyse the key issues. They will probably have a clear piece of analysis at the end of each paragraph. While this analysis might be good, it will generally relate only to the issue discussed in that paragraph.

Excellent essays will be analytical throughout. As well as the analysis of each factor discussed above, there will be an overall analysis. This will run throughout the essay and can be achieved through developing a clear, relevant and coherent argument.

A good way of achieving sustained analysis is to consider which factor is most important. Here is an example of an introduction that sets out an argument for question 1:

Within two years of Mao Zedong's death in 1976, Deng Xiaoping had returned to become the dominant force in China [1]. This was shown by his domination of the Third Plenum in 1978[2]. The resolution 'to restore Party democracy' confirmed Deng's leadership of China. However, Deng did not merely wish to re-establish himself politically. His main aims were economic. He wanted to abandon Mao's unproductive policies and turn China into a major industrial force. To achieve this, he persuaded the Plenum to accept his expansive Four Modernisations (reform of industry, agriculture, defence and education) as the basis for China's development [3].

1 The introduction begins with a claim.
2 The introduction continues with another reason.
3 Concludes with an outline of the argument of the most important reason.

- This introduction focuses on the question and sets out the key factors that the essay will develop.
- It introduces an argument about which factor was most significant.
- However, it also sets out an argument that can then be developed throughout each paragraph, and is rounded off with an overall judgement in the conclusion.

Complex essay writing: resolution and relative significance

Having written an essay that explains argument and counterargument, you should then resolve the tension between the argument and the counterargument in your conclusion. It is important that the writing is precise and summarises the arguments made in the main body of the essay. You need to reach a supported overall judgement. One very appropriate way to do this is by evaluating the relative significance of different factors, in the light of valid criteria. Relative significance means how important one factor is compared to another.

The best essays will always make a judgement about which was most important based on valid criteria. These can be very simple, and will depend on the topic and the exact question. The following criteria are often useful:

- Duration: which factor was important for the longest amount of time?
- Scope: which factor affected the most people?
- Effectiveness: which factor achieved most?
- Impact: which factor led to the most fundamental change?

As an example, you could compare the factors in terms of their duration and their impact.

A conclusion that follows this advice should be capable of reaching a high level (if written, in full, with appropriate details) because it reaches an overall judgement that is supported through evaluating the relative significance of different factors in the light of valid criteria.

Having written an introduction and the main body of an essay for question 1, a concluding paragraph that aims to meet the exacting criteria for reaching a complex judgement could look like this:

Since the early 1960s, Deng had regarded Mao's Great Leap Forward as essentially wrong; it had produced not growth but stagnation. At the Third Plenum in 1978, Deng began the process of removing the remnants of Maoism that blocked China's economic progress. However, to avoid disruption in China, Deng adopted a subtle approach. Careful to suggest that he was developing, rather than abandoning, Mao's policies, he nonetheless used his Four Modernisations programme to redirect China on a new path. By dismantling Mao's legacy and adopting economic reconstruction, Deng had made a change of huge extent. China had entered the modern world. This was truly a significant turning point in the history of the People's Republic of China.

Sources guidance

Whether you are taking the AS exam or the full A level exam for AQA Component 2: Depth Study: The Transformation of China 1936–97, Section A presents you with sources and a question which involves evaluation of their utility or value.

AS exam	A level exam
Section A: answer question 1 based on two primary sources. (25 marks)	Section A: answer question 1, based on three primary sources. (30 marks)
Question focus: with reference to these sources and your understanding of the historical context, which of these two sources is more valuable in explaining … ?	Question focus: with reference to these sources and your understanding of the historical context, assess the value of these three sources to a historian studying …

Sources and sample questions

Study the sources. They are all concerned with the Great Leap Forward and its impact between 1958 and 1962.

SOURCE 1

Extract from a report by Yin Zeming, a Chinese Communist Party official in Shaoyang, 1958.

Iron smelting and steel making in Shaoyang, Hunan Province, are rapidly developing on a mass scale. In a short period in the autumn of 1858, 12,378 local blast furnaces were built in this area. The strength of the masses is tremendous. In honor of the anniversary of the Communist Party 67,000 people in Hsinhua County worked for three days and nights on end and built 1,025 blast furnaces. Many people hearing the news came to join in the work, carrying their food and clothes. Within a few days this county collected a fund of more than 1.6 million yuan. The people contributed 1280 pigs, more than 700,000 catties [350,000 kg] of vegetables, and 180,000 pairs of straw sandals for the people who were taking part in this industrial construction project. To solve the housing problem, the people of Tienping Township, in one morning, spontaneously vacated more than 500 rooms. The contributions from the masses became a mighty torrent, and the blast furnaces were set up very quickly.

SOURCE 2

From an account by a Westerner, Jasper Becker, in Liaoning province in 1960.

A peasant woman, unable to stand the incessant crying for food of her two-year-old daughter, and thinking perhaps to end her suffering, had strangled her. She had given the girl's body to her husband, asking him to bury it. Instead, out of his mind with hunger, he put the body in the cooking pot with what little food they had foraged. He had forced his wife to eat a bowl of the resulting stew. His wife, in a fit of remorse, had reported her husband's crime to the authorities. Although there was no law against cannibalism in the criminal code of the People's Republic, the Ministry of Public Security treated such cases, which were all too common, with the utmost severity. Both husband and wife were arrested and summarily executed.

SOURCE 3

A Tibetan famine victim describes her personal experiences in 1961.

Every day five or six people would be found dead in the morning. The bodies of the children and old people were always swollen with hunger. We could collect grasses from the fields, boil them and force this mixture down our throats. If you didn't, then you would die. We still had to keep working and then we would try and pick up grain or grass to eat. But you had to keep an eye out for the guards. If they caught you, then they would grab you by the throat and make you spit out the grass seeds. They would body-search all of us when we returned from the fields. There were also special teams which searched people's homes for grain and fodder. If they discovered even a few grains, then they would organize a big meeting of 500 or 600 people. The guilty person would have a big wooden sign hung on him.

AS style question

With reference to Sources 1 and 2, and your understanding of the historical context, which of these two sources is more valuable in explaining why the Great Leap Forward led to famine?

A level style question

With reference to Sources 1, 2 and 3, and your understanding of the historical context, assess the value of these sources to a historian studying the impact of the Great Leap Forward.

The mark schemes

AS mark scheme

See the AQA website for the full mark schemes. This summary of the AS mark scheme shows how it rewards analysis and evaluation of the source material within the historical context.

Level 1	Describing the source content or offering generic phrases.
Level 2	Some relevant but limited comments on the value of one source *or* some limited comment on both.
Level 3	Some relevant comments on the value of the sources and some explicit reference to the issue identified in the question.
Level 4	Relevant well-supported comments on the value and a supported conclusion, but with limited judgement.
Level 5	Very good understanding of the value in relation to the issue identified. Sources evaluated thoroughly and with a well-substantiated conclusion related to which is more valuable.

A level mark scheme

This summary of the A level mark scheme shows how it is similar to the AS, but covers three sources. Also the wording of the question means that there is no explicit requirement to decide which of the three sources is the most valuable. Concentrate instead on a very thorough analysis of the content and evaluation of the provenance of each source.

Level 1	Some limited comment on the value of at least one source.
Level 2	Some limited comments on the value of the sources *or* on content or provenance *or* comments on all three sources but no reference to the value of the sources.
Level 3	Some understanding of all three sources in relation to both content and provenance, with some historical context; but analysis limited.
Level 4	Good understanding of all three sources in relation to content, provenance and historical context to give a balanced argument on their value for the purpose specified in the question.
Level 5	As Level 4, but with a substantiated judgement.

Working towards an answer

It is important that knowledge is used to show an understanding of the relationship between the sources and the issue raised in the question. Answers should be concerned with:

- provenance
- arguments used (and you can agree/disagree)
- tone and emphasis of the sources.

The sources

The two or three sources used each time will be contemporary – probably of varying types (for example, diaries, newspaper accounts, government reports). The sources will all be on the same broad topic area. Each source will have value. Your task is to evaluate how much – in terms of its content and its provenance.

You will need to assess the *value of the content* by using your own knowledge. Is the information accurate? Is it giving only part of the evidence and ignoring other aspects? Is the tone of the writing significant?

You will need to evaluate the *provenance* of the source by considering who wrote it, and when, where and why. What was its purpose? Was it produced to express an opinion; to record facts: to influence the opinion of others? Even if it was intended to be accurate, the writer may have been biased – either deliberately or unconsciously. The writer, for example, might have only known part of the situation and reached a judgement solely based on that.

Here is a guide to analysing the provenance, content and tone for Sources 1, 2 and 3.

Analysing the sources

To answer the question effectively, you need to read the sources carefully and pull out the relevant points as well as add your own knowledge. You must remember to keep the focus on the question at all times.

Source 1 (page 220)

Provenance:

- The source is from a report by Yin Zeming, a Chinese Communist Party official.
- He will have a particular view on the Great Leap Forward.
- It is taken from a report to his party superiors and it will therefore be addressing that particular audience to impress them.

Content and argument:

- The source argues that the people have responded enthusiastically.
- The people are eager to contribute to the rebuilding of China under Mao.
- The people have joined together in a mass movement.

Tone and emphasis:

- The tone is highly positive. Ordinary Chinese people have rushed to respond to Mao's call for a great national endeavour.

Own knowledge:

- Use your knowledge to agree/disagree with the source, for example: evidence of the Great Leap Forward often being enforced on the Chinese people, and the obvious inclination of party officials to paint as glowing a picture as possible by ignoring the dark side of the Great Leap Forward, such as the famine.

Source 2 (page 220)

Provenance:

- The source is from an account by a Western observer.
- It provides a foreign observer's account of the famine.

Content and argument:

- The source vividly describes the grim situation.
- The writer describes the hard official line the authorities take towards cannibalism.

Tone and emphasis:

- The tone is dispassionate, the writer allowing the harrowing details to speak for themselves.

Own knowledge:

- Your knowledge to agree/disagree with the source, for example: the statistical evidence that bears out the writer's account; despite the party's attempts to deny that there was famine, it was too widespread and too destructive to be kept hidden.

Source 3 (page 221)

Provenance:

- The source is from an actual victim of the famine in Tibet.
- The victim is concerned not merely to describe the suffering but to explain who caused it.

Content and argument:

- The Tibetans were helpless victims.
- The famine was deliberately made worse by the brutal way in which the authorities treated the starving.

Tone and emphasis:

- There is a controlled sense of bitterness in the way in which the writer gives the plain facts of the misery to which she and her people were subjected.
- She is anxious to emphasise that the famine was intensified by callous officials.

Own knowledge:

- Use your knowledge to agree/disagree with the source, for example: knowledge that there need not have been a famine in Tibet; that the Tibetans were deliberately targeted for starvation as part of a long-running campaign by the Chinese to destroy Tibet's separate identity.

Answering AS questions

You have an hour to answer the question. It is important that you spend at least one-quarter of the time reading and planning your answer. Generally when writing an answer, you need to check that you are remaining focused on the issue identified in the question and are relating this to the sources and your knowledge.

- You might decide to write a paragraph on each 'strand' (that is provenance, content and tone), comparing the two sources, and then write a short concluding paragraph with an explained judgement on which source is more valuable.
- For writing about content, you may find it helpful to adopt a comparative approach, for example when the evidence in one source is contradicted or questioned by the evidence in another source.

At AS level you are asked to provide a judgement on which is more valuable. Make sure that this is based on clear arguments with strong evidence, and not on general assertions.

If you were answering the AS question

- Think how you can best plan an answer.
- Plan in terms of the headings above, perhaps combining 'provenance' with 'tone and emphasis', and compare the two sources.

As an example, here is a comparison of Sources 1 and 2 in terms of provenance, and tone and emphasis:

The two sources have different viewpoints. In terms of their provenance, Source 1 is very one-sided as it is totally concerned to prove the success of the Great Leap Forward. The viewpoint is based on the desire to praise Mao and the Chinese Communist Party. Source 2 is more controlled in its analysis; however, it is written from a Western viewpoint and therefore may not be totally objective.

Then compare the *content and argument* of each source, by using your knowledge. For example:

Source 1 argues that the Chinese people have responded with whole-hearted commitment and self-sacrifice to the Great Leap Forward's call for a great collective effort. As a Chinese Communist Party official, his task is to report back to the party bosses that the plans of Mao and the party are everywhere meeting with success. He allows no hint of criticism to enter his report.

Source 2, however, focuses on the grim consequence of the Great Leap Forward: famine. Except by implication, the writer does not directly criticise the authorities but he does describe the uncompromising response of the Chinese officials to cannibalism.

Which is *more valuable*? This can be judged in terms of which is likely to be more valuable in terms of where the source came from; or in terms of the accuracy of its content. However, remember the focus of the question: in this case, what the impact was of the Great Leap Forward.

With these sources, you could argue that Source 2 is the more valuable because it was written in a more objective way, by an outside observer, whereas Source 1 is more limited since it was written by a party official who was obviously partial in his attitude.

Then check the following:

- Have you covered the 'provenance' and 'content' strands?
- Have you included sufficient knowledge to show understanding of the historical context?

Answering A level questions

The same general points for answering AS questions (see 'Answering AS questions') apply to A level questions, although, of course, here there are three sources and you need to assess the value of each of the three, rather than choose which is most valuable. Make sure that you remain focused on the question and that when you use your knowledge it is used to substantiate (add to) an argument relating to the content or provenance of the source.

If you are answering the A level question with Sources 1, 2 and 3 above:

- Keep the different 'strands' explained above in your mind when working out how best to plan an answer.
- Follow the guidance about 'provenance' and 'content' (see the AS guidance).
- Here you are *not* asked to explain which is the most valuable of the three sources. You can deal with each of the three sources in turn if you wish.
- However, you can build in comparisons if it is helpful, but it is not essential. It will depend to some extent on the three sources.
- You need to include sufficient knowledge to show understanding of the historical context. This might encourage cross-referencing of the content of the three sources, mixed with your own knowledge.
- Each paragraph needs to show clarity of argument in terms of the issue identified by the question.

Glossary of terms

Agit-prop Short for 'agitation propaganda', the teaching of political ideas through entertainment.

Agronomists Agricultural scientists.

Albania Run by an oppressive neo-Stalinist regime, it was the only Communist state in Europe to recognise China rather than the USSR as leader of the international revolutionary movement.

Analgesics Painkillers.

Anarchy Often used to describe chaos, but its literal meaning is the absence of government. It was never Mao's intention to allow the situation to get out of hand; his government never lost control.

Ancestor worship The practice of paying respect to the deceased members of the family in a simple ceremony of remembrance.

Antagonistic contradiction Aggressive opposition to party policy.

Anti-rightist movement An extension of the earlier anti-campaigns; having no precise definition, rightist could refer to anyone suspected.

Applied communism Planning according to Marxist principles involving state direction of the economy and the ending of private ownership.

Asia Watch An international body concerned with monitoring abuses of human rights.

Backyard furnaces Primitive smelting devices that every family was encouraged to build on its premises.

Bamboo curtain A figurative way of describing China's hostile attitude towards the non-Communist world.

Barefoot doctors Teams of swiftly trained medics who were sent into the countryside to provide a rudimentary health service.

Beiping Meaning 'northern peace' to distinguish it from Beijing, which meant 'northern capital'.

Blue Shirts A force largely recruited from officers at the Nationalist Military Academy in Nanjing, whose main task was hunting down Communists.

Bourgeois stage The period in Marxist theory when the middle class, having overcome the previous feudal system, dominates society until the working-class revolution occurs.

Bourgeoisie Middle-class capitalists; exploiters of the workers.

Brainwashing Using a combination of physical torture and psychological coercion to disorientate victims so that they become very susceptible to suggestion and direction.

Brezhnev doctrine The demand that all international Communists should toe the Soviet line or risk being disciplined by the other Marxist states acting under Soviet leadership.

Bride-price Payment made by the bride's family to the groom's family to seal the marriage contract.

Buddhism An ancient oriental philosophy, which laid great stress on the individual's gaining enlightenment through meditation.

Cadres Dedicated CCP workers whose special task was to spy and report on fellow CCP members and the public.

Capitalist roader A reference to Deng's wish to see the economy modernised on neo-capitalist lines.

Central Cultural Revolution Group (CCRG) A sub-committee of the Politburo, established in May 1965; its seventeen members included the Gang of Four.

Chargé d'affaires Equivalent to an ambassador.

Chauvinism Exaggerated and aggressive belief in the value of one's own ideas and attitudes.

Chinese Communist Party (CCP) A revolutionary party, formed in 1921 with support from Soviet Russia.

CIA Central Intelligence Agency, the USA's espionage and counter-espionage organisation.

Class enemies Reactionaries who refused to accept the new Communist China.

Cleansing the class ranks A terror campaign to exterminate those whose social background made them real or potential opponents of Maoism.

Collectives Areas where the peasants farmed communally rather than for themselves individually.

Collectivist principle The Marxist notion that social advance can be achieved only by the proletarian class acting together as a body and not allowing individuals to follow their own interests.

Comintern The Communist International, the body set up in Moscow to organise international revolution by requiring foreign Communist parties to follow Soviet instructions.

Communes Organised regions where collectives were grouped together.

Communist Cuba In 1959, revolutionary forces had taken power on the island; their leader, Fidel Castro, later declared himself a Communist.

Concubinage The practice of men keeping women not as wives but as mistresses (concubines).

Confucian values Social harmony, as espoused by the sage Confucius (551–479BC).

Congress The US parliament.

Conjugal visits Time set aside for couples to have sex.

Conscript armies Unable to attract volunteers, the GMD became notorious for the brutality with which it rounded up peasants and forced them to become soldiers by fearsome discipline.

Corrective labour In Communist theory, a form of imprisonment that allowed a prisoner to see the error of his ways.

Counter-revolutionaries Used by hard-line Maoists to describe those in the party who favoured more moderate policies.

Cult of personality A reference to the unlimited power that Stalin had taken into his own hands at the expense of the party.

Cult status A position that entitles the holder to a special veneration among the people and puts him beyond criticism.

Decadent tendencies Clinging to bourgeois values, the most obvious examples being the wearing of Western-style clothes, jewellery or make-up.

Democratic centralism The principle, originally introduced by Lenin in Soviet Russia, that in a truly revolutionary party the members owed absolute loyalty and obedience to the leaders.

Denominations Separate groups within a faith, for example, Catholicism and Protestantism within Christianity.

Détente Easing of tensions between the Soviet Union and the Western powers.

Dialectic The dynamic force that shapes the historical development of class war.

Dialectician A believer that life is essentially a struggle between opposites in which the more powerful always wins.

Dogma Rigid belief in a particular approach.

Drip effect Letting Mao's reputation gradually erode rather than formally attacking it.

Eastern bloc The USSR and the central European countries it dominated.

Excommunication Formal dismissal from the Catholic Church.

Expatriate Chinese Chinese nationals living abroad.

Extended family Not just parents and children but all the relatives, including in-laws.

Fait accompli Something done in such a way that it cannot be changed.

Fascist Referring originally only to Mussolini's Italy, the word came to be applied to all the nationalistic, authoritarian regimes of the period.

Foot binding The tight bandaging of the feet to prevent their growth. This had two purposes: to hobble the women so that they could not get about and to make them more attractive to men, who traditionally regarded small feet as highly erotic.

Forbidden City Beijing's greatest monument, a spacious walled inner city that had been the home and court of the emperors between 1368 and 1911.

Foreign concessions International settlements within Chinese cities in which foreign laws operated and China had no authority; dating from the intrusion of the powers into Chinese affairs in the nineteenth century, they were in effect foreign mini-states.

Foreign embassies In international convention, these are especially protected areas which the host nation respects as being immune from local interference.

Gang of Four Made up of Jiang Qing and her three male associates, Zhang Chunqiao (1917–2001), Yao Wenyuan (1931–2005) and Wang Honwen (1932–92).

GDP Gross domestic product. The total value of the goods produced in a country in a year.

Gestapo The notorious Nazi secret police.

Ginger group   A supportive group whose task was to keep the party committed to the revolution.

'Going to the people'   Mao's practice of periodically travelling through parts of China, supposedly to listen to what the people had to say.

Great Hall of the People   A large parliament building overlooking Tiananmen Square.

Great Helmsman   An adulatory reference to Mao's unmatchable skill in steering the ship of state.

Green Gang   Shanghai racketeers who dealt mainly in prostitution and drug running and who were notorious for bribing police and government officials to co-operate.

Group of Five   A set of moderate party officials led by Peng Zhen (1902–97), the mayor of Beijing.

Guerrilla warfare   A hit-and-run style of fighting, avoiding pitched battles and using local knowledge of people and terrain to harass the enemy.

Guomindang (GMD)   The Nationalists. A revolutionary party created by Sun Yat-sen that wanted the modernisation of China and the ending of foreign domination. From the early 1930s, at its stronghold in Nanjing, it claimed to be the legitimate government of the Republic of China.

'Hare-brained' economic schemes   Khrushchev's unsuccessful attempts to reform Soviet agriculture and industry between 1956 and 1964.

Heavy industry   Iron- and steel-based products and constructions.

Heroes' Monument   A large shrine, commemorating the great deeds of China's revolutionary past, at the southern end of Tiananmen Square.

Hong Kong   The Chinese city-port that had been a British Crown colony since 1898 and was not scheduled to return to China until 1997.

Ichigo campaign   A sweeping Japanese movement from April to December 1944 that brushed aside Chiang's forces.

Ideograms   Pictures. Mandarin symbols had begun as pictures of the ideas they described.

Ideologues   CCP hard liners who believed in pushing Mao's revolutionary politics to the extreme and suppressing all opposition.

Inflation   A fall in the value and purchasing power of money.

Intellectual class   Those, according to Mao, who merely talked and theorised rather than acted.

International Monetary Fund   Created in 1947 with the main intention of preventing countries from going bankrupt; member states make deposits into a central fund from which they are entitled to draw in times of difficulty.

Iron rice bowl   The system that provided a worker with a guaranteed job and wage.

Khampas   The nomadic herdsmen of Tibet.

Labour-contract scheme   An agreement between employers and workers, offering higher wages for increased productivity.

Laogai   'Re-education through labour.' Came to be used to describe the prison-camp system itself.

Left GMD and the Democratic League   Made up of breakaway Nationalists who despaired of Chiang's leadership and the GMD's policies. They wanted a compromise settlement with the CCP.

Leninism   The revolutionary theories of class war first formulated by Karl Marx and subsequently developed by Lenin.

Liberated   The CCP's term for the areas brought under its military and political control.

Lift-off   Increasing output and production at such a pace as to turn China into a modern industrial power.

Local power structures   Officials, businessmen, lawyers and financiers, who administered the regions during Japan's occupation and expected to continue after the GMD's return to power in 1945.

Long March   The CCP flight from Jiangxi to Yanan in 1934–5. It began as a rout, but its eventual success turned it into one of the great formative experiences of Chinese communism.

'Loss of China'   The US State Department's term for US failure to prevent the victory of Mao's Communists in China in 1949.

Manufactured goods   Sellable products made from raw materials.

Marco Polo Bridge   An important crossing point, 16 km (10 miles) outside Beijing.

Market   The operation of supply and demand without interference by the state.

Martial law   The placing of the civilian population under military authority and discipline.

Marxist   A believer in the theories of Karl Marx (1818–83), who used the notion of the dialectic to explain history.

McCarthyism   Senator Joe McCarthy headed a Congressional Committee seeking to expose crypto-Communists supposedly working in the USA. Relying on flimsy evidence, the Committee was responsible for creating a Red Scare in the 1950s.

Middle classes   Broadly made up of professionally qualified people.

Monkeys to disrupt the palace   Mao's imagery is drawn from the practice in the imperial court of having monkeys as pets, whose uncontrolled behaviour could cause mayhem.

Morals of the Red Guards   One of the boasts of the Red Guards was that they had risen above bourgeois thoughts of sex. That was why they dressed in plain, unisex blue or khaki uniforms and made themselves look as physically unappealing as possible.

Most Favored Nation   An arrangement in which the USA offers a selected country privileged commercial and financial terms.

National capitalists   Those who had run China before 1949.

Neo-capitalism   A return to the corrupt bourgeois system based on greed, individualism and profit-making.

Nepotism   Giving position and special favours to cronies and family members.

NRA   National Revolutionary Army of the Guomindang (GMD).

Nuclear family   Mother, father and their children, considered as a unit.

Opium War   In the nineteenth century, Britain had sent warships to force China to buy large quantities of the opium produced in British Burma, a humiliation which remained a basic historical reference point for many Chinese in their distrust of the West.

Pacific Rim   The lands around the Pacific Ocean.

Packing   Controlling the membership of committees in such a way that they always contained a majority of Maoists.

Panchen Lama   Designated successor to the Dalai Lama, the spiritual leader of the Lama faith.

Panmunjong truce   The agreement ending the Korean War. It decided little since the two sides simply agreed to recognise the division of Korea at the 38th parallel.

Papacy   The Catholic Church's system of government, headed by the Pope.

Paper tigers   A dismissive term Mao often applied to anyone or anything whose power was more apparent than real.

Paramount leader   The title conferred no specific powers on Deng, which made it all the more valuable to him since it placed no restrictions on him.

People's Armed Police   Technically a civilian police force, but essentially a wing of the PLA.

Permanent revolution   The notion that revolution is not a single historical event but a developing process.

Pinyin   A modernised form of Mandarin.

PLA   The People's Liberation Army, formerly the Red Army.

Plenum   A full, authoritative gathering of the CCP.

Pogrom   A state-organised persecution of a particular group of people.

Politburo   An inner core of some twenty leading members of the CCP.

Political correctness   The requirement that people conform to a set of prescribed opinions to show that they have accepted the ideology of the leaders of society.

Post-imperial guilt   The notion that the exploitative record of the ex-colonial powers denied them the moral right to interfere in the regions they had once held.

Pragmatism   A way of tackling problems based on the actual situation rather than on abstract theory.

Pragmatists   CCP members who believed that policies should be adjusted according to circumstances rather than being slavishly followed for ideological reasons.

Prague spring   The attempt of the Czech Communist government to liberalise some of its policies and assert its independence of Soviet control.

Price index   The cost of a selected set of basic goods at a given date against which the cost at any other time is then calculated.

Privileged audiences   In Mao's time the best seats in the theatres were reserved for party members.

Progressive thinkers   Those with a forward-looking attitude, who were beginning to demand that power and privilege in China should not be the monopoly of the leaders of the CCP.

Proletariat   The revolutionary workers and peasants.

Public utilities   Gas, electricity and the transport system.

Purges   In theory, the purifying of the party by removing corrupt elements; in practice, a method for silencing opponents and critics.

Quality control   The monitoring of industrial production to maintain set standards.

Red Army   The name adopted for the CCP's military forces.

Red Guards   Radical students whose name derived from the red armbands they were given by Lin Biao.

'Reunification' campaigns   The CCP's euphemism for forcibly bringing the invaded provinces into line.

Reuters   An international news agency.

Revisionism   Betraying original revolutionary ideas and values.

Revisionist   Reactionary, anti-party thinking. Used by Maoists, similar to 'counter-revolutionary', to describe party members regarded as not fully committed to Mao's revolution.

Revolutionary correctness   The idea that Chinese communism (Maoism) was a body of political, social and economic truth which all CCP members had to accept and live by.

Right-wing governments   Nazi Germany and Fascist Italy, for example.

Secular bible   The Little Red Book came to have the same authority in Maoist society as the Bible had in Christian culture or the Qur'an in Islamic.

Shanghai Forum   A group of hard-line leftist radicals, who believed in the harshest measures being taken against those who opposed Mao.

Show trial   A public hearing in which the accused, whose guilt is assumed, is paraded as an enemy of the people.

Sino-centric   Having Chinese interests at the centre of things with all other considerations secondary.

Sino-Indian War   In 1962, a long-running territorial dispute, compounded by India's granting sanctuary to the Dalai Lama, led to an outbreak of fighting on the Tibetan border.

Slogan-ridden society   Stalin's USSR had used mass public propaganda to train people into conformity and obedience.

Social fascism   A term first used by Stalin to denote those Communists and socialists who were willing to compromise with their political enemies.

Socialist concepts   The structuring of the economy by the government with the aim of spreading equality.

South and North dynasties   A reference to the partition of China during the civil wars of the fifth and sixth centuries AD.

Soviet   A Communist-controlled area in which life is structured along communal, socialist lines.

Soviet forces   Stalin's armies had begun occupying Manchuria one day after the Nagasaki bombing.

Soviet–GMD friendship treaty   Chiang's August 1945 agreement to allow Soviet forces into Manchuria in return for the USSR's recognition of his party as the only legitimate authority in China.

Soviet satellites   The various countries that had fallen under Soviet control between 1945 and 1948 and now made up the Eastern bloc.

Spearheads of the erroneous line   Leaders who had tried to persuade the party to follow policies that ran counter to Mao's wishes.

Special Economic Zones (SEZs)   Areas, containing China's main export industries and companies, which were earmarked for immediate and concentrated development.

Spratly Islands   Islands in the South China Sea that are believed to have large oil deposits; the islands had also been claimed variously by Indonesia, Malaysia, the Philippines and Vietnam.

Stalin's Five-Year Plans   In the USSR, between 1929 and 1953, Stalin had revolutionised the Soviet economy by a series of government-directed plans.

Stalinist purges   During his leadership of the USSR between 1929 and 1953, Stalin had introduced a series of fierce purges to crush opposition.

State Department   The US body responsible for foreign policy.

State subsidies   A scheme of payments, introduced in Mao's time, to supplement the income of workers and companies.

Superior race   An equivalent Japanese notion to the Nazi concept of the Germans as the master race.

Superpowers   Nations that possessed advanced nuclear weapons.

Tangshan   An industrial city, 150 km (90 miles) south of Beijing.

TAR   Tibetan Autonomous Region, dating from 1965 when Mao's government tried to give a semblance of legality to its control of Tibet by declaring it to be a self-governing region.

Test ban treaty   Agreement between the USSR and the Western nuclear powers in 1963, in which the parties pledged to end their atmospheric testing of nuclear weapons.

Third Reich   Hitler's Nazi regime 1933–45.

Trading space to buy time   Giving ground to the Japanese which would both overstretch their resources and allow the Chinese the opportunity to build up their own strength.

Triads   Chinese secret societies, usually criminal, involved in drugs, gambling and prostitution.

Trotskyists   Followers of Stalin's great rival, Leon Trotsky, who believed in the necessity of world revolution at any cost.

'Twenty-eight Bolsheviks'   A group of CCP members who had been trained in Moscow and returned to China with instructions to make the party conform to Soviet concepts of urban revolution.

Uighur, Kazakh, Hui, Kirghiz   Ethnic groups, who, in regard to race, language and religion, were distinct from the Han people who made up over 80 per cent of China's population.

UN Security Council   A United Nations body set up to resolve international disputes and maintain peace; its five permanent members were Britain, France, Nationalist China, the USSR and the USA.

Unequal treaties   The one-sided agreements imposed by the European powers on imperial China.

United Front   A GMD–CCP military alliance that defeated the warlords in a series of campaigns from 1926 to 1928.

Urban proletariat   The industrial working class, destined, in Marxist analysis, to be the final victor in the dialectical struggle.

Usury   Charging exorbitant interest on money loans.

Vatican   The administrative centre of the Catholic Church in Rome, where the Pope has his official residence.

Velvet revolutions   The non-violent popular movements in the Soviet-controlled Eastern bloc countries in the late 1980s, which brought down the Communist governments and led to the collapse of the USSR itself in 1991.

Whampoa Military Academy   A military base in Guangzhou dedicated to the training of GMD army recruits.

White Terror   Chiang's 1927 campaign of annihilation of the CCP.

World Bank   A UN financial body, similar in operation to the IMF, that provides loans to developing countries to enable them to embark on growth programmes requiring large amounts of capital.

World Trade Organization   Originally formed in 1948 as GATT (the General Agreement on Tariffs and Trade), a body to oversee and regulate international trade agreements, it became the WTO in 1995, its 160 member states representing over 96 per cent of global trade.

Xiang   The original village or township.

Yasukini Shrine   A traditional site in Tokyo dedicated to the remembrance of Japanese war dead.

'Yellow peril'   A term, with strong racist overtones, first used in the nineteenth century to suggest that China's vast population was preparing to swamp Europe, with Russia as the first victim.

YMCA   Young Men's Christian Association, a welfare organisation brought to China by Western missionaries.

Yuan   Worth 10p in 1950 values.

Yugoslavia   Under its leader Marshal Tito, it was the one Communist country in Eastern Europe that successfully resisted all efforts by the USSR to control it.

Zhongnanhai   The building compound off Tiananmen Square, the historic centrepiece of Beijing, which housed the government offices and ministers' residences.

Glossary of names

Chinese names in their *Pinyin* and Wade–Giles forms

Pinyin	Wade–Giles	*Pinyin*	Wade–Giles
Anhui	Anhwei	Peng Dehuai	Peng Teh-huai
Beijing	Peking	Peng Zhen	Peng Chen
Bo Yibo	Po Yipo	Quemoy	Jinmen
Chen Boda	Chen Po-ta	Qin Shi Huang	Shi Huang-ti
Chen Duxui	Chen Tu-hsiu	Qinghai	Tsinghai
Chongqing	Chungking	Rao Shushi	Jao Shu-shi
Daxing	Tsa-hsing	Shaanxi	Shensi
Deng Xiaoping	Teng Hsiao-ping	Shandong	Shantung
Duan Qirui	Tuan Chi-jui	Shantou	Swatow
Fang Lizhi	Fang Li-chih	Shanxi	Shansi
Feng Xuxiang	Feng Yu-hsiang	Sichuan	Szechwan
Fujian	Fukien	Sun Yatsen	Sun Yat-sen
Fuzhou	Foochow	Taiwan	Formosa
Gao Gang	Kao Kang	Wang Dengxing	Wang Tung-hsing
Gansu	Kansu	Wang Hongwen	Wang Hung-wen
Guangdong	Kwangtung	Wang Jingwei	Wang Ching-wei
Guangxi	Kwangsi	Wang Jinxi	Wang Ching-hsi
Guangxu	Kuang Hsu	Wuhan	Wuchang
Guangzhou	Canton	Xiamen	Amoy
Guizhou	Kweichow	Xian	Sian
Guomingdang	Kuomingtang	Xie Fuzhi	Hsieh Fu-chih
Hangzhou	Hangchow	Xinhua	Hsinhua
Hebei	Hopei	Xinjiang	Sinkiang
Hefei	Hofei	Xizang	Hsi-tsang
Heilongjiang	Heilunkiang	Xu Shiyou	Hsu Shih-yu
Henan	Honan	Yan Jioqi	Yan Chao-chi
Hu Yaobang	Hu Yao-pang	Yan Xishan	Yen Hsi-shan
Hua Guofeng	Hua Kuopfeng	Yanan	Yenan
Hubei	Hupei	Yangzi	Yangtze
Jiang Jieshi	Chiang Kai-shek	Yao Wenyuan	Yao Wen-yuan
Jiang Jingguo	Chiang Ching-kuo	Ye Jianying	Yeh Chien-ying
Jiang Qing	Chiang Ching	Zhang Chunqiao	Chang Chun-chiao
Jiangxi	Kiansi	Zhao Ziyang	Chao Tzu-yang
Lin Biao	Lin Piao	Zhou Enlai	Chou En-lai
Liu Shaoqi	Liu Shao-chi	Zhu De	Chuh The
Mao Yuanxin	Mao Yuan-hsin	Zhuhai	Chuhai
Mao Zedong	Mao Tse-tung	Zunyi	Tsunyi
Nanjing	Nanking		

Further reading

Books of overall relevance

S.A.M. Adshead, *China in World History* (Macmillan, 1995)

An absorbing study of China's development as a modern state

P.J. Bailey, *China in the Twentieth Century* (Blackwell, 1988)

A short but very informative coverage

Pei-kai Cheng and Michael Lestz, editors, *The Search for Modern China: A Documentary Collection* (W.W. Norton, 1999)

A documentary companion to Jonathan Spence's book of the same name

Pamela Kyle Crossley, *The Wobbling Pivot: China Since 1800* (Blackwell, 2010)

A sympathetic study of China's difficult path to modernity

John King Fairbank, *China: A New History* (Belknap Press, 1994)

An insightful narrative by one of the Western pioneer scholars of Chinese history

Jonathan Fenby, *The Penguin History of Modern China 1850–2008* (Allen Lane, 2008)

A lively account of China's transition to modernity with an excellent bibliography

Jack Gray, *Rebellions and Revolutions* (Oxford University Press, 2002)

A hard but rewarding read, strong on the interplay of Chinese politics and economics

Immanuel C.Y. Hsü, *The Rise of Modern China*, sixth edition (Oxford University Press, 2000)

An established major work from a Chinese perspective

Graham Hutchings, *Modern China* (Penguin, 2001)

An indispensable reference book

Alan Lawrence, *China Since 1919 – Revolution and Reform* (Routledge, 2004)

A very accessible selection of documents covering the period

Roderick MacFarquhar, editor, *China Under Mao: Politics Takes Command* (MIT Press, 1972)

An important selection of articles from the *China Quarterly*, the leading journal on Chinese studies

David J. Pyle, *China's Economy, 1949–94: From Revolution to Reform* (Macmillan, 1997)

An informed tracing of China's economic development from Mao to Deng

R.J. Rummel, *China's Bloody Century: Genocide and Mass Murder Since 1900* (Transaction Publishers, 2007)

The grim data of China's suffering in the twentieth century

Jonathan Spence, *The Gate of Heavenly Peace: The Chinese and Their Revolution 1895–1980* (Faber, 1982)

An illuminating study by the leading Western authority on China's modern history

Jonathan Spence, *The Search for Modern China* (W.W. Norton, 1990)

The same writer's masterly narrative of the development of modern China

Jonathan Spence and Annping Chin, *The Chinese Century: A Photographic History* (HarperCollins, 1996)

A combination of clear analysis and graphic illustrations

Jeffrey Wasserstrom, editor, *Twentieth Century China: New Approaches* (Routledge, 2003)

A very useful guide to some of the major Western reappraisals of modern China

Chapter 1

Iris Chang, *The Rape of Nanking: The Forgotten Holocaust of World War II* (Penguin, 1998)

A harrowing analysis of the Japanese occupation of China

Lloyd Eastman, *The Nationalist Era in China, 1927–37* (Cambridge University Press, 1991)

A study of the period when Chiang Kai-shek and the nationalists were at their strongest

Jonathan Fenby, *Generalissimo: Chiang Kai-shek and the World He Lost* (Allen Lane, 2008)

A very readable analysis of the failure of Chiang and the Nationalists

Michael Lynch, *The Chinese Civil War 1945–49* (Osprey, 2010)

A graphically illustrated account of the CCP's victory over the GMD

Tony Saich, editor, *The Rise to Power of the Chinese Communist Party* (M.E. Sharpe, 1995)

A voluminous set of documents and analysis, well worth dipping into

Odd Arne Westad, *Decisive Encounters: The Chinese Civil War 1946–50* (Stanford University Press, 2003)

The most authoritative analysis of the CCP–CMD struggle

Chapter 2

Frank Dikotter, *The Tragedy of Liberation: A History of the Chinese Revolution 1945–57* (Bloomsbury, 2013)

The most up-to-date account of the methods used to establish the PRC

Anne Freemantle, editor, *Mao Tse-tung: An Anthology of his Writings* (Mentor, 1971)

An interesting set of documents covering Mao's career until 1966

Sergei N. Goncharov, John W. Lewis and Xue Litai, *Uncertain Partners: Stalin, Mao and the Korean War* (Stanford University Press, 1993)

An exploration of Mao's involvement in the Korean War

Peter Lum, *Peking, 1950–1953* (Hale, 1958)

A first-hand account of the creation of the PRC

Chapter 3

Jasper Becker, *Hungry Ghosts: China's Secret Famine* (John Murray, 1996)

The first major Western study of the Great Famine

Timothy Cheek, editor, *A Critical Introduction to Mao* (Cambridge University Press, 2010)

A set of scholarly essays, covering Mao's ideas, policies and legacy and examining the historiography that has developed around him

Frank Dikötter, *Mao's Great Famine: The History of China's Most Devastating Catastrophe, 1958–62* (Bloomsbury, 2010)

A harrowing account of the disastrous results of Mao's Great Leap Forward

Stuart Schram, *Mao Tse-Tung Unrehearsed: Talks and Letters: 1956–71* (Penguin, 1974)

Mao in his own words

Chapter 4

Delia Davin, *Mao Zedong* (Sutton, 1997)

A little gem of a biography that says a great deal in a very short space

Lee Feigon, *Mao: A Reinterpretation* (Ivan R. Dee, 2002)

A sympathetic study of Mao from a left-leaning American scholar

Michael Lynch, *Mao* (Routledge, 2004)

A combination of narrative and analysis, written with students in mind

Philip Short, *Mao: A Life* (Hodder & Stoughton, 1999)

A biography whose balance stands in marked contrast to Jung Chang's unrestrained attack on Mao

Chapter 5

Gregor Benton and Lin Chun, editors, *Was Mao Really a Monster?* (Routledge, 2010)

A critique of Jung Chang's biography, which seeks to present a balanced alternative assessment of Mao's impact on China

Jung Chang and Jon Halliday, *Mao: The Unknown Story* (Jonathan Cape, 2005)

A strongly committed and very readable account of Mao's policies, but criticised by other historians for its heavy bias against Mao

Roderick MacFarquhar and Michael Schoenhals, *Mao's Last Revolution* (Belknap Press, 2006)

Traces the origins, course and consequences of Mao's extraordinary attempt to leave his permanent mark on the revolutionary China

Michael Schoenhals, *China's Cultural Revolution, 1966–1969* (M.E. Sharpe, 1996)

An informative combination of analysis and documentation

Chapter 6

Richard Evans, *Deng Xiaoping and the Making of Modern China* (Viking Books, 1993)

A fascinating assessment of Deng by the British ambassador in Deng's China

Wu Jie, *On Deng Xiaoping Thought* (Foreign Languages Press, 1996)

A member of the CCP gives a Chinese insight into Deng's significance

Harrison Salisbury, *The New Emperors: Mao and Deng – A Dual Biography* (HarperCollins, 1992)

Arranged in short, punchy chapters, this dual biography offers fascinating insights into the careers of its subjects

Ezra F. Vogel, *Deng Xiaoping and the Transformation of China* (Harvard University Press, 2011)

A very detailed but rewarding study of Deng's revolution

Benjamin Yang and Bingzhang Yang, *Deng: A Political Biography* (M.E. Sharpe, 1998)

An assessment by two Chinese writers of Deng's achievements

Michael Dillon, *Deng Xiaoping: The Man Who Made Modern China*, I.B. Tauris, 2015

Draws on Chinese sources to explain Deng's reforms and the motives behind them

Websites

www.youtube.com/watch?v=TfJy_wduFy4

BBCs' twentieth-century history file: *Mao's China – One Man's Revolution*

http://chineseposters.net/themes/mao-cult.php

Collection of propaganda posters in Mao's PRC

Index